D0900345

DUE DATE

◆ALTERNATIVES *is a series under the general editorship of Eric S. Rabkin, Martin H. Greenberg, and Joseph D. Olander which has been established to serve the growing critical audience of science fiction, fantastic fiction, and speculative fiction.*

Other titles in this series are:

Bridges to Science Fiction, edited by George E. Slusser, George R. Guffey, and Mark Rose, 1980

The Science Fiction of Mark Clifton, edited by Barry N. Malzberg and Martin H. Greenberg, 1980

Fantastic Lives: Autobiographical Essays by Notable Science Fiction Writers, edited by Martin H. Greenberg, 1981

Astounding Science Fiction: July 1939, edited by Martin H. Greenberg, 1981

The Magazine of Fantasy and Science Fiction: April 1965, edited by Edward L. Ferman, 1981

The Fantastic Stories of Cornell Woolrich, edited by Charles G. Waugh and Martin H. Greenberg, 1981

The Best Science Fiction of Arthur Conan Doyle, edited by Charles G. Waugh and Martin H. Greenberg, 1981

Bridges to Fantasy, edited by George E. Slusser, Eric S. Rabkin, and Robert Scholes, 1982

The End of the World, edited by Eric S. Rabkin, Martin H. Greenberg, and Joseph D. Olander, 1983

No Place Else: Explorations in Utopian and Dystopian Fiction, edited by Eric S. Rabkin, Martin H. Greenberg, and Joseph D. Olander, 1983

Coordinates: Placing Science Fiction and Fantasy, edited by George E. Slusser, Eric S. Rabkin, and Robert Scholes, 1983

Robots, Androids, and Mechanical Oddities, edited by Patricia S. Warrick and Martin H. Greenberg, 1984

Shadows of the Magic Lamp: Fantasy and Science Fiction in Film, edited by George E. Slusser and Eric S. Rabkin, 1985

Hard Science Fiction, edited by George E. Slusser and Eric S. Rabkin, 1986

MIND IN MOTION
THE FICTION OF
PHILIP K. DICK

by
Patricia S. Warrick

Southern Illinois University Press
Carbondale and Edwardsville

Library of Congress Cataloging-in-Publication Data

Warrick, Patricia S.
  Mind in motion.

  Bibliography: p.
  Includes index.
  1. Dick, Philip K.—Criticism and interpretation.
  2. Science fiction, American—History and criticism.
  I. Title.
PS3554.I3Z92 1987   813'.54   86-14634
ISBN 0-8093-1326-X

"The Eyes Have It" is reprinted by permission of Scott Merrill Literary
    Agency.
Earlier versions of chapters 2 and 9 appeared in:
    "The Encounter of Taoism and Fascism in *The Man in the High Castle*,"
        Science Fiction Studies, July 1980.
    "Philip K. Dick's Answers to the Eternal Riddles," in *The Transcendent
        Adventure*, ed. Robert Reilly, Westport, CO: Greenwood Press, 1984.

To the memory of my parents

No single thing abides; but all things flow. Fragment to fragment clings—the things thus grow until we know and name them. By degrees they melt, and are no more the things we know.
                                                        —Titus Lucretius Carus

Contents

Figures   xi

Preface   xiii

Acknowledgments   xix

Chronology   xxi

1. Introduction   1

2. Power Struggles and *The Man in the High Castle*   32

3. Madness, Schizophrenia, and *Martian Time-Slip*   62

4. Holocaust, Survival, and *Dr. Bloodmoney*   80

5. Illusions, Reality, Evil, and *The Three Stigmata
   of Palmer Eldritch*   95

6. Mechanical Mirrors, the Double, and *Do Androids
   Dream of Electric Sheep?*   117

7. Entropy, Death, and *Ubik*   133

8. Drugs, Hallucinations, and *A Scanner Darkly*   152

9. The Search for God and the *Valis* Novels   166

10. Philip K. Dick's Moral Vision   194

    Bibliography   207
    Index   213

Figures

1. Fomalhaut Cosmos. 18

2. Dick's dynamic four-chambered metaphor. 30

3. Diagram of double-plot line in *Do Androids
   Dream of Electric Sheep?* 124

Preface

In 1972 Philip K. Dick delivered a speech titled "The Android and the Human" at the University of British Columbia. Toward the end of the speech he made reference to the memo that appears ahead of the text in *The Three Stigmata of Palmer Eldritch*, saying: "This statement is for me my credo—not so much in God, either a good god or a bad god or both—but in ourselves. It goes as follows, and this is all I actually have to say or want ever to say:"

> I mean, after all; you have to consider we're only made out of dust. That's admittedly not much to go on and we shouldn't forget that. But even considering, I mean it's a sort of bad beginning, we're not doing too bad. So I personally have faith that even in this lousy situation we're faced with we can make it. You get me?

The memo is written by the protagonist Leo Bolero after he survives his encounters with the evil Palmer Eldritch. It seems an appropriate summary statement that will bring Dick's speech to a nice conclusion—.

But not so. Listen to Dick's very next sentence: "This tosses a bizarre thought up into my mind." The bizarre thought in this instance was that perhaps some day a giant automated machine would roar and clank that it had come not from dust but from rust. Dick then set off to pursue this new thought.

The episode catches the essence of Dick's mind. It wrestled an idea to its conclusion, stated that conclusion, and just when he could settle back in contentment, another idea—always a bizarre one—sprang up and he galloped off to chase this new one to its conclusion, only to discard it once he had caught it. Ideas were alive for Dick, and they always appeared first in his mind and then in his fiction in metaphorical form. Joseph Adams, a character in *The Penultimate Truth* describes the process: "In his mind the metaphor, growing, became visual and frightening; he actually experienced the doorway ahead, felt the darkness breathed by it—." The quotation from Lucretius used as an epigraph for this book seems particularly fitting, catching as it does the essence of motion and change. "No single thing abides; but all things flow." It appears in *Counter-Clock World* as the epitaph on the tomb of the visionary Anarch Thomas Peak.

A comprehensive critical study of Dick's vast body of fiction would require a very long book. I have not undertaken such a work here. Instead, I have elected to give extensive treatment to the major science fiction novels, to make only minor reference to the lesser novels and the short stories, and to ignore the mainstream novels. Dick wrote at least a dozen of the latter, but only one, *Confessions of a Crap Artist*, was published while he was alive—and that one not until fifteen years after it had been written. Others of his mainstream novels have been published since his death, and they testify to the good judgment of the editors who originally turned them down for publication. Dick was at his best when he wrote the novels for which he gained recognition in his lifetime—a strange, mutant science fiction haunted by the yearning to be another kind of fiction. These are the novels to which this study will give primary attention. That I applaud the novels I discuss does not mean that I applaud all the novels Dick wrote. My choice is to devote my attention to the great novels and to ignore the others.

My acquaintance with Philip Dick began in 1977 when in doing research for an article on *The Man in the High Castle* I wrote to ask him about his sources for the castle metaphors so important in that novel. An ongoing correspondence developed. At that time he said he planned to write no more fiction because he had nothing left to say. In 1978 he telephoned me and we began conversing by phone, a practice that continued until his death four years later. The next year I decided to do a book length study of his fiction, and while I was on sabbatical I spent a month at the Special Collections Library at California State University-Fullerton, where his manuscripts are housed. During that time I met and talked with him on three occasions. At the beginning of the first conversation I made the decision not to use a tape recorder. I was more interested in having him relax and talk freely to a friend about his work than in collecting material to publish as an interview. Each conversation lasted six or seven hours and each was very different.

I went to his modest condominium at 408 Civic Center Drive in Santa Ana where he lived alone with his two cats. The living room furniture was shabby and nondescript, the coffee table covered with dust and cluttered with books and papers. An expensive stereo set was the focal point of the living room. On the first occasion he was very shy, almost embarrassed, and played the role of a sycophant, a mannerism I found irritating as he pretentiously called me Professor Warrick. He almost immediately offered me a glass of wine, which turned out to be of very poor quality. He apologized, explaining it had been a Christmas gift. Then abruptly he said, "God, I'm so embarrassed, I'm going to get a bottle of good wine." He bolted out the door. A half hour later he returned with an excellent bottle of Mondavi red. Later he pushed aside the clutter on the coffee table and served TV dinners with yogurt for dessert.

During this first visit, we talked about his work, discussing his ideas, his plots and characters, and his writing techniques. He gradually relaxed, lost his obsequious attitude, and came to life intellectually as I probed and queried him about his vast body of fiction. He typically delivered a long monologue in response to a question. He was a man who loved to talk more than to listen, and to punctuate and puncture a serious discussion with wry humorous asides.

On the second visit, I met another Phil, this one the man whose mind had been invaded by a transcendentally rational mind in 1974. His mystical experiences were the only subject of conversation on this second visit, and he gave me much the same account that Charles Platt has recorded in *The Dream Makers*. Because I am a realist with an undergraduate major in science, I listened with great skepticism. Yes, I thought to myself, what they say about his being crazy, his having burned out his brain with drugs, is true. Yet I was nonjudgmental in my responses—an easy accomplishment since the conversation was primarily his. When I went home at the end of that long and exhausting evening, he handed me a manuscript and said, "I've ended my writing silence. Would you like to take this along with you and read it?" The manuscript was *Valis*.

I stayed up late that night reading with a feeling of *dèjá vu*. For there in the novel I saw the cynical disbelieving comments that had run silently through my mind earlier that evening as Phil had told me about his visionary experiences. The comments this time were made by the character Phil Dick in *Valis* as he listened skeptically to Horselover Fat's tale of his visionary experiences. On the third evening I encountered still another Phil Dick. This time no reference was made to his mystical voices, the focus of our previous conversation. This Phil was the pure intellectual: he discussed mainstream fiction, talked about having first understood double worlds when he read Proust's *Remembrance of Things Past*, constantly referred to Greek philosophy, ran to the bookshelf to get his copy of *Finnegan's Wake* so he could read a favorite passage to me. We had arranged that on this last visit I would take Phil to dinner, and upon my arrival he called a restaurant and made reservations. But when the dinner hour approached, he could not be persuaded to go out. Once again we sat around the cluttered coffee table and ate TV dinners and yogurt.

When I returned to Wisconsin from California, his phone calls became more regular and the letters less frequent. He began to write only when he was struggling to work out another theory that would explain his 1974 visionary experience. He called to report his excitement at visiting the movie studio where *Blade Runner* was being filmed and his fear that the film might focus only on the violent elements of the novel. He called to discuss his uncertainty about whether he should allow *Do Androids Dream of Electric Sheep?* to be rewritten to match the text of the movie. He was tempted by the huge sum of money he was offered, but recognized that the price he would pay would be to allow the bastardizing of one of his fine novels. He decided against it. He was always helpful in answering my questions about his life and his writing. Our last conversation was on February 17, 1982. When I called he said he was not well and would have to call back later when he felt better. The next day he suffered a massive stroke.

Of the many persons who have been of aid to me in writing this book none was more helpful than Phil Dick himself. He was always generous, if not always consistent, in his answers to my questions. Ideas, opinions, and information he gave me at one time sometimes contradicted what he said on another occasion or what he told another person. Did he lie? Probably not. His mind constantly invented new possibilities and for him the line between fact in the real world and fiction in his mind was so insignificant that I suspect he often ignored it.

Dick gave many interviews and wrote numerous letters and commentaries about his work, and I have found this material extremely useful. Often he is his own best critic as he points out how a metaphor or an idea works in a novel. In my study of his fiction I have included plot summaries as an aid to the reader who may not be familiar with the novel I am discussing. Phil, aware of my method, laughed uproariously, saying that it was impossible to summarize his plots. He was right! The plots are intricate, complex, contradictory, full of surprises, sometimes maddening—but never dull. The same description fits precisely the mind of the man who wrote those novels. Were I given to hyperbole, I might call him a genius. Instead, with more restraint, let me say that his was a fascinating intelligence. To read his fiction is to go exploring in his vast inner cosmos where ideas race, chase, pirouette, leap, and dance in ceaseless intellectual motion.

Acknowledgments

I wish to thank various people for their help as I researched the material for this book. Linda Herman, Head Librarian in charge of Special Collections at the library at California State University-Fullerton, was most gracious as I worked with the Dick papers located there. Anne Dick provided a great amount of biographical material on Dick's life. Paul Williams, the literary executor of the Dick estate, also made material available. I found the appendix to his *Only Apparently Real*, which lists the novels in the order in which they were written, very useful since in several significant instances the date varies considerably from the publication date. Daniel Levack's bibliography, compiled with Dick's help, is an invaluable tool for any Dick scholar. To my fellow scholars who joined me in dialogue as we struggled to penetrate the mysteries of Dick's massive and complex body of fiction I am grateful, especially Merritt Abrash, Willis McNelly, and Martin H. Greenberg. And finally, my thanks to James F. Welch, a scientist who reads literature and who was always available as a consultant to make certain that the science in my science fiction criticism was accurate.

Chronology

1928   Born December 16 in Chicago, one of twins, to Joseph Edgar Dick and Dorothy Kindred Dick.

1929   Twin sister, Jane, dies January 26. Dick family moves, first to Johnstown, Colorado, and then to the San Francisco Bay area.

1933   Parents are divorced. Dick remains with his mother in Berkeley; his father moves to Reno.

1935   Moves with his mother to Washington, D.C.

1938   Returns with his mother to Berkeley where he attends Hillside Grade School and then Garfield Junior High School (now Martin Luther King Junior High School).

1942   Attends California Preparatory School at Ojai.

1943–46 Attends Berkeley High School. Has part-time jobs working at University Radio and also Art Music, stores owned by Herb Hollis.

1944   Writes the "Aunt Flo" stories, short fantasies in the mode of Edgar Allen Poe, which are published in The Young Author's Club column in the *Berkeley Gazette*.

1947   Briefly attends the University of California—Berkeley.

1948   Marries Jeanette Marlin, a marriage lasting only a few months.

1950   Marries Kleo Apostolides. Works briefly for Tupper and Read, a music store.

1952   Begins writing full time. First published short story, "Beyond Lies the Wub," appears in *Planet Stories*. Becomes client of the Scott Meredith Literary Agency, his agency for the remainder of his life.

1953   Continues to publish short stories. Writes *The Cosmic Puppets*, his first science fiction novel. Also writes first mainstream novel, *Voices from the Street* during this period.

1955   First published novel, *Solar Lottery*.

1958   Moves with Kleo to Point Reyes Station, Marin County, in September. Meets Anne Rubenstein in October. Asks Kleo for a divorce in December.

1959   Marries Anne Rubenstein in Mexico in April. Writes *Confessions of a Crap Artist*.

1960   Daughter Laura Archer born February 25, Dick's first child, Anne's fourth. Dick continues to write mainstream novels for which his agency can find no publisher.

1962   *The Man in the High Castle* published. It wins the Hugo Award as the best novel of the year.

1963–64   Gives up writing mainstream novels, turns to science fiction full time and writes ten novels in two years.

1964   Leaves Anne in March after months of disharmony in their marriage. Lives briefly with his mother in Oakland, then with Grania Davidson. Begins romance with Nancy Hackett in the autumn. Becomes friends with Ray Nelson and they begin collaboration on *The Ganymede Takeover*.

1964   *Martian Time-Slip* published.

1965   *Dr. Bloodmoney, or How We Got Along After the Bomb* and *The Three Stigmata of Palmer Eldritch* published. Formally divorced from Anne in October. Moves to San Raphael area. Meets and becomes friends with Bishop James Pike.

1966   Marries Nancy Hackett on July 6. Bishop Pike attends the ceremony, which is performed by the Episcopal priest at Point Reyes Station. They live in San Raphael.

1967   Daughter Isolde (Isa) born on March 17.

1968   *Do Androids Dream of Electric Sheep?* published.

1969   *Ubik* published. Bishop Pike dies in the Israeli desert.

1970   Nancy leaves, taking daughter Isa with her. Dick writes the first draft of *Flow My Tears, the Policeman Said*.

1971   House burglarized and manuscripts destroyed November 17.

1972   Delivers the Guest of Honor Speech at the science conven-
        tion in Vancouver in February. Attempts suicide in March
        and is admitted to X-Kalay, a drug rehabilitation center.
        Moves to Fullerton, California, in April, where Professor
        Willis McNelly befriends him. Desperately needing
        money, sells papers to Special Collections, California
        State University—Fullerton.

1973   Marries Leslie (Tessa) Busby in April. Son Christopher
        born July 25. Begins writing fiction again after two and a
        half years, working on *A Scanner Darkly*.

1974   Has mystical visionary experiences in February and
        March. Begins writing his exegesis. *Flow My Tears, the
        Policeman Said* published. It wins the John W. Campbell
        Jr. Award for Best Novel of 1974.

1975   *Confessions of a Crap Artist* published.

1976   Tessa leaves him in February. Dick moves to Santa Ana
        and again attempts suicide.

1977   *A Scanner Darkly* published. Guest of Honor at the Sec-
        ond International Festival of Science Fiction at Metz,
        France.

1978   Mother dies in August. Writes *Valis*.

1981   *Valis* and *The Divine Invasion* published. Film rights for
        Do Androids Dream of Electric Sheep? sold.

1982   Suffers stroke at his home February 18. Admitted to West-
        ern Medical Center at Fullerton. Dies March 2 with-
        out regaining consciousness. Cremated and his ashes bur-
        ied beside his twin sister at Fort Morgan, Colorado.
        The Transmigration of Timothy Archer published post-
        humously.

I
Introduction

Philip K. Dick—a Romantic rebel born too late. A man at odds with his age when rebellion—except for a brief decade of active college students—was no longer in style. A man who had to hide his love of the classics under the tattered cover of science fiction. A man unable to find a publisher for the literary novels he regarded as his best writing. A man constantly struggling with the devil of chaos that threatened to devour him. And yet—A great science fiction writer, one who continues to gain recognition both outside and inside the genre.

How is this possible? How did he manage, despite all his difficulties and disappointments, to publish thirty-four novels and 112 short stories in the thirty years from his first story in 1952 to his death in 1982 at the age of fifty-three? How did he achieve his reputation as one of the most intellectual, profound, and inventive of writers while at the same time collecting labels like crazy, mad, spaced out? What elusive, charismatic quality in his fiction turned readers into such passionate admirers that he became something of a cult figure?

My critical study of Dick's writing searches for answers to these kinds of questions, even knowing as I begin that the chances of success are slim. Dick possessed, or perhaps more aptly, was possessed by a powerful restless intellect driving him to seek answers to the big philosophical questions: What is reality? How can we explain evil? What makes us human? Is there a God? But for Dick an answer found was an answer to reject. His mind was a mind in motion. It constantly churned forward to seek another possibility that he had not yet explored. Nevertheless, when we consider his corpus of writing, one conclusion can be reliably drawn. Dick's work fascinates and instructs because it embodies in miniature all the complexities, contradictions, hopes, and anxieties of our post-World War II world.

1

Like a giant eye in the sky, his consciousness observed all and caught it in a net of words.

We live in an age of cultural transition. The modern world at the beginning of the twentieth century imagined itself on the threshold of utopia. But after two devastating wars, it awakened to find itself instead on the very edge of an abyss. The explosion of the atomic bomb at Hiroshima on August 5, 1945, that brought World War II to an end also ended our simple faith in science as a servant to carry us into the promised land of peace and abundance. We learned with terror that nuclear warfare could in a brief moment, unleash enough power to annihilate thousands upon thousands of people. Given long years, chemicals could destroy the ecological balance maintaining our environment. Medical discoveries improved health and simultaneously created overpopulation. We seemed to be living in a world nightmare as one international crisis followed another. Social institutions and value systems began to fall apart. And we were afraid.

Dick's fiction captures the patterns and processes of the American collective psychology in the last thirty years. He has a remarkable power of abstracting the essentials from the chaotic array of events and ideas occurring in the decades of the fifties, sixties, and seventies, and then thinking about them imaginatively and, finally, expressing them in powerful, bizarre metaphors. He shares the anxieties of the American psychology as it leaps, often irrationally, from one stance to another—sometimes rebellious, sometimes reactionary, but always divided and uncertain. Dick's fiction can thus be seen as a microcosm of our cultural macrocosm during the past thirty years. Yet oddly his fiction is fiction set in the future, usually the twenty-first century, and often on other planets than Earth.

The yoking of opposites characterizes Dick's novels. We have just noted one—the present caught in the future. Other antinomies abound. Mundane California artifacts on planets in outer space, metaphysical speculation carried on in street vernacular, tragedy and farce, the possible and the impossible, logic and madness. The oxymoron is his mode. Typically he likes to use skeptical detachment to examine his insanities. His tension-riddled union of genius and madness gives birth to visions, insight, and metaphors a more sane writer could not achieve.

His imagination seems to tap some dark sun breeding energy that relentlessly fuels its journey away from mundane or consensus reality. Our daily world interests him only momentarily because he believes it is inauthentic and not to be trusted. He constantly turns to dreams, madness, drugs, death, religion—all of which fascinate him because they promise to lift him out of our world of commonsense reality. The risk involved in his journeys does not frighten but rather fascinates him, for it permits him to escape from the prison house of the everyday world. What is already known no longer interests him. He is a pilgrim of the unknown.

Critics have long recognized the contradictory elements in his writing. Depending on which aspect they choose to note, they may describe him as "the wildest imagination in science fiction . . . a creator of mad worlds" or as a writer who presents "a large scale portrait of the incursions of technological advance on the psyche of the West." While one critic notes that "the novels mimic madness," he admits this does not necessarily mean they were written by a madman. Another critic concludes that Dick was a very shrewd analyst of the American political scene whose creative instincts were firmly rooted in reality.

Contradictory as these comments seem at first glance, they are all true. Dick did find consensus reality dreary and meaningless. Because he could not escape it in his life, in his fiction he transformed it, creating one imaginary world after another. He was deeply alarmed at the direction of political events and the possibility of a third world war because he suspected the world might be run by madmen. His method of coping with his demons of anxiety was to make metaphors of them; thus in his fiction he created imaginary worlds where political leaders really are madmen, and ironically, with his strange gift for prophecy, he captures today's real world. He sees the terror at the bedrock of our social order; he sometimes suspects that even the cosmic order may be malicious and cruel. Yet he never loses his ability to laugh. While his grotesque dark humor is present and easy to spot, the warmth and wryness and delight with which he often greets the unexpected should not be overlooked merely because it is often less obvious. Bright laughter counters the dark. Those who knew him always commented about the comic spirit that often outshone his darker side.

Dick's writing delights us with its wild inventiveness and it provides wisdom with its astute social and political comments. But his novels can also be read as a phantasmal form of biography.

Because Dick was a private man, few details of his personal life were available until after his death. Now biographers have been at work, and their findings are startling. The fabric of his fiction is a patchwork quilt stitched together from the people, places, and events of his personal life, transformed just as he transformed the events of our national life with his wildly inventive and distorting imagination. A brief look at those two sources—our shared social world and his personal life—provides a useful tool for studying his fiction. Dick was a depression child and the poverty of the United States in the 1930s left deep scars. Because he was poor for so many years, his allegiance was always to the little man struggling to survive. (In fact he called his early realistic fiction proletariat novels about the working class.) The next national event to affect him powerfully was World War II, which began when he was just eleven. He studied German in high school and became fascinated with Nazism, German literature, German music—all aspects of the German mentality. He felt a particular love for Beethoven's music because they shared the same birthday, December 16. He read Schiller and Goethe and other writers of the German Enlightenment and never stopped asking how Germany could fall so tragically—from men like that to the Third Reich and Hitler. As a young man he attended college for only a few weeks, so his wide knowledge was self-acquired through reading, and that reading was primarily in literature, psychology, and philosophy. He apparently had almost total recall of anything he read. He did little reading in the physical sciences, although it seems he almost intuitively had a good understanding of scientific principles. New technologies interested him, particularly in the field of electronics, but of more concern were the social and political consequences of those technologies.

When Dick finished high school in Berkeley, California, World War II had ended. The decade that followed was the era of the cold war between the Western democracies and the East bloc of Communist countries and of the Joseph McCarthy witch hunts. Everyone agreed that another nuclear war was unthinkable, but limited conflict was accepted as a necessary evil. In 1950 the United States engaged in a war in Korea that lasted three years. Soon after its conclusion, we became involved in the Vietnam conflict as our military forces replaced the defeated French there. In 1959 a Communist government was established in Cuba. Kennedy's assassination occurred in 1963, the first and most poignant in a death march of terrorism that has made political violence a way of life. The wars that hover over so much of Dick's fiction mirror the wars in his own world when he was coming of age. In contrast, however, the assassins so common in all his political fiction began appearing in the novels of the 1950s, and thus are a foreshadowing rather than a reflection of assassinations in the real world.

Technological progress during the 1950s was stunning, drawing as it did on all the research and military inventions accumulated during World War II. Both Russia and the United States exploded hydrogen bombs in testing programs as the cold war between them deepened. Transcontinental television began, jet passenger service was instituted, the contraceptive pill was developed, Sputnik—the first Earth satellite—was launched by the Russians, machines for use in heart and lung surgery were announced. The government acquired mainframe computers. The American public responded with uncertainty to this chaotic milieu of constant change. New technology had always been hailed by a country which prided itself on its Yankee ingenuity in tinkering and making gadgets. But the horrifying memories of the nuclear holocaust and the continuing international crises made it impossible to ignore the destructive powers of modern technology. Not surprisingly, much of Dick's early fiction mirrors this world of military unrest and technological mistrust. The ubiquitous anxiety gnawing at his characters is our own anxiety.

The sixties was the decade of the counterculture—a decade of minority rebellion against conventional American values, which were now identified as the values of the military and of large corporations. The seeds of this rebellion first sprouted in the radical soul of the Berkeley campus, and the general public became conscious of this new growth when they read about the Free Speech movement of 1964. Its goal was to fight against what its leaders identified as the greatest problem of our nation—depersonalized, unresponsive bureaucracy. Flower children walked the streets of Haight-Ashbury and their cousins, the hippies, hitchhiked through the nation. One needed only a few items to qualify for membership: long hair, a backpack, drugs, an enthusiasm for the Beatles, and a rebellious attitude. The youth of America responded, rushing for the record stores and avoiding the barbershop. Soon other minority movements followed, most significantly blacks and women. Dick was well aware of the influence of this environment. He wrote in 1980, "Basically I am not serene. I grew up in Berkeley and inherited from it the social consciousness which spread out over this country in the Sixties."[1] Many of the charges of the counterculture were vindicated with the Watergate scandal and Nixon's exposure in the seventies. The Vietnam war ended in failure. It was a time of exhaustion when America lost faith in its leaders, its political system, and its religious establishments. Pop psychology responded with a deluge of self-help books that earned for the decade the title of the Me First age. Self concern replaced community responsibility.

Dick's fiction is a cultural history of this thirty-year period. He is an astute social observer with an antenna of awareness that catches and reports the first faint murmuring of critical social changes. His writing in this area is often prophetic. He is particularly sensitive to the significant political changes that will result from new communication technologies. A reading of his work today often seems more like a look in the daily newspaper at the political events, both national and international, than the reading of science fiction.

In a 1981 letter to me, Dick said, "I guess I have become multiple personalities and I like it that way." His statement summarized what his close friends already knew; he was a very complex, complicated, and contradictory man. Thus I cannot even attempt to deal comprehensively with his biography nor with the often bizarre modes and movements of his complex personality. But neither can I entirely ignore biographical material since he drew on it so heavily in his writing. The five periods of his writing correlate precisely with five distinct phases of his life. To provide a background, I want to sketch briefly those phases and also some influences in his life that affected his work.

Philip Kindred Dick was born December 16, 1928, to Dorothy and Edgar Dick, natives of Colorado who were then living in Chicago. He was born at home prematurely, the first delivered of twins. He was blonde and his sister, named Jane, was very dark. She died six weeks later. The loss, he would later lament, had inflicted a wound on his psyche so deep that he never recovered. When he was a year old, the family moved to the San Francisco Bay area. Five years later,

1. Introduction to *The Golden Man*, ed. Mark Hurst (New York: Berkley), 1980.

in 1933, his parents divorced—apparently unable to resolve their personality differences. His father was tall, rugged, and athletic—a tennis player who was also interested in football and other sports. He had volunteered for military service in World War I and fought with the marines in France in the Second Battle of the Marne. Phil's mother, in contrast, was a pacifist—a highly refined and intellectual woman who was ambitious to become a writer for the women's magazines. She also suffered from poor health most of her life. After the divorce his father moved to Reno, while Philip and his mother remained in Berkeley.

The following year, 1934, the two of them moved to Washington, D.C., where Mrs. Dick worked for the next five years in the Department of Labor. Their finances were so meager that on occasion they were forced to stay with various friends. Phil developed emotional problems and was sent for a time to a boarding school run by the Quakers that specialized in disturbed children. Years later as an adult Phil would attribute his emotional distress to his anxiety at being separated from his father. But he had other reasons to be anxious. A half century before it became common, he lived out the role of today's latchkey child, coming home from school and watching at the window for his mother to return from work.

In 1939, when he was eleven, his mother returned with him to Berkeley, where she took a job with the Forest Service. She was not strong physically and constantly took prescription drugs for her health problems. But she had a powerful and dominating personality which generated conflicting emotions in Phil—sometimes loving and protective but more often rebellious and resentful ones, although he apparently rarely expressed the latter. When she came home from work, she usually retired to bed to read and rest, leaving Phil to take care of himself. At this time he began his deep interest in classical music, both listening to records and playing the piano. He did not participate in sports or learn to drive a car. (He would be twenty-five years old before he began driving.)

The family finances continued to be meager, and so at age fourteen Dick began working as a janitor at University Radio, a radio and TV store in downtown Berkeley. He also worked at Art Music, a classical record store a few blocks away. Both stores were owned by Herb Hollis, a warm-hearted man who treated his employees like an extended family. Hollis is the prototype for many Dick characters, as are the various radio and TV repairmen who worked in the store. Later, because of Dick's uncanny ability to identify a classical composition by hearing a bit of melody, he was employed as a salesperson at Art Music. It was here he met and became friends with science fiction writer Anthony Boucher, a regular customer. The world of Art Music attracted intellectuals interested in classical music. Its antithesis was University Radio where the repairmen were from the working class. Dick learned that he could shift easily from one world to the other, altering his speech patterns as he moved. He continued to work for Herb Hollis throughout high school and for several years afterward.

In 1948 Dick briefly attended the University of California at Berkeley but soon dropped out, probably because of the agoraphobia, which had begun to trouble him in high school (although in an autobiographical sketch he wrote years later he said that he was kicked out for refusing to attend ROTC classes). In the same year he married Jeanette Marlin, but the marriage lasted only a few months. In 1950 he married Kleo Apostolides. During this period Dick became involved in Anthony Boucher's writing workshops. He soon sold a fantasy story, "Roog," and by 1952, with Kleo's encouragement, he was confident enough to quit working in the music store and begin writing full time. During the next three years he published sixty-two science fiction stories while at the same time writing realistic fiction (or as he called it, literary fiction), which he was unable to sell. Probably one of the earliest novels was *Voices from the Street,* an unpublished manuscript of 547 pages written about 1952–53.

As the decade of the fifties advanced, the paperback market grew and Dick discovered that publishing science fiction novels produced an income a bit better than the meager amounts he was receiving in the pulp magazines for his short stories, and so he turned to science fiction novels and published his first one, *Solar Lottery,* in 1955. Four more science fiction novels followed rapidly, while at the same time he continued to write realistic novels, although he still could find no publisher for them. In the little part of the Berkeley intellectual world he inhabited, everyone admired literary writers but few people read science fiction and certainly no one regarded it as literature—a situation which caused the overly-sensitive, shy young writer great pain. He was, Kleo said, embarrassed to admit that he wrote science fiction.

In the fall of 1958 the Dicks moved to the country because Phil felt he would enjoy gardening and returning to the soil. They bought a tiny house in Point Reyes Station, a rural community in Marin County. Within a short time Dick met and fell in love with Anne Rubinstein, a newly widowed neighbor of thirty who had three small daughters. Kleo soon returned to Berkeley, and after Christmas Dick moved in with Anne. They were married in April after his divorce became final. One of the first novels he wrote after he married Anne was *Confessions of a Crap Artist,* a literary novel which did not find a publisher until 1975. Many of the events, characters, and settings of *Crap Artist* are drawn from his life in Point Reyes although often significantly distorted and recombined in new patterns. The house, for example, is identical with the one where he lived with Anne, and she served as a prototype for the character Faye, although his marriage was serene as he wrote the novel of domestic turbulence. He continued to write mainstream novels for the next two years, still finding no editors willing to recommend publication. The family survived economically from the sale of his science fiction and from Anne's income.

The marriage, according to Anne, was a happy one for the first few years. He experienced none of the periods of depression his high school friends had noted, nor the agoraphobia which during his marriage to Kleo made him prefer to remain at home and avoid concerts and social events. He now altered his writing schedule so that he worked all day rather than all night. He participated happily as father to Anne's three daughters and his own daughter Laura, who was born in 1960. The only discouraging element in his life was his failure to find a publisher for his realistic fiction. For a short period he became so disheartened that he gave up writing entirely and worked with Anne in the handcrafted jewelry business she started. He helped make and market the jewelry just as Frank Frink does in *The Man in the Highcastle,* the novel Dick began to write later in the year. It received immediate recognition when it was published in 1962, and it was honored with the Hugo Award for the outstanding science fiction novel of 1962. Finally Dick had become successful as a writer and he had also found his mode—a complex novelistic pattern merging science fiction and realistic elements. During the next few years, driving himself on a relentless schedule of two novels per year, he wrote some of his greatest works, *Martian Time-Slip, Dr. Blood-*

money, or How We Got Along After the Bomb, and *The Three Stigmata of Palmer Eldritch*. But by 1963 his marriage to Anne had developed severe problems and he finally terminated it with a divorce in 1965, after a long period of unpleasantness.

Now he began a vagabond period, moving restlessly around the San Francisco and Oakland area, living with various persons, and relying more heavily than ever on the amphetamines he had used for some years to maintain his prodigious writing schedule. Finally he began to experiment with harder drugs. He became paranoid and erratic in his behavior and his writing suffered. In 1966 he married Nancy Hackett, a beautiful dark-haired girl half his age who had been diagnosed as schizophrenic. Through her stepmother he became friends with Bishop James Pike. Dick and his new wife had a daughter Isolde, born in March 1967, and they settled into a house they bought in San Raphael. Although for a time the novels he had written earlier continued to be published, he spent less and less time writing new work. Instead, like moth to flame, he flew desperately into Nancy's rebellious world of youth, drugs, and emotional illness. Only two works written during these years achieve real artistic success—*Do Androids Dream of Electric Sheep?* (a revision of an earlier work that had found no publisher) and *Ubik*.

He became heavily depressed and increasingly paranoid. Events worsened in his personal life and his income dwindled. In 1970 Nancy left him and his house became a haven for the young people of the street drug culture. In November 1971 his house was burglarized and many of his manuscripts were destroyed. He was now desperately poor, filled with anxieties, and frightened that someone wanted to kill him. This dreary period of his life ended when he left San Raphael and went to Vancouver. After a few weeks there he made an unsuccessful suicide attempt and was admitted to X-Kalay, a drug treatment center.

Two months later a rebirth occurred in his personal life, although it was not matched by a parallel birth in his creativity. He left Canada and went to Fullerton, California, where Professor Willis McNelly of California State University befriended him for a time. Before many months he met and married Leslie (Tessa) Busby, another very young girl, and in 1973 they settled in Santa Ana, where Tessa gave birth to a son, Christopher. For Dick the single most important event of this period was his mystical experience in March

1974. His writing output was small, only *Flow My Tears, the Police-man Said* (1974) and *A Scanner Darkly* (1977).

Now forty-six years old, he suffered from arrhythmic tachycar-dia, and other health problems and was often depressed, irascible, and paranoid. As his health worsened he took an increasing number of prescription drugs (but no street drugs except occasionally mari-juana). Tessa finally left him and obtained a divorce in 1976, and once again Dick followed the departure of a wife with a suicide attempt. He was hospitalized for a time and when he was released he declared that he would never write again. Many who heard his tale of the 1974 visionary experience now obsessing him thought that he really was crazy, albeit a gentle and harmless craziness.

Eventually, as with all his other experiences, he transformed this religious epiphany into fiction, publishing *Valis* and *The Divine Inva-sion* in 1981. In the last few years of his life, his finances improved as his reputation grew and royalties from reprints and foreign editions began to pour in. His sale of the film rights for *Do Androids Dream of Electric Sheep?*, which became the movie *Blade Runner,* also helped to augment his income and he began to feel almost affluent, although he did not change his modest life style.

He died unexpectedly of a massive stroke on March 2, 1982. He never saw the movie *Blade Runner* nor the publication of his final novel, *The Transmigration of Timothy Archer*, a work that returns to the mode of realistic fiction as it draws a thinly-disguised picture of Bishop James Pike's life and death. At his father's direction, Dick's ashes were buried beside the grave of his twin sister at Fort Morgan, Colorado.

Chronologically Dick's writing divides into five periods. The divisions between these periods are somewhat arbitrary, determined as they are primarily by new phases in his thinking. These develop-ments do not always match precisely the dates of publication of the novels because occasionally a novel was not published in the order it was written and mailed to his literary agency, Scott Meredith.[2]

---

2. Paul Williams in Appendix I of his *Only Apparently Real* lists Dick's novel's in their order of composition. His primary source for these dates is the records of Scott Meredith Literary Agency, which indicate the dates on which they received each of the manuscripts. The first novel the agency

Nonetheless, the broad shapes of the periods emerge as clearly as mountains and valleys on a bright day and they coincide with his various marriages (except for the first marriage, which was brief and of little significance).

In his first or Apprenticeship Period when he was married to Kleo, he practiced his science fiction art primarily in the short story form—coached by Anthony Boucher and imitating those stories published in the pulps, especially those favoring soft science fiction and fantasy. He published in *Galaxy, Imagination, Fantastic Stories,* and *Fantasy and Science Fiction.* This period extended from 1952 to 1960. In addition to the science fiction short stories that were selling well, he wrote a number of realistic novels for which, to his great disappointment, he could find no publisher. He had better luck with the science fiction novels he began writing in 1955.

In his second, or Mature Period, when he was married to Anne, he wrote some of his greatest novels, beginning with *The Man in the High Castle* and including *Martian Time-Slip, Dr. Bloodmoney,* and *The Three Stigmata of Palmer Eldritch.* His output was almost beyond belief—over twelve novels in six years, including his main-stream novels that were always returned when he sent them off to his agent.

The third or Entropic Period extends roughly from 1966 to 1973, and for the first half of these years, he was married to Nancy. *Do Androids Dream of Electric Sheep?* and *Ubik* are the great novels of this Entropic Period—a time when generally his fiction began to decline both in amount and quality until for a time he ceased to write entirely. His mental and physical health deteriorated as his use of drugs increased.

The fourth or Regenerative Period began when he remarried once again, this time to Tessa, and wrote his brilliant drug novel, *A Scanner Darkly,* a nearly biographical account of the persons and events encountered when he had been a part of the street drug scene.

It is worth noting that in the fifth or Metaphysical Period when he wrote his religious novels, he was living essentially alone and had been for a rather prolonged period, the first in his writing career.

Dick's creative method is interesting. In a 1969 letter to his

---

received was *The Cosmic Puppets* in 1953 and they handled all his work from that time.

editor, Dick outlined the steps he went through in composing a novel. First, a premise, or idea, popped into his head for no reason. For example, he suddenly found himself thinking, "What if there were only nine men in the world and all were blind except one. And an attempt is being made by the other eight to see which one of them is becoming sighted." The premise would lie in his head for a period while he would continue to play with it imaginatively. Minor details would begin occurring to him and he would start taking notes. Then came the most difficult step, the creation of the characters:

> By now I would have a premise, a world deduced from the premise . . . but without the absolutely right characters I would have nothing. First, I would cast around for the protagonist, the viewpoint character through whom either all or most of the novel is seen. I would review protagonists from earlier novels which I had written, trying to avoid merely duplicating one of them. Basically, I would consider various people in real life whom I know; I constantly ask myself, when I meet people, "How would he be in a book?" Ultimately, the protagonist would emerge as a composite of several actual persons . . . but he would need to have certain traits in order to act as the protagonist; to cite one aspect, I would have to be sure he would understand events well enough, and act logically enough, for the reader to go along with what he says and does. To a lesser extent, the other characters would be put together in the same way, but their natures would tend to be designed by the plot of the book, rather than intrinsic considerations.[3]

Dick used an intuitive or, as he called it, gestalting method which caused him to "see" the whole work at once. "Evidently," he explained, "there is a certain historical validation to this method; Mozart, to name one particular craftsman, operated this way . . . . According to me, my work consists of getting down that which exists in my mind." When Dick did begin the actual writing process, he wrote with unbelievable speed, producing as many as forty to sixty pages in a single day—pages that were essentially free from typographical errors.

Dick's massive body of fiction is uneven and all the novels do not deserve equal attention. I have therefore elected to concentrate on those novels I consider to be his outstanding accomplishments, the novels most likely to survive when the sieve of time has lifted up the

3. Dick to Ray Brown, at Bowling Green University, March 21, 1969.

great ones and let the others trickle away into oblivion. Dick was a man obsessed by a number of ideas. Each novel I have selected concerns one of that handful of ideas that are particularly important to him—ideas that never disappear from his texts in his entire thirty-year writing career. The novels I have chosen almost coincidentally arrange themselves in a semblance of chronological order, primarily because at any one period of his life he would wrestle with all the implications and permutations of a particular idea. Then, feeling he had at least temporarily exhausted the possibilities of its meanings, he would move on to skirmish with another idea, although all the other ideas still lurked in his head, ghosts forever haunting the house of fiction where he lived.

Ideas have a life of their own, Dick once said. They seem to seize you and insist on being put down on paper. His fiction glitters and writhes with ideas; they flash out from page after page, at first glance as numerous as stars in a night sky. But actually, only a handful of big ideas obsesses Dick and constantly demands his attention. Like leitmotifs in the Wagnerian opera he loved, the ideas weave through all his writing, sometimes sotto voce, other times booming out with such fortissimo that little else can be heard. Dick repeatedly announced that his grand theme was the nature of reality and how we can distinguish it from illusionary worlds. His second theme, he declared, was how we can tell an authentic human being from one who merely masquerades as a human. Actually, when one reads all the fiction carefully, one finds that several other ideas are tightly related and almost equally as important as the two Dick designated in his comments. I have chosen to devote a chapter to each of the eight ideas that form the central threads holding together the network of his vast fictional cosmos.

The early fiction, both short stories and novels, focuses on the use and misuse of power—be it political, military, religious, or economic. Individual freedom is sacred above all else for Dick, and so his keen eye always looks for those who would violate it. He finds power monsters everywhere. His most successful study of the misuse of power is *The Man in the High Castle*.

As Dick ponders about the irrational use of power to destroy life, he begins to wonder if perhaps the sensitive individual cannot remain sane in this ruthless immoral world. So he begins an exploration of madness in its various forms—schizophrenia, paranoia, autism. *Martian Time-Slip* synthesizes his ideas about the sane who must live in an insane world.

The greatest insanity, Dick says again and again, is to go to war and risk another nuclear holocaust. For him it is the ultimate horror. Usually when he writes on nuclear war, he describes a world where the monstrous disaster has already occurred. Only in one novel does he actually picture the falling of the bomb—*Dr. Bloodmoney*.

As the decade of the sixties advanced, a turning point occurred in Dick's writing career. He became less interested in writing about conflicts of the political and economic world, and more fascinated with what happens within the human mind. He declared he had discovered that terror and violence do not fall down from the sky but explode out from the human heart. How are good and evil to be understood? What is reality? Only by trying to understand the human heart and mind can these questions be answered, he concludes. One of the best records of his struggles with these ultimate questions is *The Three Stigmata of Palmer Eldritch*.

How can we tell who is an authentic human being? In a novel following soon after *Palmer Eldritch*, Dick gives his fullest definition. *Do Androids Dream* makes a statement he had been devising and revising for at least two decades. It evolved from his insight that a man takes on the very qualities of the evil he fears and hates when he goes to war with his enemy to destroy the evil. When man fights and kills, he destroys himself spiritually.

Kipple or *gubbish* is the metaphor Dick uses to picture the entropy that ubiquitously slithers through the universe, fills desk with junk, lives with chaos, and even unravels the lines of his text, destroying pattern and meaning. And Death is a cormorant perched at the edge of his fictional worlds, ready to fly down and tear out the heart of any character who has erected even a small shield of serenity and faith. In the Entropic Period that begins in the mid-sixties, Death spreads dark wings over most of the novels—*Counter-Clock World*, *Galactic Pot-Healer*, *A Maze of Death*, and *Ubik*. This Entropic Period ends with his suicide attempt in 1972.

We have noted Dick's fascination with the nature of true reality and his quest for the mental powers able to rend the veil of illusion obscuring our vision so that, at best, we see only as a glass darkly. All quests to find reality are painful, like the schizophrenic journey of Jack Bohlen in *Martian Time-Slip*. Two other possibilities besides mental illness exist for achieving true vision. One is the use of drugs, a method that obsessed Dick for a number of years and nearly destroyed him. *A Scanner Darkly* contains his final reflections on drug-induced reality and is one of the two books written in his fourth Regenerative Period between 1972 and 1980.

The final period is Dick's Metaphysical Period. The *Valis* novels, when they were published, shocked many readers who had never thought of religion as an important theme in Dick's fiction. Knowing about his 1974 mystical experience, many of us suspected that his drug experiences might have burned out his brain. Rereading all his fiction after those religious novels were published, I for one discovered I had been wrong in my suspicions. From the earliest short stories, clues and questions about God lie everywhere, "like beer cans in the trash," to use one of his own phrases in commenting about evidence for God's existence in the contemporary world.

Dick was a complex man with a prodigious imagination, and he was also a man driven to write. Writing seems to have served as his one sure hold on reality. While he wrote he was blessed with emotional stability and thus he almost compulsively generated words. The massive opus he produced is not easily handled in a study as short as this book must be. One is forced to generalize about his fiction, ever aware that such an approach ignores the myriad rich and varied details that make each of his novels a journey into a strange new country. He never repeats, he always invents. However, all his works share the complex universe that was Dick's mind and they are most rewarding when studied as a single gigantic Gestalt. The settings in many of the novels are similar, as are the characters. One is reminded of William Faulkner, who created an imaginary fictional world, Yoknapatawpha County, and used this mythical postage-stamp kingdom as the setting for all his novels. Dick has a similar mythical world, and although it is drawn on a gigantic scale, it is a single universe. As Faulkner writes about the pastoral world as it is invaded by industrialism, so Dick describes the transformation of the modern world to a postindustrial society. I have chosen to call Dick's mythical kingdom the Fomalhaut Cosmos, a name I discussed with him before I settled on it. *Fomalhaut* means whale's belly, an appropriate name for Dick's imaginary universe, since Jonah's famous biblical adventure, read metaphorically, led him on an inner journey, and one need read very little Dick fiction to understand that his journeys into the outer realm are in truth journeys within the mind.[4]

At the near side of the Dickian cosmos lies Terra, where the West Coast of the United States provides the setting for a number of the novels and many short stories. In the barren urban landscape a handful of people struggle to recover from a worldwide nuclear holocaust. Strange shapes creep through the radioactive dust and mutant humans hide in deteriorating buildings, sharing their environment with electronic constructs as strange as the new organic forms of life. Suitcases talk, androids threaten, taxicabs offer advice, mechanical bugs shrill out their commercials as they buzz about like demonic flies.

At the next level out from the Earth in the Dickian cosmos, satellites circle—the moon is one, but there are also inhabitable satellites made by men, like the one from which Walt Dangerfield sends down his news and music. The next orbital leap from Terra and its satellites takes us to Mars, a barren desert where a few colonists struggle to build a new life. The colonies remind one of the Jewish kibbutzim in the Negeb Desert. Two of the great novels, *The Three Stigmata of Palmer Eldritch* and *Martian Time-Slip* use this Martian setting. Moving further out in the Fomalhaut Cosmos, the moons of both Jupiter and Saturn serve as settings for novels. Usually characters travel back and forth between Terra and these outer locations.

Finally, Dick's imagination breaks from the planetary system and travels deeper into space for settings in other star systems in the galaxy: Alpha Centauri for *Clanes of the Alphane Moon*, Sirius 5 for *Galactic Pot-Healer*, and Fomalhaut for *The Unteleported Man*. Beyond even that, from the unexplored depths of space come strange entities like Palmer Eldritch and Morgo. Figure 1 (not drawn to scale) locates the various novels in Dick's imaginary cosmos.

Dick's landscapes are sketched in so sparsely that they are often interchangeable from one novel to the next. Two words define them

4. I discussed this cosmos with Dick in 1980, pointing out that different novels were set in different parts of it. He agreed that this was true and considered, at my request, mapping it as Faulkner had mapped his Yoknapatawpha County. He said it would be difficult because he had not consciously created this cosmos and thus the task would require him to review all the novels, but that he might try. He never did.

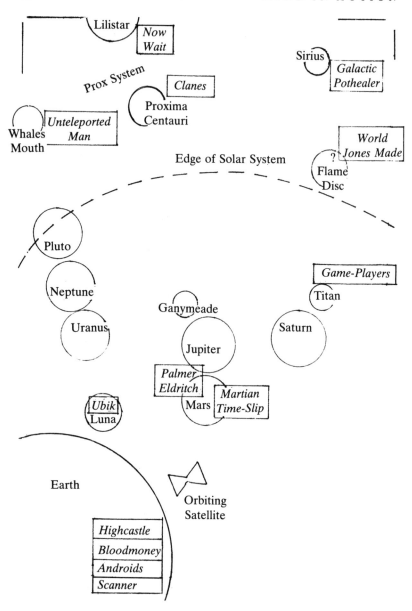

Fig. 1. Fomalhaut Cosmos.

all: barren and decaying. Earth's Edenic lushness has been lost for so long that it is almost forgotten. Men must live in a physical and spiritual wasteland, Dick says with his settings, and having made the point with abbreviated description, he moves on. He works as an impressionist, not a realist, in creating settings.

The characters who inhabit Dick's ash-gray cosmos represent a rich and varied array of humans, near humans, and alien oddities. But certain types appear again and again, even though they are usually renamed and given new faces and new clothes. Dick's attitude toward each type, and also the traits he chooses to emphasize, change from novel to novel.

Contrary to much science fiction written in the fifties and sixties, Dick's work gives substantial attention to the relationships of women and men—relationships that are always troubled. Characters never fall in love, marry, and live happily ever after. Instead they grate on each other. Generally the man in the relationship is an Everyman, and although he may be successful in his work, he is a schlemiel in his love affairs, bumbling and uncertain in his attempts to cope with the competent and castrating females who always attract him. Dick's females are never weak; they are often unpleasant.

Pris and Rachael in *Do Androids Dream* are typical of the darkhaired ruthless females who haunt the pages of so many of the novels. They are like machines or insects with dark chitinous eyes—incapable of emotions and often programmed to destroy. Occasionally the female may also be an earth mother or chthonic spirit like Juliana in *High Castle*, or she may be creative like the potmaker Emily in *Palmer Eldritch*. Only in his final novel does he create a fully realized female, Angel Archer; she is by no means angelic, but she is a warm and caring human.

Children appear in many of the novels, but they are never normal, happy children; rather they are unusual: precocious as Edie Keller in *Dr. Bloodmoney* and Marion Fields in *Vulcan's Hammer*, or emotionally disturbed, as Manfred Steiner in *Martian Time-Slip* and Jory Miller in *Ubik*, or mutant forms, as Bill Keller and Hoppy Harrington in *Dr. Bloodmoney*.

The males tend to fall into two categories: those who possess power—be it military, political, economic or religious—and the little people who are without power but who are usually outstanding craftsmen and artisans. Those with political power may use it responsibly, as do Leon Cartwright and William Barris, or they may be tyrants like Hitler or Stanton Brose. Those with military or police power also use it or abuse it; for example, Reinhart in "Variable Man" is a ruthless commissioner, but in contrast, Rick Deckard of *Do Androids Dream* recognizes the moral responsibility that rests with his job. Religious figures and industrial tycoons, too, are one half of a Janus character—either evil or good. Dick is generally less balanced in his portrayal of scientists—none fares much better in characterization than the evil mad Bruno Bluthgeld.

Another stock character is the psychiatrist, who comes in so many different forms that the reader tends not to recognize the repetition; for example, there is Dr. Stockstill, Dr. Glaub, Dr. Malperto, and Dr. Smile, the psychiatric suitcase. Dick uses the psychiatrist as the voice declaring what society regards as the norm—a position Dick usually does not espouse.

Finally, the characters Dick loves best—the little men of conviction, be they little businessmen like Frank Frink or Stuart McConchie, or repairmen like Jack Bohlen, and Father Fields. They are the ones who really hold society together. Often one of these average men serves as the moral center of the story. He is a man confused, divided, under terrible stress, sometimes nearly suicidal; but a man who finally manages to pull himself together and do the ethical thing. Three of the finest examples are Tagomi, Jack Bohlen, and Joe Chip.

Another character less common but perhaps most cherished by Dick is the idiot savant—J. R. Isidore in *Do Androids Dream* is the best example. The idiot savant first appears in *Confessions of a Crap Artist*, and we see him for the last time as Bill Lundborg who thinks he is Timothy Archer.

Dick's rich canvas of characters does not end here. His imagination spills out a variety of alien forms—the vugs from Titan; Count Runnymeade, the slime mold; live vermin traps; commercial bugs. Finally, we must not fail to note the cats. Dick was a cat lover who always owned one or two cats and they, too, find roles to play within the pages of his fiction.

This quick naming of characters suggests a flipping through the pages of the funny papers, just glancing at all the shapes and oddities, and to an extent, this is a fair analogy. Dick's method is to sketch stick figures rapidly; he never does in-depth oil paintings. Once their shape is blocked in, he can get on to what they say to each other and what they think. The bulk of any Dick text is conversation, both exterior and interior.

Nor can Dick be commended for elegance in writing style. His is pedestrian—intentionally so, I believe. He never forgot he was writing about little people, and that he was forced to use an inelegant fictional mode. He needed to sell books to make a living and we must never underrate the powerful shaping force of economic necessity. His market was the science fiction market. The ideas that interested him, however, were the big philosophical questions, and yet he had to present them in a form he tended to consider as trash writing. This necessity of yoking the loftiest metaphysical speculation with the most mundane fictional form forced him to innovate.

Dick works metaphorically and when he is at his finest, he writes as a prose poet. Like the metaphysical poets whom he admired so much, he is driven to fit together pieces that have never settled down side by side before. Donne and Marvell and Vaughan were caught between two intellectual worlds: an old authoritarian medieval world view and a new model of scientific skepticism. An analogous paradigm shift is taking place in the twentieth century, when the universe defined by Newtonian physics is challenged by the model of reality offered by quantum physics. Dick's fiction pictures the struggle between these two views. To fully comprehend Dick's innovative metaphorical mode, we need to interrupt our study of his fiction long enough to outline briefly the paradigm shift from classical to modern physics. The roots of the change lie in the paradigm shift in physics which is taking place during the twentieth century. Dick was well aware of it. An understanding of quantum physics contributes to our recognition of Dick's significance as a major literary figure.

The paradigm shift in physics started in the early twentieth century. Its seeds were sown when late in the nineteenth century physicists began to investigate the nature of atoms and encountered a strange and unexpected reality. Their findings caused them to challenge the very foundations of classical physics, forced them to think in entirely different ways, and eventually led them to establish a new view of reality based on quantum physics. An international group of physicists worked together in the research and the mathematical formulation of quantum theory. Among them were Max Planck, Albert Einstein, Werner Heisenberg, Niels Bohr, Erwin Schrodinger, Louis de Broglie, Wolfgang Pauli, and Paul Dirac. In the beginning they were bewildered by their findings and wondered if nature could actually be as absurd as their experiments seemed to indicate. For there began to emerge a picture of reality totally different from the one Newton's physics had given them.

The Newtonian, or mechanistic, model of reality—established in the seventeenth century—fits commonsense logic. According to this model, the universe is a three-dimensional space, always at rest and unchangeable. Material particles move in this space—small, solid objects out of which all matter is made. Physical events are reduced to the motion of material points in space, caused by the force of gravity. Newton developed mathematical equations for the motion of bodies and they became the basis for classical mechanics. These laws of motion permit the accurate prediction of everything that will ever happen in the future on the basis of what can be known at one instant. There is a rigid network of cause and effect, which led Pierre de Laplace (1749–1827) to declare that if indeed the position and motion of every particle in the universe at one instant really could be known, the entire past and future history of the universe could be calculated. All is determined. Eventually the medieval view of reality—which saw the world as full of mystery and magic— disappeared, and the world came to be conceived as a Great Machine. With enough study science could determine exactly how that Great Machine worked, and once understood, it could be controlled. For every effect, a cause existed. Another important aspect of classical physics is that the scientist is regarded as a detached observer of the phenomenal world he studies. His is a nonparticipating consciousness and the phenomena he observes remain the same even when he is not present.

By the end of the seventeenth century this mechanistic view of reality was established, and it was accepted by scientists for the next two hundred years. Thus one can understand the distress of quantum physicists in the twentieth century when, as they studied subatomic particles, the major tenets of their new theory emerged. For example, one tenet is Heisenberg's Principle of Uncertainty or Indeterminacy, which states that because of the interaction between the observer and what is observed, there is a fundamental inexactness in all measurements connected with elementary processes. Matter acts both as a wave and as a particle. If we determine one, determination of the other becomes impossible. We can undertake a precise measurement of one, but then we must remain ignorant about the other. Further, if a particle has a precise position, it simply does not have a well-defined momentum, and vice versa. Similar relations hold between other quantities, for example between the amount of time an atomic event takes and the amount of energy involved.

Niels Bohr introduced the notion of complementarity to aid in understanding this paradoxical relationship between pairs of classical concepts. According to Bohr, both the particle picture and the wave picture are necessary descriptions of the same reality, each of them only partly correct. Both pictures are needed to give a full account of the atomic reality, and both are to be applied within the limitations of the uncertainty principle. The concept of complementarity has become an essential part of the way physicists think about nature.

Quantum physics has other bewildering views of reality. Let me summarize: At the subatomic level, particles seem to have only a tendency to exist; atoms switch suddenly from one quantum state to another; matter is not discrete matter in empty space as mechanistic physics held, but there seems to be an essential interconnectedness of all atomic phenomena. Because everything is interconnected, reductionism—the present method of traditional science—gives a false view of reality. Within this web of reality, the behavior of each particle seems to be a chance event. Probability statements can be made, but not statements about the behavior of individual particles.

Quantum theory even shatters our commonsense view of time and space because it announces that time is not absolute and universal. Relations between events, such as past and future, become functions of the person who perceives them. In the same mode, space, while observable as time is not, nevertheless depends for its existence on the act of observation. Thus what we once conceived as an objective world viewed by a subject turns out, according to quantum physics, finally to be the creation of the subject.

A view of quantum reality begins to emerge that stands at total odds with the view of classical physics. One researcher calls it quantum weirdness. As Niels Bohr said, "Those who are not shocked when they first come across quantum theory cannot possibly have understood it."

This brief summary of the paradigm shift in physics is sketchy at best. For a fuller consideration, one can read any of a half dozen good books that began appearing on the market some years ago. Now the second wave of books is bringing to us discussions of the philosophical implications of a quantum view of reality.[5] Fritjof Capra devotes *The Tao of Physics* (1975) to exploring relationships between the concepts of modern physics and the basic ideas in the religious and philosophical traditions of the Far East. He is struck by the fact that the view of reality held by one is so similar to the other. *The Reenchantment of the World* (1981) by Morris Berman points out that reality as described by quantum physics is strange and mystical and incomprehensible.

The philosophical implications of quantum reality are just beginning to emerge, so they are not yet well defined. But a few points are worthy of note. First is the dynamic character of matter. All particles can be transmuted into other particles. They can be created from energy and vanish into energy. The concepts of classical physics like elementary particle and isolated object have no meaning. Instead of being orderly, stable, and equilibral, matter seems to be seething and bubbling with change, disorder, and process. It is never quiescent but always restless, always in a state of motion. Reality seems to be a web of interconnections that are dynamic and not static.

Another implication is that all laws are creations of the human mind. In contrast, classical physics held that God had constructed nature according to divine law, and Newton saw as his highest work to discover these laws that were impressed on nature by God. Quantum physicists believe that all their theories of natural phenomena, including the "laws" they describe, are creations of the human mind; properties of conceptual models of reality, not reality itself. Thus the role of human consciousness in creating reality takes on great significance. Increasingly researchers think that it may well be a fundamental part of the reality we experience. Perhaps, strangely enough, the universe is brought into being by the participation of those who participate. While not all quantum physicists would accept those positions, most do agree that objective reality is an illusion. No objective external world exists that we can observe, measure, and

5. Several recent books are *The Cosmic Code*, by Heinz R. Pagels (1982), *Order out of Chaos*, by Ilya Prigogine (1984), *Star Wave*, by Fred Alan Wolf (1984), and *In Search of Schrodinger's Cat*, by John Gribbin (1984).

speculate about without changing it. To isolate and examine each little piece of reality gives at best a very distorted picture of how the whole functions.

Because the conventional concepts of time, space, and causality must be discarded in quantum thinking, the systems of logical thought built on those concepts must also be discarded; one must come to think of quantum nature as irrational. Perhaps it is less that quantum nature is irrational than that our grammar and language, based on the concepts of classical physics, are inadequate to talk about it.

Most distressing of all to those who relished the certainty of a machine universe operated by the immutable laws of nature is the fact that we can never reach the ultimate truth. Physicist Fred Alan Wolf observes in *Star Wave* (1984):

> We learn and order experience through observation. Each act of observation attempts to control and manipulate the universe. We cannot observe without some idea of what it is we try to observe. This thought contains within it the seed of the control and manipulative ability we must have to gain any knowledge at all. Each act depends on how we choose to think about what we think is out there. Our living observations disturb the physical world and thereby increase disorder. We cannot help doing it. We can neither avoid nor stop doing it. We cannot become passive observers. We are active even when we think we are passive.
>
> This paradoxical aspect of human learning means that we can never completely understand the universe. The very attempt at understanding creates situations we cannot depend on for certain. Thus any process we believe to be fundamental will turn out to be only one way of seeing the truth, not the truth itself. There is no "truth itself," except the fact that there is no truth itself. . . . No one will ever know "the truth, the whole truth, and nothing but the truth."[6]

To turn back now to Dick, more often than not we discover as we read his fiction that he works from a quantum view of reality, particularly as his thinking and his writing mature. Those adjectives one finds describing quantum reality are the same ones often applied to Dick's fiction: *weird, bizarre, quirky, illogical.* Commonsense reality, with its familiar time, space, and cause-effect events, is continu-

6. Fred Alan Wolf, *Star Wave* (New York: Macmillan, 1984), p. 17.

ally smashed apart in the novels, just as quantum reality has destroyed the logical, mechanistic reality of classical physics. Dick's
plots are always in process, in motion, and never seem to arrive at a
solution as does the plot in conventional fiction. Often each character
lives in the private reality or *idios kosmos* that his consciousness has
created for him. Time runs backward, alternate universes exist,
acausality reigns. Mere accident cannot account for the view of
reality Dick shares with quantum or modern physics. Probably he
became fully aware of his method only after he had used it; as he
repeatedly said, he was an intuitive writer. But as early as 1955 in
Solar Lottery the protagonist speaks of studying Heisenberg's Principle and everything related to randomness and prediction, cause and
effect. In an interview Dick said he encountered Pauli's idea of
syncronicity through the writings of Carl Jung. Dick's jumbled Metz
Speech attempts to explain the orthogonal view of space currently
held by quantum physics. And in my conversations with Dick during
the last years of his life, we discussed the philosophical implications
of the quantum view of reality. He expressed amazement that the
mystic and the physicist, one starting from the inner realm and the
other from the outer world, should arrive at essentially the same view
about ultimate reality. He had read Fritjof Capra's *Tao of Physics*
and Gary Zukav's *Dancing Wu Li Masters,* and felt his mature fiction
worked as a metaphor for quantum reality.

Long before he was conscious of the metaphorical mode he used
to explore inner states, Dick intuited the dynamic relationship between the literal and the metaphorical. In 1953 at the beginning of his
career, he wrote a delightful little piece of foolishness that is worth
reprinting here both because it exemplifies so well his yoking of the
metaphors of the mind to outer reality and because it demonstrates
the whimsical humor so typical of Dick.

"The Eyes Have It"

It was quite by accident I discovered this incredible invasion of
Earth by lifeforms from another planet. As yet, I haven't done anything
about it; I can't think of anything to do. I wrote to the Government, and
they sent back a pamphlet on the repair and maintenance of frame
houses. Anyhow, the whole thing is known; I'm not the first to discover
it. Maybe it's even under control.

I was sitting in my easy-chair, idly turning the pages of a paper-
backed book someone had left on the bus, when I came across the

reference that first put me on the trail. For a moment I didn't respond. It took some time for the full import to sink in. After I'd comprehended, it seemed odd I hadn't noticed it right away.

The reference was clearly to a nonhuman species of incredible properties, not indigenous to Earth. A species, I hasten to point out, customarily masquerading as ordinary human beings. Their disguise, however, became transparent in the face of the following observations by the author. It was at once obvious the author knew everything. Knew everything—and was taking it in his stride. The line (and I tremble remembering it even now) read:

. . . *his eyes slowly roved about the room.*

Vague chills assailed me. I tried to picture the eyes. Did they roll like dimes? The passage indicated not; they seemed to move through the air, not over the surface. Rather rapidly, apparently. No one in the story was surprised. That's what tipped me off. No sign of amazement at such an outrageous thing. Later the matter was amplified.

. . . *his eyes moved from person to person.*

There it was in a nutshell. The eyes had clearly come apart from the rest of him and were on their own. My heart pounded and my breath choked in my windpipe. I had stumbled on an accidental mention of a totally unfamiliar race. Obviously non-Terrestrial. Yet, to the character in the book, it was perfectly natural—which suggested they belonged to the same species.

And the author? A slow suspicion burned in my mind. The author was taking it rather too easily in his stride. Evidently, he felt this was quite a usual thing. He made absolutely no attempt to conceal this knowledge. The story continued:

. . . *slowly, calmly, his eyes examined every inch of her.*

Great Scott! But here the girl turned and stomped off and the matter ended. I lay back in my chair gasping with horror. My wife and family regarded me in wonder.

"What's wrong, dear?" my wife asked.

I couldn't tell her. Knowledge like this was too much for the ordinary run-of-the-mill person. I had to keep it to myself. "Nothing," I gasped. I leaped up, snatched the book, and hurried out of the room.

In the garage, I continued reading. There was more. Trembling, I read the next revealing passage:

. . . *he put his arm around Julia. Presently she asked him if he would remove his arm. He immediately did so, with a smile.*

It's not said what was done with the arm after the fellow had removed it. Maybe it was left standing upright in the corner. Maybe it was thrown away. I don't care. In any case, the full meaning was there, staring me right in the face.

Here was a race of creatures capable of removing portions of their anatomy at will. Eyes, arms—and maybe more. Without batting an eyelash. My knowledge of biology came in handy, at this point. Obviously they were simple beings, uni-cellular, some sort of primitive single-celled things. Beings no more developed than starfish. Starfish can do the same thing, you know.

I read on. And came to this incredible revelation, tossed off cooly by the author without the faintest tremor:

. . . outside the movie theater we split up. Part of us went inside, part over to the cafe for dinner.

Binary fission, obviously. Splitting in half and forming two entities. Probably each lower half went to the cafe, it being farther, and the upper halves to the movies. I read on, hands shaking. I had really stumbled onto something here. My mind reeled as I made out this passage:

. . . I'm afraid there's no doubt about it. Poor Bibney has lost his head again.

Which was followed by:

. . . and Bob says he has utterly no guts.

Yet Bibney got around as well as the next person. The next person, however, was just as strange. He was soon described as:

. . . totally lacking in brains.

There was no doubt of the thing in the next passage. Julia, whom I had thought to be the one normal person, reveals herself as also being an alien lifeform, similar to the rest:

. . . quite deliberately, Julia had given her heart to the young man.

It didn't relate what the final disposition of the organ was, but I didn't really care. It was evident Julia had gone right on living in her usual manner, like all the others in the book. Without heart, arms, eyes, brains, viscera, dividing up in two when the occasion demanded. Without a qualm.

. . . thereupon she gave him her hand.

I sickened. The rascal now had her hand, as well as her heart. I shudder to think what he's done with them, by this time.

. . . he took her arm.

Not content to wait, he had to start dismantling her on his own. Flushing crimson, I slammed the book shut and leaped to my feet. But not in time to escape one last reference to those carefree bits of anatomy whose travels had originally thrown me on the track:

. . . her eyes followed him all the way down the road and across the meadow.

I rushed from the garage and back inside the warm house, as if the accursed things were following me. My wife and children were playing Monopoly in the kitchen. I joined them and played with frantic fervor, brow feverish, teeth chattering.

I had had enough of the thing. I want to hear no more about it. Let them come on. Let them invade Earth. I don't want to get mixed up in it.

I have absolutely no stomach for it.

Dick's technique to make the metaphorical literal is one he used again and again in creating his imaginary characters and events. As his thinking and writing matured over the years, he developed a much more complex understanding of the function of the human mind and its use of metaphor. A metaphorical pattern evolved that is dynamic, that moves. It is an expanded metaphor like that of the metaphysical poets, but it constantly oscillates both between the two polarities of the metaphor and between its negative and positive forms. I have chosen to call it Dick's four-chambered metaphor. I first noticed the dynamic quality of his metaphors some years ago; and when I called the technique to his attention he agreed, that it was indeed how his fiction worked, although he had not been aware of his technique until our discussion. In *The Golden Man*, an anthology published in 1980, he wrote the following story note for "Precious Artifact":

I insisted that this story be included in this collection. It utilized a peculiar logic which I generally employ, which Professor Warrick pointed out to me. First you have Y. Then you do a cybernetic flipflop and you have null−Y. Okay, now you reverse it again and have null − null Y. The question is: Does null − null Y equal Y? Or is it a deepening of null − Y? In this story, what appears to be the case is Y but we find out the opposite is true (null − Y). But then *that* turns out not to be true, so are we back to Y? Professor Warrick says that my logic winds up with Y equals null − Y. I don't agree, but I'm not sure what I do wind up with. Whatever it is, in terms of logic, it is contained in this particular story. Either I've invented a whole new logic or, ahem, I'm not playing with a full deck.

As I continued to study his fiction, I realized that his metaphorical method is not linear, as the comments just quoted seem to suggest. It evolves to a more complex form. *Do Androids Dream of Electric Sheep?* makes full use of this mature four-chambered metaphor, and my analysis of that novel in chapter 6 provides an example of the brief generalizations I want to make here.

The human mind, according to Dick's metaphorical mode, works in a complementary mode. Two is the smallest number; the mind cannot think of the one without thinking of its complement, the other. Thus doubles or twins achieve great importance in Dick's writing. The human mind also assigns values: a person or an action may be good but it may also be evil. Dick's heroes, his little men like Joe Chip and Mr. Tagomi, are always aware of their moral responsibility to make right choices when they must decide on a course of action.

The person who lives successfully must somehow balance his mind on the invisible edge between polarities and also between the inner and the outer view. He must be able to flip out of his head, break through the glass of darkness that locks him in a solipsistic universe, and see himself from the point of view of the other. The power that makes this journey possible is the power of empathy, which is closely related to the imagination. Mastery of empathy defines the true human being and differentiates him from the android individual whose mechanical, uncaring existence brings destruction to those around him and ultimately to himself. In addition to empathy, which allows one briefly to experience the view of the opposite, the individual must choose between good and evil. Dick

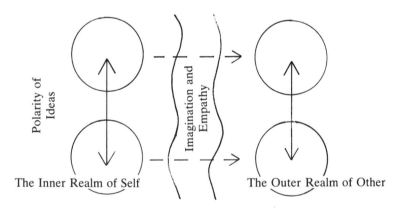

Fig. 2. Dick's dynamic four-chambered metaphor.

provides a criteria for this choice: Good is that which creates and unites; evil is that which destroys and isolates.

The individual must constantly work to maintain his balance between the pull of opposites. No place of rest exists because the universe is restless, is always in motion. Thus the mind in harmony with the creative forces must always be in motion, building and evolving new forms. To cease to move is to fall into the entropic powers that destroy form.

Dick is a prose poet. An understanding of his complex metaphor in motion, while no simple task, is essential to probing the rich meanings of his fiction. Because this four-chambered metaphor must be grasped intuitively—sensed in its entirety at a glance—an attempt to explain it as I have done here must ultimately fail. Such a discursive approach can do no more than point the way. Finally we must turn to the novels, and as we read, re-create for ourselves the metaphors Dick paints as he dips the brush of his imagination into the rich pallette of language.

2
Power Struggles and *The Man in the High Castle*

To be fully human, Dick maintains, individuals must take responsibility for their actions, but this is a difficult task because everywhere oppressive authoritarian forces try to wrestle our freedom from us. Dick identifies strongly with little people, and he is the eternal freedom marcher working on their behalf. The struggle against oppressive power is one of the most important themes for Dick. People struggle in all his fiction—struggle to survive economically while doing rewarding work, to find some meaning in life beyond mere consumerism, to escape violence, to practice political freedom, to find loving relationships. Many of the short stories written in his early period examine the misuse of power, and most of his novels in the ten-year period from 1955 to 1965 focus on various power struggles. None, however, is more successful than *The Man in the High Castle*. The novel deserves the reputation it has earned as one of his most brilliant works, and in fact it is probably the most widely read of all his novels.

Any kind of institutionalized power is anathema to Dick. *High Castle* portrays the deadly political struggle of nation against nation and demonstrates Dick's astute understanding of political processes. The use and misuse of political power never cease to fascinate and often to horrify him. But hand in hand with political power goes military power, and so war hovers in the background of many Dick novels, while the secret police often move into the foreground as they do in *High Castle*. Equally oppressive is the economic power wielded by giant corporations; for example, *Simulacra, The Penultimate Truth,* and *The Unteleported Man* all describe worlds where little people are exploited by massive industrial bureaucracies. Palmer Eldritch personifies this economic oppression. Finally, ideology—

either political or religious—is another force attempting to enslave the little man. Perhaps it is the most insidious because its fanatic leader urges the little man to submit in the name of spiritual salvation.

High Castle fascinates and dazzles the reader as it brilliantly weaves into a single tapestry images of all these powerful institutions which constantly attempt to smother the individual. The Nazis are the primary oppressive force, with their ruthless military and political power. The fanaticism of the Nazis' inner circle grows from the soil of religious conviction because they see Hitler as the savior god who ushers in a new Millennium. And finally, Frank Frink, the little man, works or starves according to the economic whims of the giant Wyndam-Matson Corporation.

High Castle is so far superior to any of Dick's previous works that one wonders what forces provided the creative matrix from which the novel arose? We can only speculate. He had achieved a technical mastery through ten years of writing experience and experimentation. Apparently also at this time he had a manageable level of frustration in his personal life. He was now happily married to Anne Rubenstein Dick, a widow whose husband, a minor Jewish poet, left her a large house and an income. She found Dick fascinating, not only because of his charismatic personality but because she recognized his genius and she encouraged his writing even when he could find no publishers for his mainstream novels. Dick had always been a Civil War buff, and his interest was heightened in its centennial year, 1961. He and Anne read Ward More's *Bring the Jubilee,* a novel portraying an alternative universe where the South wins the Civil War. Suddenly Dick hatched the idea for a novel. He would draw on his deep interest in and knowledge about the Nazis and write an alternate history of World War II. At the time he wrote *High Castle,* he considered it primarily a literary, not a science fiction, novel.

Dick had now mastered the complex narrative structure that would become a trademark of all the novels written in his great second period. To achieve this structure, he layered one story over another, and he often went back to the short stories of his first period for material. He also used multiple points of view so that the reader saw the same events from several vantage points. He was now able to write very rapidly once he had thoroughly thought out the story, and he did little revision. As he wrote his publisher in 1960, his method was to "do forty to sixty pages a day for days on end, until I'm exhausted, and then not uncover the machine for several months. But 'inspiration' is not involved; it's more that I'm unwilling to engage in wasteful work. I wait until I am sure of what I want to put down, and then away I go."

Dick delighted in his family life during the first few years of his marriage to Anne, and he knew a stability he would never again find in his personal life. He cheerfully helped with the housework, fathered his four little daughters, played games with them regularly (Monopoly was one of their favorites). He continually listened to classical music. He and Anne read widely, and among the books that interested them most were the *I Ching,* the writings of Carl Jung, the Bardo Thol, the existential psychologists, and the Absurdist writers, particularly Samuel Beckett. They picnicked and hunted mushrooms together, they participated in school activities, and they worked to improve the water supply of Point Reyes Station. The people and events of the little community provided material which served as fuel for Dick's prodigious imagination. This imagination needed to consume everything it encountered in order to meet the schedule Dick had set for himself—two books each year. He received only $750 per novel during this period and felt he could produce no less if he were to survive financially. He worried constantly about having enough money.

Before examining *High Castle,* a brief discussion of Dick's apprenticeship novels will be useful. In these novels he first used the multiple-narrative technique that made the novels of his mature period so powerful. Taken as a whole, these early novels also demonstrate his use of the antithetical creative mode that carried his restless mind forward from one idea to its opposite. He was suspicious of anything that smacked of completeness and certainty, even his own ideas. Once he had developed and expressed an idea in a novel, he was driven to counter it with another novel formulating a different possibility.

Solar Lottery (1955) is an ambitious first novel. In it are found the ideas that will leaven all his political novels and the devices and characters that will be key elements of his mature novels. His multiple narrative strategy uses three plot lines, and a favored narrator—a little man named Ted Bentley—who serves as the moral center of the novel. Other significant characters are an electronic repairman, a corrupt political leader, a vicious head of the police, a multiple-personality killer robot, and a visionary religious leader.

In the future world of *Solar Lottery* social and economic systems have gradually failed until nothing remains that is stable or dependable. People have lost faith in their ability to control their environment. To survive, they must give up all power, become serfs, and swear loyalty to one of the five large economic systems. The political system seems to promise equality since its leadership is supposedly determined by chance, but the system turns out to be corrupt.

Totalitarianism, violence, economic exploitation of little people, control of media to manipulate information, loss of moral values—these building blocks are the ones Dick will use to construct all the novels that explore the use and misuse of power. These ideas predominate in his novels from 1955 to 1965 and still stir feebly in a late weak novel like *Our Friends from Frolix 8* (1970).

The pattern of the plot in *Solar Lottery* also appears again and again in later novels. First, little men are enslaved in a corrupt situation controlled by an authoritarian figure who uses his power immorally even though he holds it legally. He may be a military, an industrial, or a religious leader. Next, the little men rebel and struggle to break the hold of the power figure, using intelligence, technological expertise, and courage. Finally they succeed.

In *Solar Lottery* Dick creates a political system that is a game. He takes the quiz game popular on television at the time and marries it to John von Neumann's game theory, which had been instrumental in developing military strategy in World War II, and comes up with an imaginary society whose ruler is the Quizmaster. Then the Challenge Convention selects a man whose task is to try to assassinate the Quizmaster. If he succeeds, he is the new Quizmaster. Thus the violence of the political game is not only obvious and legal but provides entertainment for the masses since they watch the pursuit on television. John Preston, a religious man appalled at the political situation, establishes the Preston Society and then sets out to find the mythical tenth planet, Flame Disc. He hopes to establish a colony free from the decadence and violence of Terra, where everything is "thin and empty and metallic. Games, lotteries—a bright kid's toy! All that holds it together is the oath. Positions for sale, cynicism, luxury and poverty, indifference . . . noisy tv sets shrilling away. A man goes out to murder another man and everybody claps their hands and watches. What do we believe in? What do we have? Brilliant criminals working for powerful criminals. Loyalty we swear away to plastic busts."[1]

Dick emphasizes the ruthlessness of the men in power. Society may seem to be run by game theory, but underneath that apparently impersonal approach lies something else that relentlessly drives the man who craves power. It is "another level, a submarginal syndrome of hate and desire and terrible fear: jealous . . . , a ceaseless terror of death, involved schemes and plans, a complicated gestalt of need and goal-oriented drive actualized in an overpowering sledge-hammer of ambition."

The powerless man like young Ted Bentley, the favored narrator, faces a dilemma. He wants his work to mean something and he wants to act morally. What is he to do? Bentley anguishes when he discovers he has been carrying out the orders of corrupt leaders. He muses, "But what are you supposed to do in a society that's corrupt? Are you supposed to obey corrupt laws? Is it a crime to break a law that's a rotten law, or an oath that's rotten?"

There is a solution. Take power away from the corrupt rulers. Leon Cartwright, electronic repairman, uses his intelligence and expertise to gain the position of Quizmaster and then he turns it over to young Bentley who feels power will not corrupt him because he owes allegiance to no one. "I'm probably the first person who was ever under oath to himself. I'm both protector and serf at the same time. I have the power of life and death over myself" (179).

The ending of *Solar Lottery* offers hope for mankind. Under Bentley's leadership, things will change for the better on Terra. Out in space, the representatives of the Preston Society have landed on Flame Disc where they find a tape left 150 years earlier by their leader, John Preston. His recorded voice says:

> It isn't a brute instinct that keeps us restless and dissatisfied. I'll tell you what it is: It's the highest goal of man—the need to grow and advance . . . to find new things . . . to expand. To spread out, reach areas, experiences, comprehend and live in an evolving fashion. To push aside routine and repetition, to break out of mindless monotony and thrust forward. To keep moving on. (188)

1. *Solar Lottery* (New York: Ace, 1955), p. 81.

The novel is bright and upbeat in its ending, almost old-fashioned in the values it reaffirms and its conviction that faith, courage, and hard work can undo all the political and economic corruption that has just been described. Dick was only in his mid-twenties as he wrote this first novel and not yet living under the shadow of pessimism that awaited him in the next decade.

Dick followed *Solar Lottery* with an unending string of permutations on the power theme, never writing the same tale again, but restlessly exploring the myriad ways that tyrannous structures—political, military, economic, and religious—violate the freedom of the individual. The favored narrator is always an unheroic hero—a little man—and his world is always puzzling, complicated, and dangerous. He struggles to find his way out of the maze of confusion and onto the straight path of understanding. But each turn of the plot that seems to lead out to the answer becomes instead yet another turn down into even greater complications. The legacy his hero seeks to find is freedom, choice, selfhood, spirit, hope. He never possesses it but neither does he ever stop pursuing it.

No man, Dick holds, has a natural authority over his fellow men. Granted, a community is necessary, but this need creates a problem. How does the individual maintain his freedom and still participate in the community? Not easily, Dick's fiction answers. Those in political power tend to reduce to slaves those they are meant to serve. When this happens, the slave must rebel, but unfortunately, most rebels are merely people trying to exchange one set of chains for another. Ethics is the keystone, the override switch that forestalls abuse and tyranny, but rarely do those in power operate ethically.

Given Dick's view, we can understand why stability is anathema to him because it represents a master-slave situation (since true equality seems impossible, at least at this point in history). Thus only in the struggle to free themselves are men truly free. Any system that comes to power represents a thesis. Because this thesis has been achieved, rebellion against it must begin—the antithesis must be asserted.

Dick is dedicated to this dialectical process and uses it regularly in his creative method. Once he has asserted an idea in a novel, he tends to follow it with a counterassertion in another novel. Thus *Solar Lottery,* where a religious visionary is the hope of Terra, is followed by *The World Jones Made* (1956), where a religious visionary rises to power and becomes—Hitler fashion—a dictator who must be overthrown. This second novel, granted it is rough in spots, ·is like an incendiary bomb in the ideas it shoots up. Jones, evil though he becomes, still gains our sympathy as we understand what a curse it is to be a visionary and see the future before it happens. The touching description of Jones as a child foreshadows Manfred in *Martian Time-Slip*; each child is imprisoned in a pocket of time moving at a rate different from that most people experience. Thus each must exist forever isolated and alone.

In *The World Jones Made,* Cussick, a secret service man, is the favored narrator. He lives in a world of relativism, where a police state makes certain every individual is able to express his own opinion. Into this world comes Jones, a religious fanatic. Cussick abhors any absolutism, be it religious or political. Such a faith leads to wars. He explains, "The danger . . . is in the attitude that makes war possible. To fight, we have to believe we're Right and they're Wrong. White versus black—good versus evil."[2] He maintains that "the spectacle of demagogues sending millions of people to their deaths, wrecking the world with holy wars and bloodshed, tearing down whole nations to put over some religious or political 'truth' is obscene" (33). Dick will develop this view more fully in *High Castle,* where we witness the horrors of a post-Hitler world that has been created by the fanaticism of leaders like Jones.

In his third novel, *The Man Who Japed* (1956), Dick invents a world antithetical to the relativism of *The World Jones Made.* Now moral and ideological absolutism prevail. Major Jules Streiter, another Nazi figure, had established a system called Moral Reclamation (Morec), under which peace, prosperity, and conformity are compulsory. Telemedia constantly bombards the population with propaganda to ensure "right thinking," and block committees, robot informers, and youthful goon squads make certain no deviant thinking occurs. Allen Purcell, the favored narrator, creates media packets to brainwash the masses into accepting conventional morality.

But one night in a dream state he acts out his inner rebellion by beheading a statue of Major Streiter. Later, with the aid of a psychoanalyst, he explores his inner world and discovers he is a secret social rebel, compelled to speak out against any system that claims to

2. *The World Jones Made* (New York: Ace, 1956), p. 82.

have the final truth. When this act of "japing," or parodying, Streiter by defacing the statue is discovered, Allen Purcell is forced to defend his rebellious act. He accomplishes this by a Swiftian "Modest Proposal," which he presents over telemedia. He suggests that Major Streiter had originally solved the postwar problems of starvation and food shortages by cannibalism and that perhaps the way to handle present-day rebels is to return to cannibalism, to get rid of the enemy by eating them. He notes: "Boiled enemy was a gourmet's delight"; Major Streiter toward the end of his life "ate only boiled enemy. It was a great favorite of his wife's and her recipes are regarded as among the finest." Purcell admits later that Streiter did not literally eat people, but that "in a sense, a very real sense, it was true. Morec had gobbled greedily at the human soul." Purcell concludes that surely this is cannibalism and each individual has a social responsibility to rebel against a system when it demands absolute acceptance from all its members.

The Man Who Japed, like the other early novels, is of interest because of the shower of ideas that spew from it—ideas that will serve Dick well in his mature novels. Here, he carelessly tosses out ideas from his apparently inexhaustible supply, as he goes down the street where his plot leads him. In addition to political ideas, he gives us dream worlds, fantasy experiences induced by drugs, the divided mind of the protagonist, the psychiatrist as a means of probing the unconscious, parody as a device for social criticism, and cannibalism as a metaphor for mind control.

The next novel, *Time out of Joint* (1959) pictures Raggle Gumm, who unknowingly aids the government in its war against rebelling colonists on Luna. He thinks he earns a living by being a consistent winner in a newspaper contest, but eventually discovers he does not even own his reality. He lives in a world totally fabricated by the government—which needs his puzzle solutions to anticipate where the next bombs from Luna will fall.

In *Vulcan's Hammer* (1960), a world government reigns and control is maintained by a giant computer. Once Unity, the world government, has achieved hegemony, an antithetical power arises, led by a religious visionary. In the war that erupts, one of the rebel leaders is named Chai—probably a tribute to Che Guevara, whom Dick claimed as one of his great heroes. This novel attests to Dick's keen understanding of the political processes he repeatedly metaphors. The little people resent and resist political tyranny. One of the characters in the novel explains the reasons: the masses when they "lack sufficient property to be firmly rooted are more concerned with gain than with security." He continues, "The dissatisfaction of the masses is not based on economic deprivation but on a sense of ineffectuality. Not an increased standard of living, but more social power, is their fundamental goal."[3]

The practice Dick gained in these apprenticeship novels gave him competence in handling the complex, a skill he needed for *The Man in the High Castle* (1962). In this novel he uses a large cast of characters and four different narratives that dramatize power struggles in the political, military, and economic world. He also pictures the antithesis of those who strive to dominate—the artist or the craftsman whose only desire is to do his work well.

High Castle is generally read as a political novel exploring Nazism. But Nazi ideology—one that became a religion for its followers—is balanced by another worldview, that of Taoism. The richest reading of the novel sees it as an encounter of fascism with Taoist philosophy. Dick himself emphasized the importance of both Taoism and the *I Ching* in an interview published in *Vertex* in 1974. He said he used the *I Ching* as a plotting device just as Abendsen does in the novel. Indicating he had used the *I Ching* for a number of years "to show me a way of conduct in a puzzling or unclear situation," he concluded: "If you use the *I Ching* long enough and continually enough, it will begin to change and shape you as a person. It will make you into a Taoist, whether or not you have ever heard the word, whether or not you want to be."

In the alternative history of *High Castle,* Germany and Japan have won World War II and occupy the United States. Hitler, now insane, is confined to a mental institution, and Martin Bormann is the Chancellor. This much is science fiction. But all the details of the German political and military factions are accurate. To verify this, one needs only to consult works like William Shirer's *Rise and Fall of the Third Reich* and *The Goebbels Diary,* texts Dick acknowledges he used in the extensive research into Nazism he did before beginning the novel. His interest in the Nazis began during World War II when he studied German in high school.

3. *Vulcan's Hammer* (New York: Ace, 1960), p. 65.

High Castle describes the German mind as having "an unbalanced quality," "a psychotic streak." Dick suggests this characteristic is not limited to the Germans, however. They are not alone: we all live in a psychotic world where the madmen are in power.[4] The Germanic temperament, as Dick dramatizes it, contains elements of romantic idealism, and when these are coupled with a powerful urge to dominate as they are under Nazism, the imminent destruction or twilight of civilization is at hand. Nietzsche's "splendid blond beast" becomes a giant cannibal, devouring the world. In the novel a group of Nazi officials—Goring, Goebbels, Heydrich, and von Schirach—embody these Fascist totalitarian drives, and while the reader never directly encounters the high officials in the party, he hears commentary from a variety of characters about the ideas and actions of the Nazi leaders. They have drained the Mediterranean and turned it into tillable farmland. They have disposed of the African aborigines in just fifteen years. They have taken the lead in space exploration and made the first flights to the Moon and Mars. The Germans' ability to create a grandiose "dream that stirs one" plus their fabulous talent for hard work and efficiency coupled with science and technology, have plunged the whole globe into chaos. And yet they are unaware of "what they do to others, and the destruction they are causing" (42).

The complex structure of *High Castle* uses four narratives, each with its own set of characters, which are tightly knitted to each other. The San Francisco plot contains three of the narratives and can best be understood as containing the *outer level* of meaning—picturing as it does the social reality of existence. The fourth narrative—set in Colorado—proceeds without impact on the events of the San Francisco plot, and can most meaningfully be understood as the *inner level*. It provides a commentary on the San Francisco text, offering illuminations on the inner meaning of those events. We will find that the inner meaning of the outer events of reality is the primary concern of the novel. In this pattern of text with commentary, Dick follows the structure of the *I Ching*.

The three narratives of the San Francisco plot portray: (1) *The political events,* with Tagomi—head of the Japanese Trade Mission of the West Coast—as their narrative center. He indirectly encounters

---

4. *The Man In the High Castle* (New York: Putnam, 1962), p. 42.

the Nazi power elite in a moment of crisis when Chancellor Bormann has died and the Nazi factions in Germany are struggling for control. Baynes-Wegener mediates between the Oriental and the Fascist positions; (2) *the economic events* with Robert Childan as their focal center. He represents the businessman who sells the products manufactured by society. This productivity takes two forms—mass production and individual creativity; (3) *the events of artifice* with Frank Frink as the focus for the narrative describing the creation of artifices by the individual. Frink first produces destructive artifices, Colt .44s, and then turns to creating jewelry, his most interesting artifice being the silver triangle that plays such a key role in Tagomi's moment of crisis. Each of the three characters who function as narrative foci in the San Francisco narrative—Tagomi, Childan, and Frank—regularly questions the *I Ching* and uses its answers for guidance in situations where a choice must be made.

In the inner, or Colorado, narrative, Juliana Frink is the focal character, and she also uses the *I Ching*. She is "a daemon, a little chthonic spirit," a mysterious creature who Frank Frink believes is a "direct, literal invention of God's, dropped into his life for reasons he would never know." These allusions ask us to understand her symbolically, beyond the literal level. Literally she is Frank's wife, now separated from him and teaching judo in Canon City, Colorado. She forms a liaison with the Nazi assassin, Joe Cinnadella, who is bent on destruction of the creative artist, Hawthorne Abendsen. After she destroys Joe to save Abendsen, she thinks she may return to Frank, who now creates artifacts in metal. It is she alone, among the readers of Abendsen's novel, *The Grasshopper Lies Heavy,* who intuits the inner, or true, meaning of the book. She mediates between the reader and the universe of *High Castle* and provides the key to the inner, or true, meaning of Dick's novel.

Juliana understands the destructive nature of Nazism. She muses about the ideas that came from Hitler's diseased brain and developed "first into a political party, then a nation, then half the world" (31). Like evil spores, the blond Germans spread the contamination through the universe. Upon first meeting Joe, she immediately identifies the element of death emanating from this fanatical assassin who is urged on by a powerful destructive drive. The problem lies in the fascination of the German mind with the ideal and the abstract, and its divorce from the reality of the social world around it. Baynes, himself a German, provides the deepest insight into their destructive urge:

> Their view; it is cosmic. Not of a man here, a child there, but an abstraction: race, land. *Volk. Land. Blut. Ehre.* Not of honorable men but of *Ehre* itself, honor; the abstract is real, the actual is invisible to them. *Die Gute,* but not good men, this good man. It is their sense of space and time. They see through the here, the now, into the vast black deep beyond, the unchanging. And that is fatal to life. Because eventually there will be no life; there was once only the dust particles in space, the hot hydrogen gases, nothing more, and it will come again. This is an interval, *ein Augenblick.* The cosmic process is hurrying on, crushing life back into the granite and methane; the wheel turns for all life. It is all temporary. And they—these madmen—respond to the granite, the dust, the longing of the inanimate; they want to aid *Natur.*
>
> And, he thought, I know why. They want to be the agents, not the victims, of history. They identify with God's power and believe they are godlike. That is their basic madness. They are overcome by some archetype; their egos have expanded psychotically so that they cannot tell where they begin and the godhead leaves off. It is not hubris, not pride; it is inflation of the ego to its ultimate—confusion between him who worships and that which is worshiped. Man has not eaten God; God has eaten man. (42–43)

The Nazi horror depicted in *High Castle* is brought to a climax when Chancellor Bormann dies and the various fanatical factions in Germany begin a power struggle to claim the chancellorship. Tagomi, the little Japanese official who becomes involved in the intrigue, finds it difficult to comprehend the Fascist temperament because it is so foreign to his Taoist mentality. He concludes that the Nazis seem determined to exult and immolate themselves and that German totalitarian society resembles some faulty form of life. Frank Frink, also trying to comprehend the German mind, decides it is atavistic, it represents a kind of "prehistoric man in a sterile white lab coat . . . experimenting with uses to which other people's skulls, skin, ears, fat could be put" (15). It horrifies him that this ancient gigantic cannibal near-man should reappear to rule the world once more after mankind has spent a million years escaping him.

The reader only hears by indirection about the ideas and actions of the top officials in the Nazi hierarchy who represent fascism in the novel. In contrast, he encounters the Taoist philosophy directly.

Tagomi, Frank, Childan, Juliana, and the Japanese couple named Betty and Paul all serve to define aspects of the Taoist view, and each uses the *I Ching* as an aid in deciding the right action in an uncertain situation.

At least a rudimentary understanding of Taoism and the *I Ching* is essential to appreciate the complexity and comprehend the meaning of *High Castle*. Taoism is a Chinese philosophy containing concepts also found in Hinduism, Buddhism, and Confucianism. The two main texts of Taoism are the *Lao-tzu* (or *Tao-te Ching*) and the *Chuang-tzu,* written about 300 B.C. The texts are collections of sayings, stories, and allegories, often ambiguous, that point to the meaning of Taoism. Because the Taoist perception of the real world differs essentially from our usual Western one, an easy grasp of its view is not possible. Nor is there a single school of Taoism. Many cults with a variety of doctrines have produced a large body of literature. Consequently, no comprehensive definition of Taoism will be attempted here; we can do no more than note those important elements differentiating it from the ontology of Western rationalism.

The concept of the Tao lies at the heart of Chinese philosophy. In its narrowest sense, Tao means a way or a road, and beyond that, the proper way to go or the way of nature. In the broader view of Tao given by Lao-tzu in the *Tao-te Ching,* Tao is the all-controlling principle of the universe. The natural world and all its creatures are created by and are part of the Tao. Because man is "in" the Tao, he cannot separate himself from it to define it. The first three lines of the *Tao-te Ching* say:

> *The Tao that can be told is not the eternal Tao*
> *The name that can be named is not the eternal name*
> *The nameless is the beginning of Heaven and Earth.*

The cosmology of Taoism does not see matter as discrete building blocks in empty space which can be studied by an observer. Taoism eschews this static, discrete view of reality, holding instead a view of a mobile reality which is a continuum where movement and matter cannot be differentiated. Reality is a web of time and change, a seamless net of unbroken movement filled with undulations, waves, and patterns, or ripples. Motion is ceaseless; consequently nothing is permanent. Because every observer is himself an integral function of the reality network, it is impossible for him to define it. All the separations he claims to decipher in the web are no more than fabrications, useful though they may be, and must be understood as merely fictions in his mental stream. The constant flux and incessant transformation of nature are a universal process binding all things into the Great One and equalizing all things and all opinions. Heaven, Earth, and man constitute a single, indivisible unity governed by cosmic law.

Fundamental to the Taoist philosophy is the concept of yin and yang. This doctrine holds that all things and events are constituted by the interplay of these two forces. Yin is the negative principle: passive, yielding, destructive, cold, wet, dark, mysterious. It is the shade on the north side of a hill and the south bank of a river, the essence of shadow and water. Yang is the positive principle: active, hard, creative, warm, dry, bright. It is the south side of a hill, the north side of a river, the essence of sunlight and fire.

Taoism describes reality as a pair of opposites incessantly interacting in a process; the outlook is dynamic, not static. The end is an ordered nature rather than chaos. There is contradiction as well as harmony, and there is unity in multiplicity. The apparent dualism and pluralism are a dynamic monism through a dialectical process.

The dualism of yin and yang is essentially different from Western philosophical dualism in the fact that no conflict between the two is involved. There is no struggle between light and dark, good and evil. They are complementary aspects of the Great One and both necessary to the order of the universe. The path of virtue is the way, embracing harmony between the two opposites, and the Tao—the origin of all things—is the source of that order. The aim and task of everyone, then, is to find the Tao, or way of harmony balancing opposites. Action contrary to nature (known as *wei*) is to be avoided, and its opposite (*wu wei*) to be desired. But one does not strive for *wu wei*; quite the opposite, it is attained by nonaction or nonattainment. Spontaneity, an effortless flowing with the moment, achieves harmony. All the major elements of the Taoist view are shared by Dick except on the subject of the existence of evil. Here he varies from the Oriental view because he holds that evil is real, not merely an imbalance of opposites. "Regarding evil," he says, "I am basically Zoroastrian in my theology. I believe in the Gnostic dualism, that this world was created by an evil or false deity who is being over-thrown by the Wise Mind."[5]

The *I Ching (Book of Changes)* is a classic text of Confucianism cherished by the Taoists. The incessant movement of the cosmos is not random and chaotic, but proceeds in orderly patterns and cycles. The *I Ching* outlines a rationalistic approach to a well-ordered and dynamic universe. It represents these patterns of change in a series of sixty-four hexagrams. Each hexagram is made up of combinations of six yin and yang lines (yin is represented by a broken line and yang by a solid line). Each hexagram in turn is based on combinations of the basic Eight Trigrams, all the patterns possible when combining three units of two kinds of lines. This triangle, the basis of the sixty-four hexagrams, is a key symbol in *High Castle* and is the form Frink uses when he makes the silver jewelry containing wu.

The *I Ching* discusses the sixty-four hexagrams, each of which is given a title and represents a cosmic archetype, or pattern, of the Tao in nature and in human situations. The *I Ching* is made up of several texts. One, called the Judgment, indicates the course of action appropriate to the cosmic pattern in question. Another text, the Image, elaborates the meanings of the hexagram, and these mean-ings are often expressed in poetic lines. A third text interprets each of the six lines in the hexagram. The user of the *I Ching* brings a question to the book. To determine which hexagram contains the appropriate answer, he constructs the hexagram, using either yarrow straws or coins to sequentially define each of the six lines as either yin or yang (broken or solid). Once the pattern of the prevailing hexa-gram is ascertained, he consults the *I Ching* to discover the disposi-tion of the present situation so that he will be able to take the proper action. The *I Ching* for the Taoist is not primarily an aid in knowing the future; more important, it is a book of profound wisdom, point-ing to the way of harmony between men and between men and nature. All the characters in *High Castle* who serve as focal centers for their part of the narrative network question the *I Ching* regularly.

Returning now to our study of *High Castle* as an encounter of the Fascist and the Taoist world views, we find that Dick's narrative form, characters, symbols, and themes all combine to describe a world where the harmony of complementary process has been forced

5. Dick to Warrick, October 27, 1977.

to the precarious edge of an abyss by the fanatical quest of the Nazi Fascists. Dick draws on the Taoist philosophy but—we will discover—he seems to suggest that a revision of this world view is required. The introduction into the contemporary world of a new technological element, the nuclear bomb, makes possible a nuclear holocaust. This is a development so radical and so unanticipated by the seers of earlier ages that the Taoist world view denying evil as a reality in the universe must be revised. According to Dick's view in the novel, German technological expertise and the work ethic have produced the atomic bomb. Further, romantic idealism and Fascist fanatical action have combined in an overwhelming drive to dominate the world—by nuclear war if that is the requisite price. This is a unique development in the history of mankind; consequently, *High Castle* suggests, the ancient Chinese cosmological views must be revised. The narrative traces the process of Mr. Tagomi's consciousness, which is the central focus for the Taoist view, as he encounters, grapples with, and is changed by the Nazi drive for national, world, and finally cosmic domination.

The narrative network with multiple points of view which Dick practiced in his early novels works perfectly to model the Taoist world view. This world view holds that everything in the universe is connected to everything else and no part is fundamental or superior to any other. An omniscient or a first-person point of view would not have been adequate to the narrative needs of *High Castle,* but the use of multiple narrative foci allows Dick's fictional universe to model the real universe as he understands it. Frank Frink, maneuvering his yarrow straws to determine the proper action in his situation, is aware that he is:

> rooted in the moment in which he lived, in which his life was bound up with all other lives and particles in the universe . . . . He, Juliana, the factory on Gough Street, the Trade Missions that ruled, the exploration of the planets, the billion chemical heaps in Africa that were now not even corpses, the aspirations of the thousands around him in the shanty warrens of San Francisco, the mad creatures in Berlin with their calm faces and manic plans—all connected in this moment of casting the yarrow stalks to select the exact wisdom appropriate in a book begun in the thirtieth century B.C. A book created by the sages of China over a period of five thousand years, winnowed, perfected, that superb cosmology—and science—codified before Europe had even learned to do long division. (18)

Thus in this passage early in the novel Dick describes for his reader the characters and events of his narrative network. They are set in motion when Frank, a little man in a little job, does nothing more than speak out of line at work and lose his job. As Frank grimly notes: "You can't fart without changing the balance of the universe. It makes a funny joke with nobody around to laugh" (41).

In addition to the narratives and the characters, several symbols function to carry the insights Dick wishes to suggest in *High Castle*. Two are artifices created by Frank, the Colt .44 and the silver triangle of jewelry. Although Frink never encounters Tagomi directly, his jewelry comes into Tagomi's hands and serves Tagomi creatively in a moment of emotional crisis, while earlier a Colt .44 (whether it is authentic or a facsimile possibly made by Frink is never spelled out) saves him in a moment of physical crisis. Two books are also important symbols, the *I Ching* and *The Grasshopper Lies Heavy,* the science fiction novel written by Abendsen that describes an alternative future where Japan and Germany lose the war. The characters who read *The Grasshopper Lies Heavy* are generally different from those who consult the *I Ching,* the major exception being Juliana. On the surface, the two books, one very old and one very recent, seem to have little resemblance. On a deeper level, similarities exist. Both science fiction and the *I Ching* are concerned with transformations and changes; in the view of neither are reality and matter fixed, defined, and static. The *I Ching* suggests a cyclic pattern of ebb and flow, a shifting between the yin and the yang. The connotations of the title, *The Grasshopper Lies Heavy,* propose a similar pattern. The title is a phrase taken from Ecclesiastes (chap. 12), a biblical text describing a universe where time and change come to all men, reversing high and low, light and dark, good and evil; a text admonishing man to recognize the vanity of taking himself too seriously. All three works of literature, the two just mentioned and Dick's novel *High Castle* suggest a view of a universe incessantly transforming itself, a world where defining statements are outdated almost as soon as they are uttered because reversals negate meanings.

Narrative events, characters, and symbols work together to assert several themes significant not only in *High Castle* but in Dick's other major novels. The themes are tightly related and defy tidy definitions, just as they refuse to provide pat answers. In an interview

Dick once described how for him there is a mysterious chaotic quality in the universe which is not to be feared. *High Castle* embodies this inexplicable quality and thus defies tidy analysis. Its meaning, finally, can only be intuited, as Juliana achieves insight about the meaning of *The Grasshopper Lies Heavy* in the last chapter of Dick's novel. As we list the themes we recognize the analysis is tidier than the actuality in the fictional reality of *High Castle*. One theme explores the *web of illusions masking reality*. Mr. Tagomi realizes that reality can only be "seen as through glass darkly . . . our space and our time are creations of our own psyche." The territory of sanity cannot, therefore, be clearly differentiated from the world of madness since the reality with which the sane man is supposedly in touch is unknowable. In his later novel, *Martian Time-Slip,* Dick will explore this theme in greater depth. In *High Castle,* the theme is present, if not overpowering. Throughout the novel, persons and events give a first impression which turns out to be only an illusion masking another reality. The Wyndam-Matson Corporation is officially in the business of manufacturing wrought iron staircases, railings, and fireplaces, but its illegal and real business is making forgeries of prewar artifacts. Baynes, apparently the representative for a Swedish firm manufacturing injection molds, is in reality a member of the Abwehr, a political faction in Nazi Germany. Mr. Yatabe, first seen as an elderly retired Japanese coming to the West Coast for medical treatment, turns out to be General Tedeki, a contact person from the Japanese government sent to meet the Abwehr representative. Joe is not a dark haired Italian truck driver but a blond Nazi assassin. Nothing is as it first seems.

A second theme closely alligned with the theme of the illusionary nature of reality is the one exploring the *relationship of the artificial and the authentic*. Man is an artificer, a maker of artifacts, both creative (the jewelry and the science fiction novel *The Grasshopper Lies Heavy*) and destructive (the gun and the atomic bomb). How is the artifact to be regarded? As with every question raised in Dick's novel, the answer is ambiguous. But the discussion about the difference between historicity and authenticity points toward the way of the answer. The discussion focuses on the authenticity of a Civil War Army model Colt .44 (chap. 4). The gun in question turns out to be a forgery made by Frank Frink, and yet it is authentically a revolver in that it can perform its function of killing, and a Colt .44

does just that in Mr. Tagomi's hands when Baynes and Yatabe are threatened by the Nazi thugs. The "real" Zippo light in Roosevelt's pocket the day he was assassinated cannot be differentiated from a fake, "unless you know." Its authenticity can only be proved with a document, a paper. But "the paper proves its worth, not the object itself." We can never get closer to reality than the words on paper by which we define it.

What, then, is the *function of the artist, the maker of artifices?* This is another important theme for Dick. Two works of art play a creative role in *High Castle,* the silver triangle made by Frank Frink and the science fiction novel written by Hawthorne Abendsen. The silver triangle contains *wu.*

It is a "blob" possessing no particular shape or form. The blob is a fundamental form in Taoism because at the very center of the universe, in the holy of holies, there is only a simple clod. It is utterly mysterious because, like everything else, it can never be understood in an absolute sense at all. Nothing can be understood absolutely. Reality for the Taoist does not lie in an ideal world elsewhere; it lies in the world of things—of clods. One is reminded of William Blake, who could see the world in a grain of sand.

The silver triangle of jewelry has authenticity, in contrast to historicity. It is alive in the now, and as Paul Kasoura explains, "It somehow partakes of Tao . . . . It is balanced. The forces within this piece are stabilized. At rest. So to speak, this object has made its peace with the universe" (163). The *wu* contained in the jewelry is another complex Taoist concept. It is letting things work out their destinies in accord with their intrinsic principles. Opposing *wu* is the concept of *wei,* forcing things in the interests of private gain, without regard to their intrinsic principles and relying on the authority of others.

Dick gives to the young Japanese, Paul Kasoura, the task of explaining how true art functions:

> To have no historicity, and also no artistic, aesthetic worth, and yet to partake of some ethereal value—that is a marvel. Just precisely because this is a miserable, small, worthless-looking blob; that . . . contributes to its possessing wu. For it is a fact that wu is customarily found in least imposing places, as in the Christian aphorism, "stones rejected by the builder." One experiences awareness of wu in such trash as an old stick, or a rusty beer can by the side of the road. However, in

those cases, the wu is within the viewer. It is a religious experience. Here, an artificer has put wu into the object, rather than merely witnessed the wu inherent in it.

In other words, an entire new world is pointed to, by this. The name of it is neither art, for it has no form, nor religion. What is it? I have pondered this pin unceasingly, yet cannot fathom it. We evidently lack the word for an object like this . . . . It is authentically a new thing on the face of the world. (164)

The science fiction novel *The Grasshopper Lies Heavy* accomplishes something similar to the jewelry. Clodlike, it still contains *wu*. One of its readers comments: "Amazing the power of fiction, even cheap fiction, to evoke." Taking one step backward in the hall of mirrors Dick builds for us, we can understand the science fiction novels of the real world, *High Castle,* for example, as having the possibility also of being a new form, a blob possessing wu and pointing to "an entire new world."

A fourth theme, and perhaps the most important one in *High Castle,* is *the necessity of faith.* Mr. Tagomi, in his individual moment of crisis, defines the situation of all the characters caught in the network of world crises when he cries out, "I have no faith, but I am currently grasping at straws" (211). He is temporarily vitiated by his dilemma because, while he has lost his faith, he knows "we must all have faith in something. We cannot know the answers. We cannot see ahead, on our own" (69). Each of the characters in the novel is looking for some kind of transcendent meaning in the face of the entropy and chaos threatening them as Germany in Operation Dandelion plans to destroy Japan in nuclear warfare.

The narrative movement or transformational process of the novel climaxes in a moment of choice for each character who is a narrative focus. In the San Francisco plot these characters are Childan, Tagomi, and Frink; in the Colorado plot the focus is Juliana. In Dick's novels, as he has commented, "there is no plot, but only a great many characters in search of a plot." Perhaps no better visual image catches the essence of a Dickian narrative structure than Chinese calligraphy, where a configuration of curved and straight lines forms a network. All parts are connected to all other parts, but not directly. By linear threads or veins, one can zigzag his way through the plot, but he is not given the hub of a central narrative view, with other characters circling a wheel connected by the direct spokes of the protagonist's vision. Difficult as this narrative technique may be to read, it is essential if Dick's fictional universe is to be a mirror catching and reflecting the essence of his vision of the real universe in all its forms—individual, economic, political, and cosmological.

In studying the narrative movement, it is helpful to see the fifteen chapters as a trigram with each of its sides comprised of five chapters. As we enter the novel, in the first five chapters, the transient balance of each central character is disturbed. All movements are connected, often not directly, but the vibrations of an event occurring in one part of the narrative network will be felt by the whole. The movement of the novel is set in motion with a minor event: Frank "spouts the wrong kind of talk" to Wyndam-Matson at work and loses his job. Childan subsequently is unbalanced when Frank, masking his identity, appears at the shop and exposes the Colt .44 as a fake. Tagomi's work as the head of the West Coast trade commission is unsettled when the Nazi, Baynes, contacts him and informs him of the intended arrival of the Japanese gentleman, Yatabe. This turn of events will plunge the little Japanese official into the center of an international political intrigue. Juliana, in Canon City, meets Joe, who "breathes death" and who leads her from her role as a karate instructor into his world of fanaticism, violence, and destruction.

In the central third of the novel, the second side of the trigram, all the narratives move forward to a moment when each central character must make a choice about which way he will go. The event pushing the moment to its crisis is the death of the Reich's chancellor, Martin Bormann, an event unleasing a power struggle by several contending political factions in Germany for the vacant position.

The last third of the novel, chapters 11 through 15, dramatizes a situation where each focal character is required to make a decision and take some action, but where the proper direction of that action is not clear. The crisis of Mr. Tagomi is the most dramatic, and the action he must take is the most extreme. His resolution of the mental crisis participated by the necessity of his killing two men is dramatized in chapter 14, perhaps one of the most powerful single chapters Dick has ever written. Chapter 15, Juliana's chapter, elucidates the inner meaning of Abendsen's novel, and by reflection—if the reader can grasp the fleeting truth—the inner meaning of *High Castle*.

Childan faces his moment of choice first, and it is an economic choice. Paul verbalizes the alternatives Childan faces: he has a chance to become extremely wealthy by mass producing Frank's jewelry. To do this, he must bastardize authentic art, turn it into trinkets sold as good luck charms for the natives in South America and the Orient. The wu, the authenticity, will be lost. The choice facing Childan is not simple; ambiguity is the key word in all the situations—ambiguity in the economic situation, the political situation, and the situation of the artist. The ambiguity will be almost more than Mr. Tagomi can bear when he has to make his choice. "I cannot face this dilemma," he will cry out. "That man should have to act in such moral ambiguity. There is no way in this; all is muddled. All chaos of Light and Dark, shadow and substance." How will the "inferior man" behave? Which way will the "superior man" go? (168).

Childan, grappling with the temptation to prostitute art for profit, has a brief moment of insight when he "rises to the surface," sees unencumbered, "splits the ambiguity of the moment," and sees the way. He decides against prostituting art: "I am proud of this work. There can be no consideration of trashy good-luck charms. I reject."

Frank, the artist, is discouraged by the lack of sales of his handcrafted jewelry. His moment of decision about whether he should continue his work as a metal artist is less dramatic than Childan's and more deeply tied to the political situation. The network of events leading Childan to complain to his dealer, Calvin, about the fake Colt .44s in turn leads Calvin to report Frank as a Jew to the authorities. His arrest interrupts his deliberation about the direction of his career. Subsequently he is released from jail because of an action Mr. Tagomi takes—a refusal to sign a paper allowing Frank's extradition to the Eastern German zone for prosecution. Frank can understand neither his arrest nor his release. He concludes that he never will understand anything, that the way is just to "keep moving." He must go back to making jewelry: "Working and not thinking, not looking up or trying to understand." Frank represents the intuitive artist who works out of the unconscious and cannot analyze or understand through logic.

In contrast, Mr. Tagomi is a man of reason. His moment of choice is the most dramatic, and his decision the most difficult to make because none of the alternatives open to him is an acceptable one for the superior man. In a letter to *SF Commentary* (January 1969), Dick described his method of plot development, which he employed in *High Castle*. "In my novel the protagonist's comfortable private world is disintegrating and an awful, mystical, puzzling, enormous world is expanding—from elements already there—to fill the void." Tagomi's values as the novel opens are clear, and they are directly opposed to those of Nazism: "No man should be an instrument for another's needs; philosophical involvement and fanaticism must not blind us to authentic human facts." He has faith in the heart of the good man, sometimes locked within two yin lines of passion, but yet flickering with the light of yang at the center. But each of his five encounters with the Nazis pushes him further from the calm balance he has displayed in the early chapters of the novel as he consulted his *I Ching*. Tagomi has explained to Baynes that it may seem absurd to live by a five-thousand-year-old book, but it *is* alive, animated by spirits, and can answer the questions put to it.

Finally the situation in which he finds himself becomes so extreme that he is driven to revise his Taoist view of evil in the universe. He is pushed from his confidence in the balanced harmony of opposites in the universe when he hears the roster of Nazis being considered for the vacant chancellorship: Goring, Goebbels, Heydrich, von Schirach, Seyss-Inquart. Each is as monstrous as the others. He thinks: "I am going mad . . . . There is evil! It's actual, like cement . . . . I can't believe it. I can't stand it. Evil is not a view" (92). That the world will be ruled by one among these evil men is beyond his comprehension. "We're blind moles. Creeping through the soil, feeling with our snoots. We know nothing," he concludes. When he consults the *I Ching*, it gives him no help, revealing only that the moment is one of static oppression.

In Mr. Tagomi's final meeting with Baynes, they are joined by General Tedeki. Baynes asks this representative of the Japanese government to intervene in the German power struggle by supporting Heydrich, the head of the Nazi SS, the most malignant of all the political factions, solely because the SS group are opposed to Operation Dandelion, the sneak nuclear attack supported by Goebbels. Mr. Tagomi cannot face "the dilemma of being forced to assist evil in gaining power in order to save our lives," of becoming involved in the monstrous schizophrenic morass of internecine Nazi intrigue. His moral chaos is total when, raised as a Buddhist for whom all life is sacred, he is forced to kill two men to protect Baynes. He has only one word for it. "Sickening."

The progress of Mr. Tagomi's moral confusion and despair is worth examining closely, as we have just done, because it is a paradigm for the Dickian view appearing again and again in his political novels. The hexagram, the Abyss, prevails in the contemporary world, and the sensitive heart is sick with horror at the bloodbath approaching. None can hide or escape, even the little man, because we all exist together in the network of reality. Later novels like *Dr. Bloodmoney* will picture the world after the nuclear horror; *High Castle* stands at the moment before the climax of horror.

For Dick, entropy is at work in the world, and it is the force destroying the protagonist's private world. Dick says: "I personally conceive the form destroyer as personified, as an active evil—the evil—force. I also conceive of it winning, at least in the short run, although perhaps not ultimately. Yes, it is an anti-God if by "God" you mean the "form creator," which is how I view him. I am with Luther in his belief in an active Satan who is at work all the time."[6] The terrible dilemma of our lives, as Dick expresses it in *High Castle,* is that "whatever happens, it is evil beyond compare. Why struggle, then? Why choose? If all alternatives are the same . . . ."

Yet Dick is not a total nihilist. He has pointed out that in each of his major novels at least one human has faith; the redeemer exists. In *High Castle* that redeemer is Mr. Tagomi, but disoriented by the Nazi evil, he is unable after the shooting to act again until his faith is restored. That healing process comes to him through the silver triangle, the art object crafted by Frank. It is made from metal, from the dark yin world below. And yet, Mr. Tagomi observes, "in the sunlight, the silver triangle glittered. It reflected light. Fire . . . . Not dank or dark object at all. Not heavy, weary, but pulsing with life. The high realm, aspect of yang: empyrean, ethereal. As befits work of art. Yes, that is artist's job: takes mineral rock from dark, silent earth, transforms it into shining light-reflecting form from sky . . . . Body of yin, soul of yang. Metal and fire unified. The outer and inner; microcosmos in my palm" (214).

Experiencing a transformation in his heart as he holds the shim-

6. Dick letter published in *SF Commentary*, February 9, 1970.

mering triangle in his palm in the sunlight, Mr. Tagomi suddenly finds his source of light cut off and looks up to see a policeman standing over him. Pained, Tagomi moans: "My chance at nirvana . . . interrupted by that white barbarian Neanderthal *yank*" (215). The image Dick creates here is very powerful, catching as it does the essence of the conflict his novel dramatizes: Western authoritarianism opposing the way of art and Taoism.

But Mr. Tagomi does not give in to despair; he now knows what he must do. Return to his world of responsibility. Restored by Frank's artifice, he will upon reaching his office refuse to sign the papers permitting Frank's extradition to the German zone, and in this act he saves Frank's physical life just as Frank's art has saved his inner life.

Juliana's moment of choice is so different from those of Frank, Childan, and Tagomi that it can hardly be called a decision. She kills Joe almost without awareness, once she realizes the act is necessary to save Abendsen. Her scene parallels the Tagomi killing scene, but he acts analytically and logically while she acts intuitively. Her intuitive awareness is one of the clues guiding us to understand the Colorado plot as a dramatization of the inner truth, the truth Mr. Tagomi cannot fully understand even when he is directed to it by hexagram sixty-one. Juliana *is* inner truth, intuitive, beyond logic: she symbolizes the Tao or animating spirit or reality of the universe, embodying both the yin and the yang, the light and the dark, the creative and the destructive. In her dialectical movement, she has lived with Frank, who creates; she joins Joe, who destroys; at the novel's end she says she may return to Frank. She is last seen walking "into the patches of *light* from the living room and then into the shadows beyond the lawn of the house, onto the *black sidewalk*" (239, italics mine).

She is the only one who understands the meaning of Abendsen's book and it shows her there is a way out: "There's nothing to be afraid of, nothing to want or hate or avoid, here, or run from. Or pursue" (234). Her understanding is confirmed when she asks the *I Ching*: What are we supposed to learn from *The Grasshopper Lies Heavy*? The answer: Inner truth, the same hexagram as Mr. Tagomi's. And what is the inner truth? That Germany and Japan lost the war (189), just as Abendsen's book describes. The winner of the war is really the loser. Dick here asks the reader to follow him through a series of reversing reflections in the artifices mirroring reality. In the world of *High Castle,* the Nazis really won the war, but in the science fiction world of *The Grasshopper Lies Heavy* (representing inner truth), they really lost it. If the reader moves back a step, he realizes that in the real world of human construct, the United States and its allies won the war, so the inner truth, contained in Dick's science fiction, is that they really lost it. An equation is established in which Dick's novel is to the real world as Abendsen's novel is to Dick's fictional reality. The winner of any war is locked into the necessity of continuing to fight to maintain his superior power position. The effort eventually destroys him. On a moral level, he has already been destroyed because of the horrendous acts he committed to win. The winner paradoxically is the loser. The reader's eyes meet Dick's in the hall of mirrors the fiction builds when he understands this meaning.

What is the function of literary art for Dick? According to the parallelism of the San Francisco and Colorado plots, it offers the same creative salvation as Frank's silver triangle. Abendsen is the artist in one plot, Frank in the other. Abendsen's name—evening and sun—suggests the same elements of dark and light as the yin and yang in the silver triangle. Further, according to the structure of the novel, science fiction can function as a kind of contemporary *Book of Changes,* pointing the way into the future. Juliana, who relies on the *I Ching,* says to Abendsen of his book: "You showed me there's a way." Granted science fiction is only "cheap popular fiction" as one character in *High Castle* describes it, it still has an amazing "power to evoke."

Books are alive, animated by spirit, Mr. Tagomi explains. They offer wisdom for those who have vision, who can catch the truth as it emerges in a fleeting moment of light and then disappears in the dark. Mr. Tagomi finds meaning in the *I Ching,* Juliana, in *The Grasshopper Lies Heavy.* Dick asks the reader to find meaning in his book, to grasp the relationship between the outer events and the inner truth. The title of the novel—*The Man in the High Castle*—embodies the best clue. The array of ideas Dick associates with the name *High Castle* is worth noting.

He says the particular castle he had in mind when he chose the name was Vysehrad, a fortress near Prague revered by Bohemians because of the role it played in the Thirty Years' War. He continues:

The Bohemian composer Bedrich Smetana wrote a musical portrait of this castle in his orchestral cycle *Ma Vlast*. When the Protestant Elector Palatine, Frederick, revolted against Ferdinant, Emperor of the Holy Roman Empire, the High Castle came to symbolize the center of religious and political freedom against the autocratic Catholic Hapsburgs. I used the mention of it in the title of my novel as a symbol of Abendsen's 'revolt' against the tyranny of the Nazis, suggesting a similarity between the monolithic rule of the Catholics in Europe before the Thirty Years War and the Nazi rule in my novel.[7]

Dick says that in his research on the Third Reich in preparation for writing the novel, he found mention of references to the Nazi castle system in several sources. He explains:

Various lofty and beautiful castles from the old days of the kings and emperors were taken over by the SS and used as places to train young SS men into an elite body cut off from the "ordinary" world. They were to be bases from which the Ubermenschen would emerge to rule the Third Reich. They became notorious, since not only were the men being trained into hideous inhuman behavior modes, but there was also the rumor that, like the Catherists of 13th century Southern France, on whom the structure was modeled, they were either asexual or downright homosexual. You can see, then, that the two castles are bipolarized in the book: the legendary High Castle of Protestant freedom and resistance in the Thirty Year War versus the evil castle system of the elite youth corps of the SS.[8]

Dick concludes his discussion of the sources for his title by pointing out that it is rumored in *The Man in the High Castle* that Abendsen lives in a high castle, but that actually "he does not live in this paranoid fashion but in fact lives like anyone else—with a tricycle in the driveway, suggesting not only a wife but a child, and no defenses. Thus there is an irony in the title, inasmuch as Abendsen does *not* live in a high castle or any sort of castle at all."

Abendsen has learned that there really is no high castle where man can safely withdraw, no abstract or ideal realm lying above the real world. As Abendsen has found that truth, so Dick asks his reader to discover it, too. Man is not *above* but *in* the universe, part of the network of existence which connects all things.

7. Dick to Warrick, October 8, 1977.
8. Ibid.

Dick's concern with the violation of individual freedom does not end with *High Castle*. True, he does, as he continues to pour out novels during the 1960s, move on to explore the nature of ultimate reality and the distortion of consensus reality by mental illness, drugs, and religious experience. But even in those novels he continues to characterize and condemn persons who misuse power. *Martian Time-Slip*, for example, pictures exploitative Arnie Kott, labor boss, and Leo Bohlen, unscrupulous land speculator. In *The Three Stigmata of Palmer Eldritch*, Dick declares the ultimate misuse of power to be the taking over or cannibalization of someone else's psyche. Always looking at an aspect that he has not previously explored, in *The Game-Players of Titan* he creates a world where the autonomy of the survivors on a severely depopulated Terra is threatened by alien vugs from Titan.

Dick published two novels in 1964 as complex in their exploration of the abuse of power as *High Castle,* although they have never attracted critical attention. They are *The Simulacra,* done in a lighthearted comic mode, and *The Penultimate Truth,* whose tone is much more serious. Each describes a world where the masters—those in power—use the media to distort reality enough so that the little people cannot comprehend the degree to which they are enslaved. In *The Simulacra* the president of the United States is a robot and his wife an actress hired to play the role. The real wielders of power are a committee who operate behind the scenes. The finger exercise preparing for these novels is "If There Were No Benny Cemoli" (1963), a brilliant little story exploring the power of the media to erect a political reality totally divorced from the events of the real world.

The Penultimate Truth creates one of Dick's richest metaphors for political exploitation and ruthless use of power. Of all his political novels, I consider it the most underrated. It contains a powerful statement of his political philosophy—a philosophy for which he is indebted to Rousseau, as he acknowledges in the novel. When the novel opens, the mass of the population have lived underground for thirteen years where they patriotically produce the weapons necessary to carry on nuclear war between Earth's Eastern and Western blocs. The war made the surface of the Earth uninhabitable, so the authorities tell them. They do not know that the ruling elite of the two blocs have ended the war years ago, restored the Earth's surface, and now live like feudal lords, served by obedient robots. The elite manufacture and send fake reports down to the masses via the media, reports about the progress of the war. Those in power must delude these little people because if the little people discover the war has ended, they will ascend to the surface and the elite will have to share with them their restored Eden on Earth. A rare moral rebel among the elite named Joseph Adams addresses the enslaved condition of those underground when he says: "Your lives are incomplete, in the sense that Rousseau had meant when he talked of man having been born in one condition, born into the light free, and everywhere was now in chains."

Adams faces the dilemma of all Dick's moral heroes: to assure the release of the underground masses, he must destroy Stanton Brose, the corrupt ruler of the elites, even though Adams holds killing to be morally reprehensible. He realizes that "to live we have to destroy; this price has to be paid, this bad bargain." Gone is the simple faith of an early protagonist like Allen Purcell in *Solar Lottery* that political evils can easily be corrected if one is willing to act. Adams recognizes that inevitably any action seems to yield a result just the opposite of the desired outcome. The world is deeply ironic.

Dick's final novels exploring the tyranny of power are weak. The bulk of them are written in his third or Entropic Period when his interest has moved to ontological questions and his creative energy is being drained by personal problems, drug abuse, and physical exhaustion. *Now Wait for Last Year* (1966) pictures a sympathetic dictator named Molinari who uses his illness as a means of preserving the hegemony of his country against the pressures of aliens.

Finally in *The Zap Gun* (1967) Dick unintentionally but with great skill parodies all his previous political fiction. The same concerns are there, the same corrupt forces hold power, but now Dick himself becomes "the man who japes" or makes fun of something. He reduces the struggle against tyranny to comedy—not important enough any more to be taken seriously. It is a funny book (although Dick later commented that when he wrote it he did not intentionally parody himself). In *High Castle*, the *I Ching* and a science fiction novel played a key role. Here, a comic book called *The Blue Cephalopod Man for Titan* serves that function. Like Lars Powderdry, the favored narrator of *The Zap Gun* who has lost his ability to design new weapons, Dick himself at this time in his life is close to depleting his previously inexhaustible power to generate new ideas and images. Entropy advances.

If an award were given for the most sterile Dick novel, *Our Friends from Frolix 8* (1970) would be one of the leading candidates. Once again he returns to the theme of power struggles. In the novel Willis Grams heads a Fascist police state so oppressive that a small group of rebels attempts to overthrow it, relying primarily on print media. Thors Provoni ten years earlier went into space searching for help that can unseat the police state and return democracy and freedom to the United States. Now he comes back with an alien—a giant blob impervious to laser rays. For this book Dick has thrown a ragged net into his previous fiction, pulled up some old characters and ideas, and hastily patched them together—in a haphazard arrangement held with staples and binder twine. There's the android-like darkhaired girl, the mad scientist, the little artisan. And not one original idea—a near impossibility for Dick. He has been cannibalized by his inhuman writing schedule, his drug use, his chaotic personal life. The creative forces that fathered *High Castle* have been devoured by his excesses.

Dick wrote *Our Friends from Frolix 8* at the end of his Entropic Period, but not before he had followed *High Castle* with a number of novels so outstanding that critics, when they later recognized Dick as one of the great science fiction writers, would hail it as his Mature Period. Our next three chapters will examine three of the finest of those novels, starting with *Martian Time-Slip*.

3
Madness, Schizophrenia, and
Martian Time-Slip

Emotional health never plays the leading role in a Dick novel.
Neither does sanity. Who could stay sane in a world like ours? Dick
asks. The cosmos itself might even be irrational, he sometimes suggests. At any rate, powerful forces are at work—be they evil, alien,
ignorant, or accidental—driving people crazy. Many of his characters
are neurotic, psychotic, paranoid, manic-depressive, compulsive-
obsessive, schizophrenic, autistic, suicidal. Besides that, they worry
a lot! And well they should; they must try to survive in a world gone
mad. A character in one of the novels says, "Whom the Gods would
destroy, they first make mad." The Gods seem to get busier as Dick's
writing career moves along, because more and more characters
appear with emotional problems, especially schizophrenia.

The finest of these novels about schizophrenia is *Martian Time-
Slip*, written in 1962, the year after Dick finished *High Castle*. In that
same year he also wrote *We Can Build You*, a much less successful
novel about schizophrenia that did not find a publisher for almost
nine years. When *High Castle* was published, many readers commented that except for its use of the technique of alternative history,
it really was mainstream fiction. The success of the book led Dick to
hope that he had bridged the gap between the experimental mainstream novel and science fiction. He had visions of an entirely new
kind of fiction, and in *Martian Time-Slip* he thought he was repeating
what had been so successful in *High Castle*. Again, he wrote about
ordinary people in extraordinary circumstances. He felt the contemporary world, with its power-mad leaders, destructive military technology, economic exploitation, and disintegrating environment, created these extraordinary circumstances, ones with which ordinary
people had never before had to cope. The tension and trauma drove

suburban housewives to drugs, teenagers to schizophrenia, children to autism. In *Martian Time-Slip* Dick borrows from science fiction a few devices like the Martian setting, but most of the other elements are those of mainstream fiction. The time distortions so critical to the power of the novel are used to dramatize the inner world of the schizoid individual, not to create a typical time-travel story.

From his childhood Dick had suffered periods of psychic distress—the first was his anxiety at the loss of his father through divorce. He had what he termed "nervous breakdowns" or periods of extreme anxiety at ages nineteen, twenty-four, and thirty-three, the last one just a couple of years before he wrote *Martian Time-Slip*. The inner world of the mentally ill he so brilliantly creates for the characters Manfred and Jack Bohlen was a world he knew well.

What does it really mean to be sane? What if those who are sane, who agree on what reality is, are wrong? Then the man who is labeled mad might come closer to the truth than those who call themselves normal. Dick built the character Jack Isidore in *Confessions of a Crap Artist* (written in 1959) on this hypothesis. In the novel, everyone calls Jack crazy or nuts or insane. And yet, as Dick commented in the introduction when it was finally published twenty years later, Jack survives, while "all the normal human beings, the sane and educated and balanced ones, destroy themselves in truly dreadful ways." The question of sanity is tightly tied to the question of reality. Those who share the same reality tend to call themselves sane and to label anyone who deviates from their view as crazy. Yet from his childhood Dick frequently had bouts when he slipped from the accepted reality into strange, distorted realms. What he saw there fascinated and frightened him and often made more sense than the reality that consensus declared to be true.

It is not surprising to find when we examine the short stories written in the early fifties that a number of them explore madness in its varied forms. Nine of the stories picture disturbed children, and several others are about paranoia and madness. "The Hanging Stranger" (1953), for example, dramatizes the horror of a quiet little man gone berserk when he discovers aliens disguised as humans are taking over mankind. The aliens need to distinguish genuine men from their own numbers in disguise. So they hang up a man for bait. Those who respond with distress identify themselves to the aliens as humans and they are then killed. Another story, "Expendable"

(1953), cited by Dick as his favorite short fantasy story from his early days, describes a man suffering from paranoia who believes the ants are plotting against him. It turns out they really are. In contrast, in "Shell Game" (1954), a group of men and women from a spaceship that crashes on Betelgeuse II suspect first that they will be attacked by someone hidden in the dense vegetation, and next that one of their group may be a spy. At the end of the story, as they begin killing each other, the reader discovers that all of them are paranoid; there is no enemy.

"The Father-thing" (1954) has often been anthologized and is one of the most chilling of the short stories about disturbed children. A little boy named Charlie believes his father's shape has been taken over by a malignant power he calls the father-thing after it has eaten his real father. With the help of his friends, he tries to kill it when he finds it in its larval form in a pile of junk, but it turns on him and tries to eat him. Commenting on the story, Dick said that when he was small he believed his father was two people, the good one and the bad one, and that in this story the bad one remains and the good one goes away. "A World of Talent" (1954) foreshadows the autistic child Manfred who is so appealing as he dances on tiptoe through *Martian Time-Slip*. In this short story a little boy has withdrawn into his own world and rarely speaks to his parents. He possesses powers of precognition and moves through time to appear both as a baby and as a grown man.

Dick once commented that going to an analyst is a way of life in California, that the psychologist has replaced the priest in contemporary culture. He counseled with psychologist-psychiatrists while he was living in the San Francisco area and later when he moved to the Los Angeles area in the seventies. He also read the literature in the field extensively, finding that first Carl Jung and then the existential psychiatrists, particularly Ludwig van Bindswangler, defined a view of the human psyche most acceptable to him. "Exhibit Piece" (1954) is the first short story in which a psychiatrist appears.

Eye in the Sky (1957), Dick's fourth novel and the first one to attract much attention, explores extensively the human psyche, both normal and psychotic—although Dick might argue that the term *normal* is inappropriate for any human psyche. In the novel eight individuals who are visiting a bevatron accidentally fall a considerable distance, passing through the highly energized beam of the machine. As a result, seven persons enter the consciousness of the eighth, a religious fanatic, and are trapped in the reality of his illusory world. Finally escaping his consciousness, the group next falls into the reality of each of the others who live in fantasy worlds: Mrs. Pritchet, a culture freak, and Joan Reiss, who suffers from paranoia. Next, they enter the illusory world of each of the realists: Marsha Hamilton, who dabbles in causes, including Communism; Law, a Negro physicist; McFeyffe, who turns out to be a real communist; and finally David Pritchet.

Two other novels written during the same period as *Martian Time-Slip* are also concerned with mental illness in its various forms. *Clanes of the Alphane Moon* (1964) describes the outcome of an experiment in which seven clanes, or colonies, are established on the Alpha moon for Terran immigrants to the Alpha system who have cracked up. Each colony houses a different type of psychosis. Twenty-five years later, the Terrans decide to see how each of these deranged colonies has developed and whether some of them may have invented technology that might be useful to the Terrans. The seven types of mental illness are the hebephrenic, the manic, the paranoid, the hyperactive, the schizoid, the depressed, and the obsessive-compulsive. A psychiatrist, Dr. Mary Rittersdorf, is sent to study the clanes. Her estranged husband, Chuck, accepts an assignment to program a simulacrum who will accompany the group. Angered by her bitterness and hostility, Chuck decides to program the simulacrum to kill her. Thus two of the themes so important to *Martian Time-Slip*, mental illness and domestic disharmony, are central to this novel, although the two works have little else in common. *Clanes* deserves more attention than it has received. It seems to have been buried in the avalanche of brilliant Dick fiction thundering into publication in the period from 1962 to 1965.

We Can Build You was apparently written during the same year as *Martian Time-Slip* and it is also concerned with schizophrenia. It provides the reader with everything he ever wanted to know about this type of mental illness, beginning with textbook definitions, with careful distinctions being made between the schizophrenic and the schizoid personality. The cold unfeeling Pris Frauenzimmer builds androids very successfully because she herself is no more than a machine, unable to feel love or empathy for anyone else. Missing is Dick's usual suspenseful plot that bumps the reader along from one surprise to the next. According to Anne Dick, Dick regarded *We Can Build You* as a literary novel; and when his agent could find no publisher, he gave up writing in this form. Some years later Dick reworked the material, shaping it into the powerful *Do Androids Dream of Electric Sheep?* which was published in 1968.[1] Eventually *We Can Build You* found a publisher in 1972 after it was first serialized as "A Lincoln, Simulacrum" in *Amazing* in 1969. A comparison of the two novels demonstrates Dick's great power as a science fiction writer and his weaknesses as a mainstream writer. In the former, his incredibly inventive imagination paints metaphors that show the reader his meaning; in the latter his characters talk and talk, driven to make certain they have told all about schizophrenia.

None of the problems of *We Can Build You* trouble *Martian Time-Slip*. It is a favorite novel for many readers, just as it was for its author. Dick often mentioned it when asked to cite a novel of which he was especially fond. It is in my opinion his most successful work artistically. Virtually without flaws, it is intricately designed, uses multiple settings, a cast of a dozen characters, and a complex plot. Yet Dick effortlessly controls his material. His writing has matured and here he works as a master craftsman. No other work, except perhaps *Dr. Bloodmoney*, captures the aura of lucidity and serenity we find in this novel. *Martian Time-Slip* flows calmly along, like a magnificent piece of Renaissance polyphonic music. Each of the four narrative lines asserts itself clearly, and yet they all harmonize. The author's control here contrasts with the situations of his characters, for almost all of them live in a world of chaotic events over which they have no power. The elusive magic of *Martian Time-Slip* may well lie in the paradox of a fictional structure built with supreme authorial mastery that creates a reality where no one achieves mastery of his life.

1. Paul Williams, *Only Apparently Real* (New York: Arbor House, 1986). This profile of Philip K. Dick contains a useful appendix which lists all the novels in the order in which they were written. Williams compiled the information from the files of the Scott Meredith Literary Agency, which maintained a record of the date on which each manuscript was received. In some instances the novel was received several years before it was published, and in the case of most of the mainstream novels, publication was post-humous.

All the characters must struggle to survive in an apparently malignant web so sterile it barely offers them the sustenance they need to stay alive physically and spiritually. Most of the characters cannot cope with the entropic demons gnawing away at the structures they have worked so hard to build, so they escape through drugs, mental illness, or death. But the reader, lifted above their despair and anguish by the author's control and craftsmanship, sees with calm clarity what life in this dry, barren world means. The Martian landscape is a metaphor for the emotional and spiritual poverty of our contemporary world. Dick in this novel and the next one we will examine closely, *The Three Stigmata of Palmer Eldritch*, moves from his usual West Coast setting to Mars. But he still writes about contemporary culture at the end of the twentieth century. The novel shows us a picture of ourselves caught up in our peculiar times, shows us our self-deceptions, our aspirations, our failures in our attempts to escape the sterility of our wasteland world.

The first concern of *Martian Time-Slip* is to explore the nature of schizophrenia and the autistic or schizoid child who has descended so far into his private world that he is totally isolated. But other concerns of importance to Dick weave their threads through the rich tapestry of the novel: problems in relationships between men and women and the difficulty of achieving marital harmony; the horror of economic exploitation so evil that the compassionate man cannot live with it; the mechanical world where even humans become like machines, without feelings; entropy and death; religious visionaries; the joy of music. All these secondary themes flow around, harmonize with, and enhance the primary theme exploring madness and the human psyche.

High Castle focused on the corruption and misuse of political power. *Martian Time-Slip* examines the misuse of economic power, and part of its dramatic tension lies in the struggle between two unscrupulous men, Leo Bohlen and Arnie Kott. Each hopes to gain from land speculation in the undeveloped Franklin D. Roosevelt Mountains lying in the Martian desert. Closer to the heart of the novel's meaning is the struggle of the favored narrator, Jack Bohlen, to resist fleeing into madness as an escape from the inhumanity of the game of economic exploitation in which Arnie Kott and Leo Bohlen glory. Their web of ruthlessness traps Jack because Leo is his father and Arnie is his boss. Each demands assistance in committing an act

Jack considers to be immoral, and yet Jack owes parental loyalty to the one and service to the other.

Dick again uses a multiple narrative structure, one with four settings. The first is the domestic domain in the outskirts of Bunchewood Park, where Jack's wife, Silvia, regularly escapes boredom by falling into phenobarbital slumbers. The second setting is Lewiston, where Arnie Kott, head of the Water Workers' Local, lives in an abundance of luxuries, the greatest being water. His dwelling is surrounded by a moat. Third is the Jewish settlement in New Israel. There Arnie's ex-wife, Anne Esterhazy, runs a gift shop. The settlement operates Camp Ben Gurion, which houses anomalous children, those unable to be educated in the Public School. In this Israeli school the psychiatrist Dr. Glaub works with the autistic child Manfred Steiner, whose parents are neighbors of Jack and Sylvia Bohlen. The fourth setting is the desert, inhabited now by a few Bleekmen, the last remnants of the indigenous population that at its peak centuries earlier had occupied a fifth of the planet. The desert has one other inhabitant, Otto Zitte, the pariah entrepreneur.

Four networks or webs interweave their strands across the Martian landscape, both sustaining and trapping the humans who live in the reality the networks create. Some are visible, like the precarious web of civilization that channels its spiderlike routes across the country along the canals bringing water and life to the settlers. The physical survival of the settlers depends on water, a scarce resource they share through the administration of the water supply by the United Nations. The little people like the Bohlens and their neighbors in Bunchewood Park barely have enough water to exist, in contrast to Arnie Kott, whose economic power buys him enough water so that he relaxes regularly in a steam bath. The native Bleekmen, pushed out by the settlers, wander the desert virtually without water.

The second web tying together the Martian settlers is an invisible network of human relationships built by emotional needs. This fragile network has broken in many places, dropping individuals into terrible isolation. Otto Zitte, the little black marketeer, has been expelled from his union for seeking solace from his loneliness in affairs with housewives. Silvia Bohlen, a lonely housewife, tries adultery with him as a substitute for drugs. Manfred, the autistic child, has fallen from the supportive web of human relationships into a terrible tomblike silence where he must live because he is unable to communicate. Even Arnie Kott, whose economic fortress should protect him, finally dies in the terrible isolation of a schizophrenic illusion. The network supports Jack in his schizophrenic attacks because he and Doreen Anderton are able to communicate.

The third web is symbolized by Manfred's vision of the decayed housing project in the mountains. He labels it AM-WEB, the shortened slogan of the co-op that built the complex: "Alle Menschen werden Bruder"—All Men Become Brothers. The slogan is ironic because AM-WEB represents the network of economic exploitation and corruption whose abusive power can destroy the network of cultural and human relations assuring the reality necessary to human survival.

Beyond these three webs lies a fourth, a mystical cosmic web spun by the world spider who designs the cosmos. It may be malignant: Manfred's glimpses of its underside when he descends into the Tomb World horrify him. But it may have another dimension, one only the Bleekmen wandering in poverty through the desert can occasionally touch. Heliogabalus at first denies to Arnie that his native Bleekman religion, which he has apparently discarded, possesses any power. Yet later he gives Arnie instructions for contacting through Manfred the spirit that animates the sacred mountain called Dirty Knobby.

All the characters are bound together by these networks, and even an insignificant twitching or trembling in one part will ripple its effects across the web and into the lives of all the others. The novel opens with such an event, the suicide of an insignificant little man, Norbert Steiner. Silvia Bohlen realizes its effect: "That little man's death has reached out and touched others, and the coldness is spreading. She felt the chill in her own heart. And I did not even like him, she thought."

The central confrontation of the novel is between Jack Bohlen and Arnie Kott. The first chapter rapidly sketches a portrait of Jack—husband, father, repairman of the machinery that keeps life on Mars going. Receiving a call from his boss, he departs to make repairs first on a refrigeration system that cools milk on a ranch and then on a teaching machine at the Public School.

The second chapter deftly characterizes Arnie Kott, head of the Water Workers' Local in Lewiston, and reported to own the town.

Arnie refers to the indigenous population, the Bleekmen, as niggers and refuses to pay them minimum wage for work in the mines owned by the union. He delights in wasting water as a symbol of status and rarely bothers to be civil to his Bleekman cook, Heliogabalus. A real villain? No, *Martian Time-Slip* has no villains. One of the joys of the novel is its rich characterization. Like Shakespeare, Dick here draws white squares of appeal beside those dark characteristics in Arnie Kott that disgust us. He loves good music and owns the only harpsichord on Mars (although it is out of tune), along with an excellent record collection that contains the largest holdings of Bach on the planet. He regards himself as a classicist, and the latest composer permitted in his collection is Brahms. He regularly reads the *New York Times*. He maintains a civil relationship with his ex-wife, Anne Esterhazy. He exhibits no jealously when his girl friend, Doreen Anderton, has an affair with Jack Bohlen.

Immediately after Jack Bohlen and Arnie Kott are presented to the reader, they are brought into a confrontation. Arnie, being flown by his pilot to talk to Anne Esterhazy, and Jack, helicoptering to make his repair calls, each hear an emergency announcement from the UN transmitter that a small party of Bleekmen are dying from exposure and lack of water in the desert. Ships in the area are required by law to go to their assistance. Jack responds immediately, while Arnie orders his pilot to disregard the call. The pilot, afraid to disobey the law, ignores Arnie's order and lands his ship. While the two men give water to the Bleekmen, the pilot tells Jack about Kott, who ordered him to disregard the call for help. Jack walks to the copter and confronts the bald, well-fed man inside:

> "Doesn't it make you feel good to know you saved the lives of five people?"
> Arnie replied, "Five niggers, you mean. I don't call that saving five people. Do you?"
> "Yeah, I do," Jack said. "And I intend to continue doing so."[2]

The Bleekmen thank Jack as they leave and give him a present, a water witch. They assure him it will bring him water, the source of life, any time he needs it. When Jack examines the water witch, he finds it has a face and vague limbs, the mummified remains of a once

2. *Martian Time-Slip* (New York: Ballantine Books, 1964), p. 29.

living creature. He shivers because "the face was oddly human, a wizened, suffering face, as if it had been killed while crying out."

This is the critical scene in *Martian Time-Slip*, a scene that Arnie Kott will live again in the final chapter of the novel when he attempts to travel to the past to remake it to his advantage. There, ironically, he learns too late that a helping hand can be given only at the moment another human cries out in need.

The multiple strands of the plot unfold with great economy following the opening section that has introduced the key characters, themes, and conflicts. As I reread *Martian Time-Slip* I am always reminded of the density and pace of a Shakespearean play. Each chapter of the novel contains several short, brilliant scenes. Only a space break on the page signals the move from one setting and its cast of characters to another. Yet so tightly related are the various threads that the story never unravels into chaos, except in the deliberately repeated scene in the middle of the novel when Jack slips out of normal time into the confusion of schizophrenia.

In suburbia, Silvia and her son David aid their neighbors, the Steiners, as best they can after Norbert Steiner commits suicide. Silvia entertains her father-in-law when he comes to visit from Earth. She allows herself to be seduced by Otto Zitte and afterwards regrets it.

In New Israel Dr. Glaub works at the school for anomalous children while he worries about money and dreams of gaining status. He is elated when Arnie Kott contacts him. Perhaps now, he schemes, a door will open to lead him from his mean, sterile life.

The central action of the story occurs in Lewiston in Arnie's luxurious quarters in the Union Hall. There he collects people useful to him: Doreen Anderton for sex and company, Heliogabalus for cooking, and Jack Bohlen ostensibly to repair his decoding machine but actually because he plans to pay back Jack for insulting him in the desert when he refused to share water. When he learns through a tip from Anne that the UN plans to buy land in the FDR Mountains, his problem is to discover the exact location. He quizzes Helio about Dirty Knobby, the oracular rock in the desert that, superstition has it, can answer questions about the future.

People suffering from schizophrenia also have precognition, he muses. So when Helio refuses to aid him in finding Dirty Knobby, he jumps at the idea of procuring a precog schizophrenic from Camp BG

through the psychiatrist, Milton Glaub. Glaub agrees and provides
Manfred Steiner, blonde ten-year-old son of Jack's neighbors, the
Steiners. But Manfred is out of phase with time as normal people
experience it and he cannot communicate. Arnie schemes to have
Jack build a machine that will alter time for Manfred and thus allow
him to talk. Jack is drawn to Manfred, recognizing in the child's
isolation a condition similar to the isolation he suffered in schizophrenic attacks back on Earth. He has no idea that Arnie's hidden
purpose is to learn about the location in the FDR Mountains. He is
equally unaware that his father's real purpose in coming to Mars is to
buy real estate.

An intuitive vision that he cannot yet understand warns Jack
about the exploitative maneuver in which he is about to participate.
He sees Dr. Glaub disappear, as his perceptions alter:

> He saw the psychiatrist under the aspect of absolute reality: a thing
> composed of cold wires and switches, not a human at all, not made of
> flesh. The fleshy trappings melted and became transparent, and Jack
> Bohlen saw the mechanical device beyond. Yet he did not let his terrible
> state of awareness show; he continued to nurse his drink; he went on
> listening to the conversation and nodding occasionally. Neither Dr.
> Glaub nor Arnie Kott noticed.
>
> But the girl did. She leaned over and said softly in Jack's ear,
> "Aren't you feeling well?" (94)

Doreen Anderton's empathetic response to his attack opens the door
to a friendship possible only because Doreen had a brother who also
was a schizophrenic. Later when they are alone she explains to Jack:

> "I used to try like hell to comprehend what it was Clay—my brother—
> saw and heard. I couldn't say. I know that his world was absolutely
> different from the rest of ours in the family. He killed himself, like
> Steiner did . . . . The existential psychiatrists often say to let them go
> ahead and take their lives; it's the only way for some of them . . . the
> vision becomes too awful to bear."
>
> Jack said nothing.
>
> "Is it awful?" Doreen asked.
>
> "No. Just—disconcerting." He struggled to explain. "There's no
> way you can work it in with what you're supposed to see and know; it
> makes it impossible to go on, in the accustomed way."
>
> "Don't you very often try to pretend, and sort of go along with it,
> by acting? Like an actor?" When he did not answer, she said, "You
> tried to do that in there, just now."

"I'd love to fool everybody," he conceded. "I'd give anything if I could go on acting it out, playing a role. But that's a real split—there's no split up until then, they're wrong when they say it's a split in the mind. If I wanted to keep going entire, without a split, I'd have to lean over and say to Dr. Glaub—" He broke off.

"Tell me." the girl said.

"Well, he said, taking a deep breath, "I'd say, Doc, I can see you under the aspect of eternity and you're dead. That's the substance of the sick, morbid vision. I don't want it. I didn't ask for it." (96)

Eventually Leo Bohlen explains the purpose of his visit to his son. His syndicate is going to buy up land in the mountains before the UN actually takes over this land. Then they will resell it to the UN for a big profit. Leo has come to Mars to stake his claim as required by law. Jack's response is immediate: "You're gypping the entire population of Earth—they're the ones who'll have to put up all the money. You're increasing the costs of this project in order to make a killing."

"But Jack, that's what's meant by land speculation," Leo replies, puzzled that Jack should question the practice.

Looking at his father, Jack thinks that Leo is insane. Yet he knows that according to the ways of the business world, his father is not insane at all. It is Jack who is insane to question the practice. Nevertheless, Jack clings to his conviction, telling his father: "I can only repeat: It's immoral, what you're doing."

Jack finally recognizes why Arnie Kott has asked him to help Manfred, that Arnie is trying to learn the location of the UN site. Arnie's only interest in Manfred has been exploitative. Again, as with his father, he is appalled. He anticipates with dread Arnie's anger when he discovers that the site has already been claimed and that it was Jack's father who staked the claim.

Chapters 10 through 12 contain the most bizarre and dramatically original section of the novel. Dick draws the scene from Jack Bohlen's point of view as he suffers a schizophrenic attack and lives through the confrontation with Arnie several times before it happens. The reader plunges into Jack's faltering, chaotic perceptions, which have in turn been dragged down into the schizoid world of Manfred. Normal perceptions of time and space, cause and effect— they all collapse into the Tomb World where the Buggler disintegrates the world with age, rot, and dust until only gubble remains. *Gubble* is the single word Manfred is able to utter. In his nightmare visions Manfred experiences himself as an old man, hardly human, kept alive with pumps and hoses and dials, lying helplessly in the decayed UN buildings. Beyond that monstrous future lies the horror of the void. While Manfred watches, great things like slugs land and begin to dig and,

> He saw a hole as large as a world; the earth disappeared and became black, empty, and nothing . . . . Into the hole men jumped one by one, until none of them were left. He was alone, with the silent world-hole.
>
> At the rim of the hole he peeped down. At the bottom, in the nothing, a twisted creature unwound as if released. It snaked up, became wide, contained square space, and grew color.
>
> I am in you, Manfred thought. Once again.
> . . . .
>
> The hole, beneath AM-WEB, waited to be all those who walked above, or had ever walked above; it waited to be everyone and everything. And only Manfred Steiner held it back. (pp. 166–68)

The reader follows Jack as he relives the scene several times in schizophrenic confusion and chaos. Later the confrontation with Arnie actually occurs, but Jack's mind blanks out, and afterward he is totally unable to recall it.

Frightening as Manfred's world is to Jack, it also fascinates him. He is drawn to Manfred as Manfred is drawn to the void. His urge to help Manfred escape from the silent Tomb World where he is a prisoner is indirectly a desire to help himself avoid that terrifying world. Its lifeless machine quality frightens him so much that he hates to go to the Public School to repair the broken teaching machines. The machines are lifeless, they are unable to respond, as humans can, to the world around them. They repeat the same routines over and over, just as Manfred must in that inner world of self where he is locked.

Jack takes Manfred to the school one day when he goes to pick up his own son, violently curious to see Manfred's reaction to the machines. Somehow, he hopes Manfred's response will give him an understanding of the numbing process within his mind that seems to be dragging him to the bottom of a great stagnant sea.

Manfred speeds ahead with excitement into the school to examine the machines—the Tiberious, the Immanuel Kant, the

Thomas Edison. Jack finally finds Manfred seated on the floor, staring into space. He can give Jack no explanation of what he is experiencing; he is locked forever into his silent world. No communication is possible.

Jack goes to the Thomas Edison Teaching Machine to ask for his son, David. The response of the machine? It is one of those Dickian shocks for which the reader is never prepared. The machine answers, "Gubble, gubble." The power of Manfred's schizoid world has even dragged the machines into it.

Another of the powerful scenes in *Martian Time-Slip* occurs at the end of the novel when Arnie encounters again, in his Manfred-distorted reality, the Bleekman to whom, in the opening scenes, he refused water. He pilgrimages to Dirty Knobby with Manfred, where he hopes to tap the primitive powers of the oracle and return to the past. He will alter it to allow him, not Leo Bohlen's syndicate, to claim the land the UN plans to build on. This time, too, he decides he will take care of Jack Bohlen for daring to criticize his refusal to share water with the Bleekmen. He pulls a gun to kill Jack, and one of the Bleekmen immediately shoots Arnie with a poisoned arrow.

Dying, he realizes how foolish he has been to attempt to alter the past. He begs Manfred to release him from his tormented time journey.

He awakens, chastized. He has lost his desire to get Jack Bohlen, and even his desire to buy the land in the mountains. He will even try to help Manfred if he can just make it from the desert back home to Lewiston.

Another copter lands, this time not a visionary one, but a real ship carrying Otto Zitte, angry at Arnie's destruction of his black market landing field in the mountains. He shoots Arnie just before Jack and Doreen arrive by copter to rescue Arnie. Arnie dies believing he is merely reliving another scene in Manfred's schizoid world, and that the bullet is no more deadly than the Bleekman's arrow had been.

Arnie's death almost achieves the dimensions of tragic death in Greek drama. He has recognized his errors and stands ready to try to correct them. His death fills Jack, to his great surprise, with grief. Arnie's death, he thinks, seems so harsh, more than he deserved for what he did. What he did was bad but not that bad. This loving compassion encircles all the characters in *Martian Time-Slip*. None of them is bad enough to deserve the sterile life each must live in the Martian wasteland. Even Leo Bohlen, master profiteer that he is, has the redeeming qualities of a sincere father and grandfather.

Jack gives up his affair with Doreen and returns home to Silvia. Manfred goes off to live with the Bleekmen in the desert where the slower pace of their primitive life may perhaps allow him to break out of his silent world and communicate with them. The quiet ending of the novel, with normal Martian routines restored, almost suggests a happy-ever-after ending. Almost. But that kind of ending is not Dick's style. Always one more twist of the unexpected pushes the plot, and us with it, away from the comforting belief that a normal world exists to which we can return. Suddenly, the Steiner's living room is filled with Bleekmen bearing an old man who is human only from the neck up. The rest is machinery to keep him alive. It is Manfred, who again tampering with time has come back as an old man to thank Jack for trying to communicate with him when he was a child. He gleefully wheezes that he escaped AM-WEB, that he is with his friends, the Bleekmen. The reader shudders with ironic horror at the grotesque shape because Manfred seems blind to his fate; he has become what he feared.

The complexity of *Martian Time-Slip* places many demands on the reader, as did *High Castle*. A single reading will not yield all its rich accomplishments, insights, and surprises, although it will fascinate and delight, and perhaps those pleasures are enough to receive from fiction. But for the reader who is willing to spend the time to probe deeper, the treasures are almost inexhaustible. As in good poetry, each rereading offers the reward of an insight or technique or symbol not noticed before.

The mastery of literary techniques strikes one first. In this novel and also in *Dr. Bloodmoney* Dick uses with consummate artistry the multiple narratives and points of view he had been practicing in his earlier fiction. Here he also uses omniscience, something new for him. His usual custom had been to enter the consciousness of several of his favored narrators, and for the other characters he presented only an external view. Now in *Martian Time-Slip* we see the world not only as it looks to the major characters like Jack Bohlen and Arnie Kott, but also as it appears to almost all the minor characters, too—Otto Zitte, Anne Esterhazy, Dr. Glaub, Silvia Bohlen. The result is a richness and depth of characterization that makes us feel sympathy and compassion for each individual. The economy in characterization is impressive—a rapid sketching with sure strokes, like an artist bringing a character to life on a sketch pad while we watch. The sure choice of details that accomplishes the transformation from words to life never falters. In a short chapter Norbert Weiner, with his tormented, guilt-ridden inner life, becomes so real that we understand the inevitability of his suicide. Dick's characterization is not always as successful in some of the novels of his next period.

The characterization of the women here is particularly rich, too. Critics have often condemned Dick for the hard, ruthless women he so often uses in his novels and have suggested he is not very successful at understanding the female psyche and drawing a sympathetic picture of it. The criticism is justified in many of the novels, but not this one. Doreen Anderton, Anne Esterhazy, and Silvia Bohlen are all appealing women.

A Dick novel is never without powerful metaphors and symbols, and they work particularly well in this novel. The desert, as we noted earlier, represents the barren contemporary world where the little canals carrying the water of human love and concern so precariously sustain our psychic lives. The teaching machines at the school are the first major use of a symbol that will later become one of Dick's most important. The machine stands for the rigid, unresponsive human who cannot or will not use his empathetic powers to make contact with others. Music, always significant to Dick, represents the harmony that can heal, and it is used in the BG camp as therapy for the anomalous children. Finally, there is that shrunken water witch, the talisman of the primitive Bleekmen. With its little shriveled face crying out, it symbolizes what has happened to the spiritual nature of man as it struggles to survive in the sterility of the contemporary world.

Dick offers penetrating insights into the nature of schizophrenia and the schizoid or autistic personality—the frozen prison house into which the individual falls when he loses contact with objective reality and becomes totally locked in his own subjectivity. Through Manfred's perceptions we listen to the sights and sounds of entropy as it decays and gobbles the structures of the universe; and we journey with him into the black horror of death that torments human consciousness when it first discovers it is not immortal. Schizophrenia continues to haunt Dick and he probes deeply into the nature of mental illness again in *Dr. Bloodmoney* and *The Simulacra*, novels he wrote within the next year.

Martian Time-Slip, even given its subject matter of decay, madness, and death, is not a work of darkness. It is saved first by its light touches, like the geographical names—the William Butler Yeats Canal and the FDR Mountains, for example. And the Public School with its teaching machines—the Aristotle machine teaches philosophy and the Sir Francis Drake machine teaches English history. This gentle humor undercuts the horror, as though Dick were saying, "Don't take all this too seriously. It's a kind of joke between us. Remember, this is only an imaginary world and neither Jack Bohlen nor I am really crazy." The Dickian black humor does not appear until later.

Finally the moral wisdom of *Martian Time-Slip* shines through all the pages, from the opening scene when Jack brings water to the final scene when he sets off in the dark with a light searching for Erma Steiner. Dick reminds us of what we have forgotten in our affluence. The resources of the Earth like water must be husbanded and shared because they are necessary to sustain physical life. Just as necessary to sustain the emotional life of humans is the flow of love between individuals.

The powerful impact of the novel lies in its terrible sincerity. The Martian world may be imaginary, but Jack's struggle to escape the Tomb World of mental illness is real. It is the struggle today of Everyman who is sensitive and intelligent and must watch the deadly fruits of human greed. It was Dick's constant struggle: How to survive after you have fallen out of the comfort of a conventional reality that assures you everything is going well and will end happily. After you have seen another reality, a vision of eternity so frightening it paralyzes you.

Jack understands the power of the vision:

> "It's designed to make you flee—the vision's for that purpose, to nullify your relations with other people, to isolate you. If it's successful, your life with human beings is over. That's what they mean when they say the term schizophrenia isn't a diagnosis; it's a prognosis—it doesn't say anything about what you have, only about how you'll wind up." *And I'm not going to wind up like that*, he said to himself. Like Manfred

Steiner, mute and in an institution; I intend to keep my job, my wife and son, my friendships . . . . Yes, and even love affairs, if such there be. *I intend to keep trying.* (97)

Philip Dick kept trying, too. He did it by writing, by creating imaginary worlds where ordinary people do survive, where unheroic people like electronic repairmen fix things and thus keep entropy at bay. He would rarely fail in the brilliance of his ideas and metaphors, but often he would not be as successful as he is in *Martian Time-Slip* in weaving all the complex parts into a whole. Here he dances along a tightrope of rationality and control stretched precariously over the chaos of insanity, and he never for a moment loses his balance.

4
Holocaust, Survival, and *Dr. Bloodmoney*

It happened when Philip Dick was seventeen years old. On the morning of August 6, 1945, a U.S. B-29 flew high over Hiroshima in southern Japan. The entire landscape was suddenly lit by a blue white flash that turned into a giant fireball. The first thermonuclear bomb in history spread death and destruction for miles around. One hundred forty thousand people died in Hiroshima, and another 70,000 died in Nagasaki three days later when a second bomb was dropped. The world was shocked into a new reality. No single individual saw what the Fall meant more immediately, more clearly, and with more horror than Dick. The barren holocaust landscape with its gray ash and devastated buildings became almost a trademark of his novels. Again and again he sketched his vision of what the world would be like if men did not learn to live peacefully together. The warning shocks us because of the technique he uses: He juxtaposes the horrors of an atomic holocaust with the trivialities of daily life in suburbia.

Almost one third of his novels and a number of his short stories use this postholocaust setting. But only in a very few works does the atomic bomb actually explode and *Dr. Bloodmoney, or How We Got Along After the Bomb* (1965) is the best of them. To understand it most fully, one should also read its twin, *The Simulacra*, written at about the same time. *Dr. Bloodmoney* has as its focal character a physicist who suffers from paranoid schizophrenia while the matching character in *The Simulacra* is an artist suffering from a similar mental derangement. *Dr. Bloodmoney* was completed early in 1963, just a few months after Dick had finished *Martian Time-Slip* (and according to him was based on an unpublished mainstream novel, *Voices from the Street*). *The Simulacra* was also written in 1963, and apparently finished about six months after *Dr. Bloodmoney*.

Most people shared Dick's extreme anxiety about nuclear warfare. But despite the horrified outcry of the world after the explosions in Japan in 1945, the U.S. government continued research and testing of atom bombs. In 1949 Russia tested its first bomb and the atomic race between the two superpowers began. Scientists split in their opinions about whether this continued development was morally acceptable. Physicist Edward Teller, who had worked on the original research under Enrico Fermi during World War II, was one of the most outspoken of those who defended the bomb. In 1952 he became a professor of physics at the University of California and director of the Livermore division of its radiation laboratory.

Teller and his hydrogen bomb were anathema to Dick, whose visions of nuclear destruction tormented him so powerfully that he held anyone must be mad to continue building bombs. Dr. Bruno Bluthgeld, the physicist in the novel, is a thinly disguised Teller, born in Hungary just as Teller was, and employed in the radiation lab at Livermore before that apocalyptic day in 1988 when the power of his mad mind hurls bombs down to destroy the world.

The devastation of the explosion occurring in urban Berkeley and rural Marin County to the north is described in the early chapters of *Dr. Bloodmoney,* and the remainder of the novel pictures life in city and country seven years later. *The Simulacra,* in contrast, focuses on the political and economic events that lead to an atomic war, and the mushroom cloud of destruction does not appear over northern California until the final chapter of the novel.

Only two other works in the whole Dick canon picture the bombs actually falling. In "Breakfast at Twilight" (1954) Tim and Mary McLean and their three children awake one morning to a strange world shrouded in fog. Soldiers crash through their front door and demand to know how their house has withstood the night's bombing. They discover they have somehow been plummeted seven years into the future and the third world war. The next night's bombing sends them back into their own time, where McLean is afraid to tell his neighbors about what he has seen because he senses they do not want to hear about the horror that awaits them.

The Man Who Japed, set in the twenty-second century, contains one brief scene where an atomic explosion is simulated in a museum exhibit of a twentieth century house complete with robot mannikins. The exhibit is labeled "How they lived and died." When a button is pushed, the house is blown up and a ruined cellar remains where the haggard mannikins now huddle, their clothing in shreds and their skin seared with radiation burns.

Although Dick rarely pictures atomic warfare, explosions do often occur in his fiction. He uses the explosion as a metaphor for the event that shatters the illusions an individual believes to be truth and reality. As an example, take the very early story "Imposter" (1953), where Spence Olham works on a research project whose purpose is to find a new means to defeat the threatening aliens from Alpha Centauri. One day he is accused of being a humanoid robot spy landed by the aliens as a replacement for the real Olham. The robot contains a bomb that will explode and ruin the research project. His accusers plan to destroy him despite his protestations that he is a human, not a robot. Desperately trying to save himself, he finds a wrecked spy ship and what is apparently the remains of the robot. But in the surprise ending, it turns out to be the body of the real Olham, and Olham discovers, just before he blows up, that he really is a robot.

What is reality? Dick asks again and again. Never what it first appears to be. When our illusions are shattered and we fall into another reality, we *may* begin to discover truth. But on the other hand, the new may be another illusion as false as the old.

Dick's prodigious output of fiction in the period from 1961 through 1965 is almost unbelievable because so much of it is of outstanding quality. But it sprang from more than pure genius and unfailing imagination. He worked long, long hours. He also constantly mined old short stories for ideas, and he occasionally got double mileage from a piece by publishing it first as a short story and then expanding it into a novel. For instance, "Novelty Act," published in *Fantastic* in February 1964 is about Americans who hope to be invited to the White House to perform for the president's wife, Nicole Thibodeaux. This material becomes part of *The Simulacra,* which was published later the same year. Ideas from several 1950s stories become part of *Dr. Bloodmoney.* "The Crawlers" describes the babies born to people working in a radiation lab. They are strange mutant forms with wormlike bodies and wizened little heads—very much like the little brother Edie Keller carries within her in *Dr. Bloodmoney.* "Null-O" (1958) is the story of Lemuel, a little boy so destructive his parents take him to a psychiatrist for help. The psychiatrist diagnoses Lemuel as a mutant form with high intelligence, complete logic, and no emotions—he has the potential for becoming a scientist. So Lemuel is sent to join a group of scientists who have planned the C bomb to blow up the surface of the Earth, the E bomb to blow up the Earth itself, the G bomb to blow up the galaxy, and finally the U bomb, which will unify everything by destroying form. The mad scientists in this little story foreshadow Dr. Bluthgeld, and—an interesting note—Lemuel reads *Mein Kampf*. Jim Fergesson, a character in "Pay for the Printer" (1956), lives in a postholocaust world where things are running down and a bloblike life form from Proxima is the only entity able to make replacements. When it dies, Jim decides he must learn to make things himself, to take responsibility in his small way for rebuilding the world. This is the course that Stuart McConchie follows in *Dr. Bloodmoney*, when his boss, Jim Fergesson, who kept the TV store going, is killed by the Bomb.

Dr. Bloodmoney glows with the same sense of control and harmony that gives *Martian Time-Slip* its charm, which is not surprising since one novel followed immediately after the other. It is generally regarded as the most utopian of all his novels, although that adjective suggests an optimism hardly consonant with Dick's bleak visions of the future. Perhaps the novel can better be described as offering some small hope that a future is possible—if we are willing to learn spiritual values as we cross over the late twentieth century sea of economic and political violence. The little group gathered in Berkeley at the novel's end have finally discovered how necessary sharing and cooperation and love are if they are to survive.

Along with mining old material for characters and ideas, Dick also used real people and events, particularly from his life at Point Reyes Station, as more bricks to shape the novel. *Dr. Bloodmoney* provides a nice demonstration of this technique so constantly used by Dick because its settings—Marin County and Berkeley—are ones Anne Dick knows well and she has been generous in pointing out the sources for his settings and also for some of the characters and events. For example, Anne and Phil were both interested in mushroom hunting. They attended school board meetings together at the school where one of the science teachers resembled Mr. Barnes. The bright and imaginative Edie is very much like one of Dick's little stepdaughters. Phil himself had briefly been a disk jockey like Walt Dangerfield, and in 1963, the year the novel was written, John Glenn first orbited the Earth in satellite. The thalidomide-damaged babies in England provided the prototype for Hoppy Harrington. The television repair store matches almost exactly the one where Phil worked in Berkeley (the street address is even the same) and Phil's boss Herb Hollis was very much like the store owner Jim Fergesson who is killed by the bomb. Phil and Anne Dick were both seeing a former psychiatrist, Dr. Anderton, doing general practice in Point Reyes Station, and he becomes the Dr. Stockstill of the novel.

These people, places, and events of course are not the whole of *Dr. Bloodmoney*. Nor are the musical and literary allusions that so abundantly enrich the novel. They are all important elements. So is the use of pairs of settings—Marin County and Berkeley; the use of pairs of times—1981 and 1988; the use of pairs of characters—Edie and Bill, Bluthgeld and Hoppy. And the use of inner and outer states, madness and sanity. And the use of mutant animals and normal animals. And the . . . . The list of doubles goes on, but finally the novel is more than a sum of the parts. Dick's remarkable inventive powers and bizarre vision combine all these elements into an intricate gestalt. The bonds between all the many parts seem strained in anguish on some occasions and relaxed in harmony on others. Thus as he finishes the book, the reader has an ambivalent response: both a dread and a hope for the future that may evolve from our present world.

The cast of characters in the novel is large—over twenty of them and even the minor ones are sketched with sure details that bring them vividly to life. At least ten characters are of major importance in the novel and each of them is fully drawn and memorable. To accomplish this feat, Dick uses the omniscient point of view as he did in *Martian Time-Slip,* a rather uncommon method for him. His usual point-of-view technique during this period is to use a favored narrator in each of his several settings and to take us into the inner worlds of only these favored narrators. But in *Dr. Bloodmoney* he takes the reader into the mind of almost every character—showing us so-called consensus reality as its events are perceived by the mind of a paranoid scientist, a bright little girl, a kindly Negro repairman, a mutant human born without arms and legs, and many others. Each time we see Marin County from another person's vantage point, it changes into another world, thus dramatizing with great power Dick's conviction that the outer reality we perceive is not fixed but rather a projection of the inner world.

Dick confidently moves in and out of the minds of a large number of characters, both sane and psychotic. He moves just as confidently back and forth between the two West Coast locations— urban Berkeley and rural Marin County. He also takes his reader to the Dangerfield satellite, the encapsulated microcosm high in the sky that daily circles the larger globe below. In pivotal chapters, short though all the fifteen chapters are, he may make as many as five or six such moves, using only the mention of another character's name as a clue to the reader that he has entered another mind. For instance, in chapter 5, the day the bomb falls, we witness the event through the perceptions of Doctor Bluthgeld, Stuart McConchie, Walt Dangerfield, Doctor Stockstill, Hoppy Harrington, and finally, Bonny Keller. Each witnesses and responds to the event in a totally different way. In chapter 13, the day the bombs again begin to fall, we experience the catastrophe from the view of Bill Keller, Doctor Bluthgeld, Walt Dangerfield, Edie Keller, and Bonny Keller.

Dick uses a dislocation of time continuity. The first three chapters describe Shattuck Avenue in Berkeley on the day the Bomb falls in 1981. Stuart McConchie, Negro repairman, and Hoppy Harrington, phocomus repairman, work in a TV sales and service store. Across the street Doctor Bluthgeld goes to visit psychoanalyst Doctor Stockstill. Bluthgeld is seeking relief from the guilt he still suffers because of the miscalculations in his nuclear tests that caused devastating radioactive fallout in the Bluthgeld catastrophy of 1972. Stockstill almost immediately recognizes that Bluthgeld is suffering from paranoid schizophrenia. A historical event has been scheduled for noon of this day; Walter and Lydia Dangerfield will begin their journey by rocket to Mars, the first couple to emigrate, a modern Adam and Eve who will found a Nova Terra. It will be a new beginning for humanity.

Chapter 4 jumps forward seven years to 1988, where a little community in Marin County has partially rebuilt itself after the Bomb. In chapters 5 and 6 we return to Berkeley in 1981 on the day of the bomb, a means of intensifying the horror of the event. Bluthgeld watches the destruction of the city with awe at his own power because he is certain he is the omphalos of this cataclysmic disruption. Godlike, he is the first cause of all. Stuart McConchie, Doctor Stockstill, and Hoppy hide together in the bomb shelter under Stattuck Street. Hoppy, psychic kin of Doctor Bluthgeld, is filled with a terrible joy at the destruction. Dangerfield, far above the earth, watches in fright as the force of the explosion diverts the path of his satellite away from Mars and into perpetual orbit around the Earth. Out in Marin County, Bonny Keller, bleeding and dazed, walks down the road after her house is destroyed. A stranger (Andrew Gill) picks her up and they make love in the back of his Volkswagen bus. From this union comes the strange child Edie. She bears within her the homunculus Bill, who alone will have the power to nullify Hoppy's attempts to take over the world. (Parenthetically, one notes this strange set of twins, one alive, one unborn and wonders about its sources in Dick's own psyche, wounded by his twin sister's death at birth.)

The concluding nine chapters jump forward again to 1988 and record the efforts of the survivors to rebuild their world after the Bomb. The pre-Bomb world cannot be precisely restored because the effects of the destruction and radiation are too great to be reversed. There are "freaks and funnies," radiation-darkies, and brilliant animals. A rat is reported to play a nose-flute, tabby cats to craft objects from tin-can lids, and dogs to talk. Of the many freaks or mutant humans, Bonny's seven-year-old daughter Edie is one of the strangest. Her unborn twin brother Bill lives in her abdomen in a wizened embryo form, and they talk regularly in private as she describes the world to him. Hoppy achieves a status he never had in the old world because now the skill of building and repairing machines and equipment is highly valued.

The post-Bomb story is told through multiple narratives—Dick's usual mode at this point in his career. In the Dangerfield narrative, Walt circles endlessly in his satellite, using his communication system to talk with those below. His is the one voice that unifies the world as he reads literature, plays music, shares advice and news—ever trying to maintain his cheerful stance in spite of depression and illness. In the Berkeley narrative, a brief one, Stuart McConchie survives by selling electronic vermin traps. He shares a close relationship with the owners of the little company that makes the traps. The major narrative pictures life in the little Marin County community. There Bluthgeld has disguised himself as a sheep farmer named Mr. Tree. He fears for his life if it is discovered that he caused two nuclear catastrophes. Only Bonny Keller knows his secret. Hoppy has achieved first importance in the community because of his technological know-how. His dreams of self-aggrandizement resemble those Bluthgeld once held. Edie Keller regularly reports events to her brother, Bill, and they try to think of a way for him to be born.

The values of the little community remain as they had been before the war. All strangers are suspect. School teacher Austurias, who comes in from the outside, is killed by the police chief because the community thinks he lied to them. Next, outsider Eldon Blaine is killed by Hoppy for trying to steal a radio. Outsider Stu McConchie is suspect when he comes from Berkeley because he is black, and the editor of the local paper thinks perhaps a "darky-killing" would be timely.

The plot is intricate and not easily summarized, but at the novel's end, Hoppy, lusting for total power, uses his technological skill to take over Dangerfield's satellite communication system. Bluthgeld, more insane than ever, uses his mental powers to begin another atomic war to "punish those who are evil." Bill is finally born as the bombs fall. The war is short lived because Hoppy kills Bluthgeld and the bombing ceases. His nearly successful destruction of Dangerfield is averted only when Bill, using his strange powers, changes bodies with Hoppy. Bill, the antithesis of Hoppy, puts Hoppy's technology to new uses and begins the task of restoring Dangerfield to health again so that mankind's voice of unity will survive.

Dr. Bloodmoney is a novel of twins, intricately patterned doubles that generate meaning by moving against each other. The function of Dick's four-chambered metaphor (discussed in chapter 1) is more complicated here than in any of his other novels. The antinomies looming the largest are the forces of Life and Death. Hoppy delights in destruction and yet fears death so much that he kills in attempting to escape it. His twin is Bluthgeld, the ultimate dealer of death. Opposing them are the child Edie and the new life form she bears within; only when Bill is finally born into the world is Hoppy destroyed. Hoppy represents a mechanical world and Bill the world of magic. Bluthgeld, a demented scientist who drops death on the world, finds his mirror opposite in Dangerfield, who, as he himself admits to Doctor Stockstill, may perhaps have a few neuroses that need improvement but at least has not lost his sense of humor. He sends down literature and music to the world, not bombs.

In conclusion, we should address the full title of the novel, which is *Dr. Bloodmoney, or How We Got Along After the Bomb*. Well, how did they get along out there on the West Coast after the paranoid, schizophrenic scientist caused the bombs to fall? Precariously, precariously! Suspicion and fear and greed and killing did not cease in West Marin, they grew to the beginning of another atomic war. Only the birth of Bill, a new form of humanity, averted the nuclear disaster. True, Stu McConchie and the Hardy Vermin Trap Company planned to cooperate with Gill's Tobacco Company—but as the novel ends, this is only a hoped-for development.

Thus, if we see Dangerfield in his satellite as a symbol for humanity locked into a new technological age, then his condition at the end of the novel is a warning. Rather than nuclear energy sending the Dangerfields to a new life on Mars, atomic war has led to the death of Walt's wife and nearly destroyed him. The fictional future Dick paints could easily come true, will come true unless something new evolves in our thinking. This reading, I grant, pictures *Dr. Bloodmoney* as a dark novel, rather than the utopia that most critics label it, but I find it difficult to make any other interpretation. I will concede that as the novel ends Dangerfield's voice is growing stronger, the result of Bill's having replaced Hoppy as the controller of technology. Hope for a world without nuclear war exists, nothing more.

Our understanding of *Dr. Bloodmoney* is enriched by looking at its twin, *The Simulacra*, finished just a few months later. As we have noted, for Dick everything that exists has complementary aspects. In the second novel he explores the other polarity of the concepts he handled in *Dr. Bloodmoney*. For example, the human mind works both in the scientific and in the artistic mode. Doctor Bluthgeld is a physicist. In *The Simulacra* the complementary character is Richard Kongrosian, a gifted pianist who suffers from schizophrenic delusions just as Bluthgeld does.

If *The Simulacra* had a subtitle, it would be *How We Got Along Before the Bomb* because it pictures the kinds of power struggles that lead to atomic disaster. The plot is crowded, kaleidoscopic, often bewildering, and out of control at the end of the novel. Here Dick's imagination seems to start at a walk down a long hill in creating plot, then it begins to pick up speed and finally runs out of control, wildly flinging out helter skelter events that bewilder and puzzle the reader and terminate only because the last page of the novel has arrived. Thus the novel is flawed in its ending, as are *The Penultimate Truth* and several other novels.

The primary focus of the plot is the portrayal of the power struggles of those in high places, those in on the secret of how things really operate. They are called the Ges, and the Ges include high level officials in the government, the military, the police, and the economic cartels. The secret they all know is that the president is a robot and his wife, Nicole Thibodeaux, an actress. A council of powerful people really runs the country from behind the scenes. Add to this a subplot: A neo-Nazi revolutionary named Bertold Goltz who is attempting to overthrow the government which he accuses of being totalitarian and corrupt. Add another subplot: The activities— business and personal—of the little people (called the Bes) who are the naïve and trusting public totally unaware of what really goes on in high places. Maury Frauenzimmer's small company makes simulacra, which serve—for those disgruntled citizens who choose to emigrate—as companions on the lonely planet of Mars. Al Miller's Loney Luke business sells cheap jalopy spaceships able, with luck, to make it to Mars. Because life on Mars is actually very dismal, he uses an advertising device, a cute little animal called a papoola (it's a simulacrum) able to hypnotize people into believing that life on Mars will be marvelous. Add still another subplot: a psychokinetic pianist named Kongrosian able to play without using his hands—he does it all with his mind. He is a great favorite of the First Lady. But he can no longer perform at the White House when so ordered because of his psychosis, and treatment is not available because the government has just outlawed the practice of psychiatry, except for a temporary reprieve given one Dr. Egon Superb. Finally, throw in one more minor plot line about a record company that travels to the rain forests of northern California hoping to record Kongrosian. Unable to find him, they record instead the primitive chants of the chuppers, or Neanderthal type men, they find living there. The novel seems crowded with far more characters and action than are necessary.

In *The Simulacra* Dick turns to biting political satire rather than the straight political criticism he wrote in his earlier novels. It is a funny book in many places, but also heavy with cynicism. For instance, listen to Chic Strikerock, a favored narrator and one of the

Bes, or little people, as on his way to work one morning he reads an article in the *New York Times* dealing with a discovery of unicellular fossils on Ganymede. He imagines what they will find as they continue to dig there:

> Old-time civilization, Chic said to himself. The next layer down, just on the verge of being uncovered by the auto-shovels operating in the airless, near-weightless void of mid-space, of the big-planet moons.
> We're being robbed, he decided. The next layer down will be comic books, contraceptives, empty Coke bottles. But they—the authorities—won't tell us. Who wants to find out that the entire solar system has been exposed to Coca Cola over a period of two million years? It was, for him, impossible to imagine a civilization—or any kind of life form—that had not contrived Coke. Otherwise, how could it authentically be called a "civilization?" But then he thought, I'm letting my bitterness get the better of me. Maury [his boss] won't like it; better curb it before I arrive. Bad for business. And we must have business as usual. That's the watchword of the day—if not of the century.[1]

When Chic arrives at work, boss Maury has another newspaper item to share which he has just read in the morning *Chronicle*, and he is not cheerful either.

> "The whole world's coming to an end. It's not us, Chic, not just Frauenzimmer Associates. Listen to this item in today's paper: 'The body of Orley Short, maintenance man, was discovered today at the bottom of a six-foot vat of gradually hardening chocolate at the St. Louis Candy Company.'" He raised his head. "You get that 'Gradually hardening chocolate'—that's it. That's the way we live."
> "Listen, Chic, this is how this terrible item in the *Chronicle* ends. You simulacra, you listen, too. It'll give you an idea of the kind of world you've been born into. 'Brother-in-law Antonio Costa drove to the candy factory and discovered him three feet down in the chocolate, St. Louis Police said.'" Maury savagely closed up the newspaper. "I mean, how are you going to work an event like that into your Weltanschauung? It's just too damn dreadful. It unhinges you. And the worst part is that it's so dreadful it's almost funny." (64)

In the novel Dick makes heavy use of the technique of taking a metaphor literally and thus changing it from a figure of speech to a concrete entity. The president of the United States has often been

1. *The Simulacra* (New York: Ace, 1964), p. 44.

charged with being a mere robot programmed by people behind the scenes. So in *The Simulacra* the president really is a robot. Another example—we've all said, "Those commercials really bug me." Starting there, Dick creates the Nitz commercials, which literally are electronic bugs. They buzz around squeaking out their sales pitch:

> "In the presence of strangers do you feel you don't quite exist? Do they seem not to notice you, as if you were invisible? On a bus or spaceship do you some times look around you and discover that no one, absolutely no one, recognizes you or cares about you and quite possibly may even—"
>
> With his carbon dioxide-powered pellet rifle, Maury Frauenzimmer carefully shot the Nitz commercial as it hung pressed against the far wall of his cluttered office. It had squeezed in during the night, had greeted him in the morning with its tinny harangue (116).

The Nitz commercials crowd into taxis and attack people. Most people regard the ubiquitous bugs as mere nuisances like mosquitoes—either to be endured or destroyed—except for Richard Kongrosian, who listens seriously to one about offensive body odor that says, "In moments of great intimacy with ones we love, especially then does the danger of offending become acute." The commercial nudges him further into the schizophrenic process that is eroding his stability. He believes he must avoid everyone because of his body odor.

A comparison of the form schizophrenia takes in Dr. Bluthgeld, the scientist, and in Richard Kongrosian, the artist, is instructive. Dick obviously had not concluded his interest in schizophrenia when *Martian Time-Slip* was finished. He is still fascinated with how the brain works in mental illness, particularly the brain of the madman who has power, be it creative or destructive. Dick develops the two characters Bluthgeld and Kongrosian by entering their inner realms and showing us how their ideas and illusions create the world for them. Bluthgeld *believes* his power causes the bombs to fall and the reader, now viewing the action from inside his mind, experiences the same conviction. Bluthgeld, a rational or left-brain thinker, is the man who acts, who causes things to happen.

Dick takes us on a parallel journey into Kongrosian's mind, but its workings are a mirror reversal of Bluthgeld's. He is an artist whose right brain dominates and he is essentially passive. Kongrosian's delusions of grandeur are similar to Bluthgeld's, but while Bluthgeld claimed to have caused the bombs to fall, Kongrosian's only claim to such power is that it is he who has caused the workman in the candy factory to fall into the vat of hardening chocolate. After his distress because of his imaginary body odors, his next delusion is that he is vanishing, becoming invisible, that nothing remains of him but his body odor. Next he concludes he has died and must await rebirth. And finally "something terrible" happens to his mind, because, as he wails, "I no longer can keep myself and my environment separate; do you comprehend how that feels? It's awful!" (224).

As Nicole Thibodeaux watches him, a vase of flowers disappears from the desk into Kongrosian's body and is replaced by an organ that appears to be part of the endocrine system. He shrieks that he is turning inside out, and literally that begins to happen:

> Nicole shut her eyes. "Richard," she moaned gratingly. "Stop it. Get control of yourself."
>
> "Yes," Kongrosian said, and giggled helplessly. "I can get hold of myself, pick myself up, the organs and vital parts all around me, lying on the floor; maybe I can stuff them back inside somehow" (225).

The scene proceeds in this mode, with the metaphorical made literal. It is a funny scene, and yet tragic because we are viewing the anguish of an artist who is suffering mental illness and it is very painful to watch because Dick has re-created the emotion so powerfully here. Kongrosian does indeed try to put things back together, and at the novel's end he uses his power of telekinesis to save Nicole. His final actions sharply contrast with Bluthgeld's—who starts another atomic war at the end of *Dr. Bloodmoney*.

Dick expresses here an idea that will grow into an obsession with him. We become what we think and one of the most important elements of thinking is metaphor-making. The metaphors the mind uses to model reality become the reality where that individual lives. The most powerful minds, however, will often drag weaker ones into their reality—another in Dick's explorations of the maps of the mind that he will undertake in *The Three Stigmata of Palmer Eldritch*.

The conclusion of *The Simulacra* is like an echo of the beginning of *Dr. Bloodmoney*. Those in power are fighting each other, unleashing destruction: "In the sky, to the north, an immense, gray, mushroom-like cloud all at once formed. And a rumble stirred through the earth, jarring Chic and making him jump. Shielding his eyes he peered to see; what had happened? An explosion, perhaps a small, tactical A-bomb. Now he inhaled the reek of ashes and knew definitely what it was" (234).

As the atomic bomb functions as the metaphor for disharmony and destruction in Dick's writing, so music is the metaphor for harmony. Allusions to music play as important a role in his texts as music did in his real life. His characters go to operas and concerts as well as listen to records and refer to music—most of it classical. One character in *The Simulacra* warns Nicole Thibodeaux, "He does not enjoy your musical evenings either, does he? That's a bad sign. Recall Shakespeare, *Julius Caesar*. Something about 'I distrust him for he hath no music.' Recall? 'He hath no music'" (48). To list all the musical allusions in Dick's fiction would be to name all his favorite composers and many of the titles in his large record collection: Mozart, Beethoven, Bach, Verdi, Wagner, Gilbert and Sullivan, Dowland, Mahler. In keeping with his satiric mode in *The Simulacra,* Dick sends two of his characters to the White House to perform Bach's "Chaconne in D" on jugs.

Literary allusions also abound in Dick's fiction, suggesting the great importance he gives to the written word. Again, to list the allusions is to list the books Dick read—and we should note how intellectually demanding these authors are: Joyce, Eliot, Kafka, Shakespeare, Goethe, Proust, Yeats, Pascal, Lucretius. The allusions work to enrich his fiction, and deserve more extensive study than is possible here. However, one does occasionally feel that Dick uses them to cover his sometimes embarrassment at writing science fiction and to signal his reader that he is well read in the great literary tradition. Dick's attitude toward science fiction is ambivalent. He seems to express it through Al, one of the jug players in *The Simulacra,* who is criticized for wasting his time in this pursuit. His attacker says: "No grown man in his right senses would be hooting into an empty bottle anyhow." Al replies: "That's where you're wrong. Art can be found in the most mundane daily walks of life, like these jugs for instance" (127).

Will mankind survive in the nuclear age? In summary, Dick is ambivalent, answering in *Dr. Bloodmoney* that it is possible and in *The Simulacra* that it is not likely. The comments of two characters in *Dr. Bloodmoney* illustrate this ambivalence. Andrew Gill is pleased

both with the plans for automating his cigarette factory that Stuart
McConchie brings him and with the character of the man himself. He
muses, "Perhaps the world, at last, was really beginning to regain
some of its old forms, its civilities and customs and preoccupations,
all that had gone into it to make it what it was. This, he thought, this
talk by McConchie; it's authentic. It's a survival, not a simulation;
this man has somehow managed to preserve his viewpoint, his enthusiasm, through all that has happened—he is still planning, cogitating,
bullshitting—nothing can or will stop him" (193).

But near the novel's end, as Dangerfield lies close to death in the
satellite, Bonny Keller also muses, "The killing, the slow destruction
of Dangerfield was deliberate, and it came—not from space, not
from beyond—but from below, from the familiar landscape.
Dangerfield had not died from the years of isolation; he had been
stricken by careful instruments issuing up from the very world which
he struggled to contact. If he could have cut himself off from us, she
thought, he would be alive now. At the very moment he listened to
us, received us, he was being killed—and did not realize it" (266).

5
Illusions, Reality, Evil, and *The Three Stigmata of Palmer Eldritch*

"There I went, one day, walking down the country road to my shack, looking forward to eight hours of writing, in total isolation from all other humans, and I looked up at the sky and saw a face. I didn't really see it, but the face was there, and it was not a human face; it was a vast visage of perfect evil. It was immense; it filled a quarter of the sky. It had empty slots for eyes—it was metal and cruel and, worst of all, it was God."[1]

Thus Dick described the vision that generated his strange novel, *The Three Stigmata of Palmer Eldritch* (1965). Readers react to it either with fascination or horror, and Dick himself said that when the galley proofs arrived, the novel so frightened him that he could not read it. It has been called his LSD novel because it re-creates so powerfully the isolated prison of shifting hallucinations where the terrified user of LSD sometimes finds himself locked alone. Dick insisted he had not yet tried LSD when he wrote the novel in the spring of 1963. His only source of information then about the effects of LSD was the description written by Aldous Huxley after his use of the drug. He said he later took LSD because he "had a cat's curiosity about the drug." The second part of *The Unteleported Man* is the single work he admitted to having written while under the influence of LSD.

In December 1963 Dick published a short story, "The Days of Perky Pat," whose idea came to him in a lightning flash of inspiration

1. Headnote written for a reprint of "The Days of Perky Pat," in which Dick describes his vision that led to writing *Palmer Eldritch* and tells how the short story served as a vehicle that he could use in developing his ideas about evil. In *Science Fiction Origins*. Ed. William F. Nolan and Martin H. Greenberg. (New York: Fawcett Books, 1980), p. 98–101.

when he saw his daughters playing with their Barbie dolls. He created a postwar setting where small colonies of survivors struggle through a dull existence on the wasted earth and brighten their drab lives by playing with dolls in miniature settings that represent their lost culture.

Early in 1964 Dick completed a novel using this story of children's toys and layering it with another telling about the devil with the leering face. He is called Palmer Eldritch (horrible pilgrim), and he is an industrial tycoon returning from a ten-year visit to the Proxima Centauri system where he went to establish an economic empire. Or is he really Palmer Eldritch? Perhaps that man was destroyed by the Proxers and what returns is a powerful alien evil force. His three stigmata—the metal Jensen eyes, the stainless steel teeth, and the metal hand—all suggest he is no longer the man who left Terra years earlier.

Dick stated again and again over the years that his grand theme was the question of who is human and who only masquerades as a human, and that he had a second theme of almost equal importance—How can we know what is true reality and what is merely illusion? In *Palmer Eldritch* he explores both of those questions in a brilliant drama that actually catches the essence of evil uncertainty about one's fellowmen, one's God, and even one's self. Reading the novel is a frightening experience. The reader stumbles into a microcosm mirroring the most horrible macrocosm Dick can imagine—a universe where nothing is certain except that God, turned cannibal, has come to consume, not save, man. And to consume each man alone in his private reality. Unless of course it turns out that each man's reality is a mere subjective illusion. But if that is true, where is our objective, common reality? Are we anchored together in a shared time and place? Or is it possible that . . . ? The fascination of *Palmer Eldritch* is that anything is possible. Dick later commented that the novel was "a dark journey into the mystical and the supernatural and the absolutely evil as I understood it at the time. . . . I wrote it during a great crisis in my religious beliefs. I decided to write a novel dealing with absolute evil as personified in the form of a 'human.'"

In my discussion of *Martian Time-Slip* and *Dr. Bloodmoney* in the two previous chapters, I noted the beautiful balance that harmonizes all the intricate parts of the novels; Dick is always in control of his material. In *Palmer Eldritch* that control begins to vanish. He still uses multiple narratives and omniscience as he did in the other two novels, but the material constantly runs away from him and seems almost to write itself. Indeed, Dick himself commented later to a friend that exactly such a phenomenon had happened. Once he had the plot under way, it exploded into its own trajectory rather than following any course he had planned for it. As we trace the journey of Dick's mind, it is useful to note the order in which these three important novels were written. First came *Martian Time-Slip* and then *Dr. Bloodmoney*, the manuscript for the latter being delivered to his agent in February 1963, although the novel was not published until 1965. About a year later, in March 1964, his agent received the manuscript for *Palmer Eldritch*.

During this time his personal life began to crumble around him and his relationship with his wife, Anne, became very stormy. In 1963 he had been confirmed in Saint Columba's Episcopal Church at Point Reyes, and it was to his priest he went for healing unction after he saw the leering vision in the sky, which the priest concluded must have been a glimpse of Satan. Dick was deeply depressed, among other things, by the assassination of John F. Kennedy in November 1963. For three years he had been driving himself relentlessly in his writing, producing at least fourteen stories and seven science fiction novels as well as several mainstream novels for which he could find no publisher. The amphetamines which he now used regularly to sustain him in his frantic writing schedule began to take their toll. After an extremely chaotic year in their relationship in 1963, Dick left Anne in March 1964. *Palmer Eldritch* was written probably late in 1963 or early in 1964 during this period of great crisis, both marital and religious. He finally filed for a divorce, which was granted October 2, 1965.

"Precious Artifact" (*Galaxy* 1964) gives a sense of the weariness he felt during this period. In this short story a Terran engineer works in reconstruction on Mars after a devastating war between the Terrans and Proxmen who both wanted Mars for expansion. Exhausted and homesick, he finally becomes depressed with his strenuous work schedule and goes for help to a psychiatrist. He is allowed to return to Terran but once there discovers the small bit of Terra he sees is a mere illusion built by the Proxmen so he will not discover that Earth is also in total ruins. Completely discouraged, he attempts suicide on his return to Mars.

The fascination of *Palmer Eldritch* is its uncanny ability to reel along from one hallucination to another, one uncertainty to another, one despair to another, and yet somehow never to collapse into total irrationality. Each of the two central characters, Barney Mayerson and Leo Bulero, struggles in his way against the evil power of Palmer Eldritch—Barney with near despair and Leo with sanguine determination. Neither man triumphs. But even at the novel's end, after having been dragged mercilessly through space and plunged erratically through time by Palmer, each man still believes he has at least a small chance to overcome the alien evil that has invaded Mars and now approaches Earth.

While *Palmer Eldritch* is the major novel in which Dick grapples with the problem of evil, it is not the first one. Mr. Tagomi in *High Castle* viewed the ruthless violence of the various Nazi factions vying for power and concluded that "there is evil, it is actual, like cement." An even earlier novel, *The Cosmic Puppets* (1957), pictures a small town which is a microcosm of the cosmic struggle of two opposed forces, Ormazd, the cosmic constructive power, and Ahriman, the destructor. Ormazd labors to build forms and give shape to reality while his cosmic opposite seeks to destroy order, truth, and law, reducing the world to darkness, chaos, and death. The townspeople see only as "through a glass darkly" the meaning of this battle between the cosmic polarities, but they do understand that one force is good and one is evil. The novel was originally published as "A Glass of Darkness" a title Dick took from Paul's 1 Corinthians. Twenty years later the phrase once again provided a story title, revised this time to *A Scanner Darkly* (1977).

Another novel written after *Palmer Eldritch* exploring the cosmic forces of good and evil is *Galactic Pot-Healer* (1969). While this novel is one of Dick's less successful attempts artistically, it does present ontological and epistemological ideas interesting and useful as we attempt to understand his view of evil. In the novel an alien supernatural power called the Glimmung has assembled a group of artisans to aid in the restoration of an ancient sunken cathedral. Sometime in the distant past the cathedral fell under the power of an evil anti-Glimmung power and was nearly destroyed. Only with the cooperative aid of human craftsmen can Glimmung repair it and raise it again from the depth of the sea where it now rests. Dick describes Glimmung as like Goethe's Faust, ever striving upward to learn more and create more. As Faust reclaims the foul swamp and turns it into a green and fruitful meadow, so Glimmung attempts to reclaim the fallen cathedral. He is like the God of Genesis, declares one of the characters, for God was also very Faustian—creating forms from chaos, separating the light from the dark, the sea from the land.

Dick freely acknowledged that Carl Jung with his theory of archetypes and the creative process was a major influence in his thinking and his writing. Nowhere is this influence more apparent than in *Galactic Pot-Healer.* The dark ocean represents the unconscious mind, and Glimmung and his Shadow represent the archetypal figures that can be raised to the surface of awareness only through the efforts of little craftsmen like Joe Fernwright. The novel so obviously works as an allegory of Jung's creative theory that it is not one of Dick's successful novels. He is at his best when he dives into his own unconscious to bring up archetypal figures rather than allegorizing the process.

During the 1950s and early 1960s Dick's mind relentlessly probed the nature and cause of violence and destruction. He watched with near despair as the world armed itself with increasingly lethal military weapons. He concluded that the only explanation lay in some evil cosmic power using men in its struggle against the form creator. He began to associate the form creator with a benign communal reality and the destroyer with an isolated, despairing private reality. His mind probes into the nature of evil are dramatized most successfully in *Palmer Eldritch,* the novel we are about to explore in depth.

Closely related to the question of evil is the question of true reality and how it can be differentiated from illusion. Dick's early short stories, written during the 1950s, first consider this problem. These stories suggest there is no constant reality out there, that each person lives his own illusion, which he labels as shared reality. The stories do not yet, however, associate faked reality, where one person manipulates another person's perceptions, with evil.

"Beyond Lies the Wub," Dick's first published story, appeared in *Planet Stories* in July 1952. The subtitle of the story might well have been "Appearances Are Never to Be Trusted." Captain Franco and his crew load Martian animals on their ship to take them back to Earth. One of the men appears with a wub, a fat animal resembling a pig. The Captain has heard wub are good to eat, despite their ugly appearance, so he orders it shot and cooked for dinner. The wub, who can talk, soon reveals himself as a highly refined intelligent life form who enjoys discussing philosophy and myths, particularly the myth of Odysseus. The wub finds "Odysseus a figure common to the mythology of most self-conscious races. As I interpret it, Odysseus wanders as an individual aware of himself as such. This is the idea of separation, of separation from family and country. The process of individuation."

Captain Franco cannot see beneath the wub's alien appearance, despite the wub's plea that he is passive and will not hurt anyone. So he shoots the wub, and thus demonstrates that his inner reality is more animalistic than the wub's, however human he may appear to be on the surface.

Other stories on this same theme rattle out from Dick's typewriter. "Roog" (1952), the first story Dick ever sold, pictures the world of garbage collectors from the alien view of the family dog who guards his owner's house. He sees a totally different world from what his owner does. In "The Commuter" (1953) the ticket agent puzzles about a man who keeps asking for a ticket to Marion Heights, a town once planned but never built. To untangle the mystery, the agent decides to ride the train, and he discovers it really does stop at Marion Heights. When he returns home, he has trouble remembering that his wife and child are real. In "The World She Wanted" (1953) Larry Brewster meets Allison Holmes as he is drinking in his favorite rundown bar. She tells him she needs him in her affluent world, where everything is just the way she wants it. She plans to fall in love and get married. She leads him into her world and he discovers her lifestyle is not one he wants. He goes back to his rundown bar, concluding that reality is a private thing for each person. He saw only one aspect of Allison and she one of him; they can never really know each other.

A particularly interesting early story is "Small Town" (1954). Verne Haskel dislikes many of the people in his town. He hates his job at Larson Pump Works, too. As an escape he builds a model train layout in his basement like the real town where he lives. But one day he gets so fed up with his job that he quits and begins working full time on his layout. His wife is appalled and calls Dr. Tyler for help. When they hear Haskel shouting, the two of them go down to the basement. Haskel has vanished but they discover he has begun making changes in the layout to convert the town to his ideal. He has replaced the Pump Works with the Woodland Mortuary, built the Steuben Pet Shop beside it, removed advertising signs, altered the wealthy district to remove the mansions, and finally made himself mayor. Dr. Tyler explains that "the mind constructs reality. Frames it. Creates it. We all have common reality, a common dream. But Haskel turned his back on our common reality and created his own. And he had a unique capacity—far beyond the ordinary. He devoted his whole life, his whole skill to building it. He's there now."

They set out for the police station to report Haskel missing. Suddenly Mrs. Haskel screams. She sees the Woodland Mortuary and the Steuben Pet Shop and realizes they are trapped in Haskel's imaginary world. The seeds of the ideas for *Palmer Eldritch* are immediately recognizable in this very early story—the power of one individual to drag others into his private reality.

Two novels written before *Palmer Eldritch* focus on the question of reality and how it can be differentiated from illusions. In *Time out of Joint* (1959) Raggle Gumm earns a living and gains fame by being a consistent winner in the "Where Will the Little Green Men Be Next Contest." Puzzling occurences begin to make Raggle suspect that the reality around him is a mere illusory fabric, not the truth. He finally escapes from the town where he lives and discovers the real world of 1998, not the world of 1959 in which he thought he lived.

He learns that he is really a rich industrialist who first worked with the government fighting Luna rebel forces, but then switched sides because he decided he was for space development rather than against it. However, the government brainwashed him, and put him in the constructed reality of the little town where in providing the answers to the puzzles, he gave them the information they needed to successfully wage the war against the Luna forces.

The Game-Players of Titan (1963), probably written not long before *Palmer Eldritch*, uses some of the same ideas but does not succeed in synthesizing all the parts with dramatic economy. The game here combines Monopoly and poker. It is played for entertainment by Pete Gardner and the other members of the Pretty Blue Fox Bind, although actual real estate is won or lost. The Hinkel Radiation

Effect used in the last war killed the bulk of the population. Of those who survived, most are sterile. Vugs, amoebalike creatures which are a silicon-based life form from Titan, are invading and taking over the Earth. They are an advanced life form that can, when they choose, mimic human forms. They can also distort reality for the humans. Finally the vugs challenge the humans to a game. Since the vugs have telepathic abilities, the humans decide on a strategy to prevent the vugs from knowing the moves they plan to make. They use a combination of drugs that will alter their brain functions, thus masking the usual patterns of their mental actions.

The stories and novels I have cited are by no means the only ones where Dick plays with the possibilities of hallucinations, illusions, and multiple realities. As he kept telling his readers over the years, the nature of reality fascinates him more than any other subject. Finally, after all these preparatory works, came the giant face in the sky, and then Dick was ready to create *The Three Stigmata of Palmer Eldritch*. Readers and critics alike hail it as one of his great novels.

The usually difficult task of plot summary becomes nearly impossible in *Palmer Eldritch* since the novel studies a shifting world where no reality is stable. The plot moves erratically through space and time, those two categories our common sense tells us we can depend on because they exist outside our perceptions. But nothing is to be depended on as authentic reality in *Palmer Eldritch*.

The novel uses a number of settings—Terra, Ganymede, Mars, Luna, Sigma-B satellite. It opens in 2016, but only temporarily does time move forward as an arrow. It soon explodes into the future, falls back into the past, dilates, collapses, until the time of common sense reality becomes meaningless.

The two major figures in the novel are Barney Mayerson and Leo Bulero. Significantly, the novel opens with Barney and closes with Leo. At the heart of the complicated plot lies the encounter of each man with the mysterious Palmer Eldritch. Leo's response to Palmer is very different from Barney's.

The first three chapters rapidly sketch in the characters, conflicts, and puzzles of the intricate narrative. In New York City, Barney and his new girl friend, Roni Tungate, work for Leo Bulero, head of the Perky Pat Corporation. Because of atmospheric overheating and environmental deterioration, life on Earth is nearly unbearable. The United Nations drafts people and sends them to colonize Mars and Venus.

Across the river in New Jersey lives Barney's former wife Emily, who is now married to Richard Hnatt. She has made a number of miniature pots that her husband hopes to sell to the P. P. Corporation. If he is successful, they will have enough money to go to Germany and get Denkmal's E Therapy, a treatment causing rapid evolution of the mind in successful cases and devolution when the treatment fails. The treatment is so expensive that only affluent people like Leo Bulero can afford it.

On Mars life for the colonists is marginal. They live in underground hovels, make occasional weary attempts at gardening in the dust above, and escape their barren reality through an illegal drug called Can-D, which gives them the illusion that they have returned to an idealized twentieth century Earth in affluent suburbia. This translating experience works only with the aid of miniaturized props—clothes, furniture, dishes, sports cars. The miniatures are made and distributed by the P. P. Corporation, which also secretly supplies the drug.

On Earth the morning papers report a crash landing on Pluto of the industrialist Palmer Eldritch, who ten years earlier had gone to Proxima Centauri to modernize the autofacs of the Proxers. Leo Bulero is disturbed at this report because rumors claim Palmer is bringing back a new translating drug that will compete with his own Can-D. He decides he must do something.

The settings and characters are blocked in by the end of the first three chapters. Action begins in chapter four. Leo, full of uncertainty and anxiety, decides to confront Palmer. He goes to Luna, where Palmer has finally been brought for treatment of his injuries. By now the head of Leo's secret police, Felix Blau, has informed him of a rival organization in Boston that will market Connie Companion dolls to compete with the Perky Pat layouts. He suspects that Palmer plans to supply the drug for this corporation.

So far the plot has proceeded in a conventional enough way and the reader is totally unprepared for the shattering event that next occurs. As Leo talks with Palmer, he is struck by a beam of light and plunged into blackness. When he returns to consciousness he finds himself tied to a chair in a barren room. Palmer is there and they continue their conversation. Suddenly the room blows up in Leo's face, and commonsense reality vanishes from the novel. He begins moving erratically through time and space, uncertain of whether what he sees is hallucination or reality. He finds himself on a grassy plain where he encounters in quick succession a child who claims she is Zoe Eldritch, Dr. Smile (the electronic suitcase that is Barney's psychiatrist), a rat, and a gluck.

He soon realizes that while he was unconscious Palmer gave him an intravenous injection of Chew-Z and he is now in a nonexistent world. The child Zoe explains that her father was forced by the Proxers to bring back the drug and that it is the agent by which the human race is to be delivered over to alien control.

Leo reverses his conviction that this world is illusionary when the gluck attacks his leg, penetrates his flesh with tubelike cilia, and begins to drink him. Abruptly Palmer appears and announces that he did not find God in the Prox system, but something superior. "God promises eternal life. I can do better. *I can deliver it.*"

Palmer explains that his power lies in Chew-Z. It frees the user from time, which is a subjective experience, and also gives him the power to reincarnate in any form he chooses—a bug, a physics teacher, a hawk, a slime mold . . . . All he needs to do is project a fraction of his essence and supply the Logos. Whatever he imagines will take material form. However, it is a subjective world he inhabits alone, in contrast to the Can-D fantasies, which are shared by the entire group.

Leo tests Palmer's claim by attempting to construct his own artifacts—first an electronic gluck trap and then a set of stairs that end in a luminous hoop. He climbs the stairs, passes through the hoop, and apparently arrives back in the real world of P. P. Layouts.

He immediately demands to know why Barney Mayerson did not come to rescue him on Luna. Barney is ashamed to admit that although he did feel a sense of responsibility, he decided not to go when his precog abilities showed him how risky the mission would be. Just as Leo is explaining that Chew-Z does not provide the genuine reincarnation it promises and that its worst aspect is its solipsistic quality, he discovers a gluck under his desk and realizes he has not escaped from Palmer's illusory world.

He decides to try his power by turning Roni Tungate into an old woman. He is horrified when she becomes first a shriveled old head in a spider web, then a mere slime puddle swimming with life. After a time Zoe appears to remind him he is trapped in Palmer's world and to inform him he will be released only if he agrees to retire and turn over his corporation to Palmer for the distribution of Chew-Z.

Leo lunges at the child and strangles her, thinking he will thus escape from this irreal world. But when she is dead, the hallucination still remains and he wanders forlornly through the barren landscape. He recognizes that once Palmer invades the Sol system, every human will end up as he has, on a plain full of dead things that have become nothing more than random fragments.

As he wanders on, he meets two strange creatures with reedlike limbs and grotesque, egg-shaped heads. They turn out to be humans living several decades in the future who have evolved with great speed as a result of Denkmal's E Therapy. They recognize him as a dawn man from the past, a "chooser." When they learn he is Leo Bulero, they hail him as a hero and take him to the monument commemorating the spot where he killed Palmer Eldritch. They throw a stone to drive off a dog defecating on the monument and the stone passes through the dog. It is not real. Leo realizes he is still trapped in Palmer's irreal world.

And then suddenly the scene vanishes and Leo is back on Luna, facing Palmer as they had been when the hallucination began. Palmer explains that the hallucination has been a little demonstration of his power, that if Leo refuses to cooperate with him, he will kill Leo. "I must, to save my own self," he concludes and then dismisses Leo.

As Leo leaves the room, he decides that he in turn has no choice but to kill Palmer. "And I have to do it not just to save myself but everyone in the system, and that's my staff on which I'm leaning."

Leo's encounter with Palmer will be balanced later in the novel with a parallel episode in which Palmer encounters Barney. He will give Barney Chew-Z and take him to a series of hallucinatory worlds. While Leo fought against being trapped in Palmer's irreal realms, Barney will go with a willing passivity.

Barney emigrates to Mars after Leo fires him for failing to make a rescue attempt when Leo was held prisoner by Palmer. Barney is weighted down with guilt, and hopes perhaps on Mars he can somehow atone for having deserted first his wife Emily and then Leo. Aboard the ship to Mars he meets Anne Hawthorne, a Neo-Christian, and they discuss religion and drugs in the colonial life they are about to share on Mars. When Barney arrives at Chicken Pox Prospect, the underground hovel where he will live, he finds the group of three couples voting on whether they should switch from Can-D to Chew-Z, and his vote tips the decision in favor of the latter.

Soon Palmer Eldritch appears on Mars and accuses Barney of participating in a complicated plan Leo has designed to trap and destroy Palmer. Barney considers attempting to kill Palmer, but instead accepts Chew-Z from him and later joins the others in the hovel to consume the drug.

Barney's hallucinations take him back in time, first to the period when he was married to Emily, and then to the time she married Richard Hnatt. Palmer fades in and out of his hallucinations, warning him he cannot really return to the past. Barney consumes a second dose of Chew-Z, this time alone, and falls deeper into Palmer's irreal worlds. He wanders forward through time and encounters his future self, who turns from him in disgust at his depressed, pathetic behavior and unwillingness to fight Palmer and his drug. Palmer's invasion of his reality continues until finally, totally cannibalized, Barney becomes Palmer. As Palmer, he encounters the despairing Barney and diagnoses Barney's problem: "What you want is death." Palmer explains that Barney's desire to become a stone so he will no longer have to feel is no more than a screen hiding his death wish from himself.

The conclusion of the novel presents a reversal of an earlier action. Barney had failed to make a rescue attempt when Leo was trapped by Palmer, but now Leo comes to Mars to try to save Barney and bring him back to Earth. By now Barney has emerged from his hallucinations. He discusses his experience with Anne Hawthorne and they try to puzzle out whether the evil Palmer can really be God. He senses that he will never be free of the stigmata of evil with which Palmer branded him when they merged and became one. He decides he will refuse to be rescued by Leo. Instead he will remain on Mars and work at gardening.

Leo returns to Earth. On the way he discusses with his police chief how best to combat Palmer. Then they notice with alarm that they both have artificial arms and steel teeth; they, too, are branded with the stigmata. But Leo vows to fight Palmer because as an evolved human, he sees himself as "the Protector of the human race."

This skeletal plot summary, ignoring as it does many elements of the plot, almost violates the essence of the novel. Yet it does outline the supporting strands of the plot through which various other threads, some bright with hope and others dark with despair, are woven. Unfortunately such a summary cannot capture the hypnotic power of the plot over the reader's consciousness. Just as he has turned the kaleidoscope of his attention on a world and focused enough to see its pattern, the lens shifts and he finds himself looking at another bizarre world. Dick's trick of dragging an element from one world into the next creates a degree of plausibility—or is it implausibility—in the journey through alternate realities. For example, Dr. Smile, the psychiatrist suitcase from Terra, appears on the satellite world of Sigma 14 and the gluck from Sigma 14 turns up in Leo Bulero's office on Terra.

The rich array of characters equals that in *Martian Time-Slip* and *Dr. Bloodmoney*. The women are sympathetically drawn; even Roni Tungate, aggressive though she is, possesses enough compassion to urge Barney to rescue Leo. Not until the novels of the Entropic Period will Dick regularly portray women as destructive androids without the capacity to respond emotionally.

Implausible as the matrix of alternative realities may be in *Palmer Eldritch,* readers never reject them as totally impossible because of Dick's skillful use of the omniscient point of view to give them credibility. We see the events of the novel primarily through the perceptions of Barney and Leo and listen to their awarenesses as each tries to puzzle out a meaning for the events. But Dick does not limit himself to these two points of view. He enters at least briefly the inner worlds of almost all the characters. Even Palmer Eldritch, evil and powerful as he is, evokes a sympathetic response when the reader along with Barney enters his consciousness and feels his helplessness in the hands of a cosmic force greater than he. His hell is that he may not be able to escape that force through death.

The ideas may well be the most powerful characters in the novel, exemplifying Dick's comment that "ideas seem to have a life of their own; they appear to seize on people and make use of them." As the idea of evil seems to have seized Dick and used him to write *Palmer Eldritch,* so Dick in turn seizes on the characters and uses them in order to express his meditations on the nature of reality and of good and evil. Five ideas weave through the novel, entangling themselves with each other as they progress. First is the theme of economic exploitation, one Dick has used so often in earlier novels that here he soon discards it for others. As the novel opens, Leo Bulero is indeed a greedy industrialist ready to battle to the death any competitor who threatens his economic empire. But when he encounters an evil force that threatens to imprison and destroy humanity, he without hesitation takes on the task of being "Protector of our race." True, in one sense he exploits the colonists on Mars, but in another sense their sterile lives are more bearable because they use the products of P. P. Corporation to "translate" together.

The second theme explores religious possibilities and it is far more important in the novel than economic exploitation. The religious crisis Dick experienced during this period of his life triggered the appearance in the sky of the huge satanic face that in turn led him to write the novel in an attempt to exorcise it. Thus we can understand the religious discussions throughout the novel. He catches in the net of his fiction—where he can examine it more closely—ontological concerns about which he is deeply troubled in his personal life. Here Dick's brilliant creative leap is to substitute a drug for the wine and wafer of the mass. This allows him, through the vehicle of the Martian settlers, to discuss the medieval doctrine of substance versus accident and whether the wine and wafer really become the blood and body of God during communion or merely stand for God's body. Dick combines the sacred and secular outrageously—adults play with dolls and consume drugs together to experience transubstantiation! Escaping temporarily from their world, they descend back to Terra rather than ascend up to Heaven. This religious experience may seem almost profane, yet it *is* a communal experience; they share their illusory world together. In contrast, one must go alone into the worlds created by Palmer's drug.

Religious allusions punctuate the entire novel. Texts and names from the Bible are mentioned, as well as theologians, philosophers, and religious figures—for example, Marcus Aurelius and his *Meditations,* Thomas a Kempis, Erasmus, Luther. Paul and his letters to the Corinthians, Dick's favorite biblical text, are discussed. So also is Buddhism with its doctrine of reincarnation. The continuing conversation of Barney and Anne Hawthorne is the focus of religious discussion, but Leo also ponders religious possibilities after he recognizes Palmer as an evil power. No definitive religious truths emerge.

Any conclusion reached by an individual is soon discarded as he considers another possible explanation for the mysteries that surround him or encounters a new situation that fails to fit his conclusion.

The religious discussions are webbed and tangled with a third theme, the question of good and evil and this leads to a fourth motif in the novel, the nature of ultimate reality. It is difficult to talk about one without the other. How can we know when we are experiencing authentic reality rather than fake, or ersatz, reality? Indeed, does an ultimate reality exist and if it does, can a human ever know it? Or must he forever be trapped in his own subjective world? This novel, and all Dick's writing, rests on the assumption that the universe has form and meaning; the problem for man is to discover what it is. In this novel, the power of evil isolates man in the *idios kosmos,* or purely private world, and he loses contact with the given, shared universe, the *koinos kosmos.* When he wrote *Palmer Eldritch* Dick seems to have been primarily drawing on his subconscious for ideas as he dramatized his ontological speculations. Later he arrived at some metaphysical conclusions about the meaning of the metaphors he had created in his fiction. The speech he gave at Metz, France, in 1977 is primarily concerned with his understanding of the nature of reality. There he said:

> I, in my stories and novels, often write about counterfeit worlds, semireal worlds, as well as deranged private worlds inhabited by just one person, while meantime the other characters either remain in their own worlds or are somehow drawn into one of the peculiar ones. This theme occurs throughout all my twenty-seven years of writing. At no time did I have a theoretical or conscious explanation of my preoccupation with these pluriform pseudo-worlds, but now I think I understand. What I was sensing was the manifold of partially actualized realities lying tangent to what evidently is the most actualized one, the one which the majority of us, by consensus gentium, agree on.[2]

What have Barney and Leo discovered about the nature of reality by the novel's end? Only clues to the answer, not the answer itself. Through the drug experience (and here drug and religious experience are synonymous), they have been dragged through a number of delusional worlds and have learned that the dividing line

2. At this date the Metz speech has not been published.

between hallucinations and authentic vision is very thin. The subjective experience of irreal worlds dislocates both the sense of space and the sense of time because they are constructs of the human mind, and the nature of hallucination—whether it is induced by religious experience, dream, drug, or mental illnesses—is to release the mind from the commonsense reality it ordinarily inhabits. To escape the world of time is to put on immortality, but if one has descended to the underworld of reality, as has Palmer, to be unable to die is to be eternally cursed.

"The evil one wears a mental face," Dick often notes. He cites the war masks of the Attic Greeks, the masks of knights in the Middle Ages, the gas masks of the soldiers in World War I. "When men wish to inspire terror and kill they put on metal faces."[3] Thus Palmer Eldritch, with his metal eyes, teeth, and hand, is an archetypal symbol and perhaps the quintessential symbol in Dick's fiction. He is Deus Irae, the God of Wrath, the God of Battle. He stands for the Form Destroyers, the entropic power of destruction, the unfeeling entity masquerading as a human, the alien force that separates the individual from his true self and from his fellow humans. His three stigmata are, Leo finally recognizes, a negative trinity of alienation, blurred reality, and despair. Evil does exist, it is the "original ancient blight," and all men are infected with it. Barney finally admits to himself that he has done evil, first in sacrificing Emily to maintain his apartment and again in refusing to go to Leo's aid when he was trapped by Palmer.[4] Everyone carries the stigma, we are reminded in the final chapters of the novel when metal hand, eyes, and teeth appear on all the characters. Evil is any thought or act that cuts us off from others, that destroys our shared reality; and all humans are guilty of having these thoughts.

Palmer, an anti-Christ, comes not to establish a community of men but to destroy it by alienating each individual and dragging him into a private or subjective reality where he must live alone. Christ came to Earth to die for men, but now two thousand years later Palmer struggles to stave off his own death (111). In the ritual of the Eucharist, man eats and drinks of the body of God, but Palmer

3. Headnote to "Perky Pat."
4. *The Three Stigmata of Palmer Eldritch* (New York: Doubleday, 1965), pp. 118–19.

reverses the process. He is a great mouth that comes to consume man.

Yet Palmer stirs at least a small sympathetic response from the reader because he is so totally isolated, and he must live alone with the absolute awareness he has gained from his unending solitary brooding in the void somewhere in space. And even his power is limited; he is mysteriously controlled by forces greater than he. In later writings Dick will return to the question of evil and try to comprehend a universe where it is such a powerful force. He will develop a cosmogony to explain it. But that will not happen for a decade. He goes no further in this novel than to identify the existence of evil—both in the outer and in the inner world.

Then Dick turns to his final concern in *Palmer Eldritch*. How does the responsible individual live in a world where evil is real? Richard Hnatt clearly sees the options as soon as he undergoes Dr. Denkmal's E Therapy:

> Below lay the tomb world, the immutable cause-and-effect world of the demonic. At median extended the layer of the human, but at any instant a man could plunge—descend as if sinking—into the hell-layer beneath. Or: he could ascend to the ethereal world above, which constituted the third of the trinary layers. Always, in this middle level of the human, a man risked the sinking. And yet the possibility of ascent lay before him; any aspect or sequence of reality *could become either,* at any instant. Hell and heaven, not after death but now! Depression, all mental illness, was the sinking. And the other . . . how was it achieved? (74)

Richard immediately intuits the answer to his question. The rising is achieved "through empathy, the grasping of another not from outside but from the inner."

Barney and Leo in their confrontations with the evil Palmer metaphor the split possibilities lying within the human heart and mind. Barney thinks; Leo acts. Barney gives in to Palmer; Leo resists him. Barney goes passively into Palmer's private world of illusions and longs for death, while Leo fights Palmer and vows on behalf of all mankind that he will kill this evil force before it consumes his fellow men. Barney offers so little resistance to the three stigmata of alienation, blurred reality, and despair that he for a time actually becomes Palmer. Leo in contrast may be cursed by the stigmata but he never ceases to fight them. His brief journey into the future reveals to him that he is a *chooser*, an early form of man whose choices will determine the evolutionary course of the human race (109-14). It *is* possible to fight against evil and win because in this alternative future he visits the marker commemorating his slaying of Palmer.

Leo is not heroic. Dick deliberately creates only antiheroes. But Leo has the capacity to act heroically when he finds himself in a situation where such action is required. As Dick once said, "certain agonizing situations create, on the spot, a human where a moment before there was only, as the Bible says, clay."[5] Thus Leo, the greedy industrialist, becomes an authentic human. He recognizes his transformation and declares it in the memo he dictates after he returns from Mars—a memo placed at the beginning of the novel although he writes it at the end.

> I mean, after all; you have to consider we're only made out of dust. That's admittedly not much to go on and we shouldn't forget that. But even considering, I mean it's a sort of beginning, we're not doing too bad. So I personally have faith that even in this lousy situation we're faced with we can make it. You get me?

Barney, the thinker who broods rather than acts, has nevertheless by novel's end, martialed his will enough to escape from the despair threatening to drag him forever into the tomb world. He decides to live on the colonial frontiers of Mars and work on his garden, building irrigation ditches to fight the desert.

What certainty has either man discovered through these encounters with Palmer Eldritch? Nothing beyond their conviction that evil exists, a powerful force in the universe. Evil comes from an alien power that aims to isolate man from the *koinos kosmos,* or shared universe, and trap him in a purely private world where he must live alone. This is enough for the two men to know with certainty. They both will resist evil, each in his way. Leo will fight it, Barney will attempt to understand its mysteries. Neither will win his quest, but that does not matter; much more important is to be on the quest.

Dick commented in his 1972 Vancouver speech that "our flight must be not only to the stars but into the nature of our own beings. Because it is not merely *where* we go, to Alpha Centaurus or Be-

5. *Philip K. Dick: Electric Shepherd*, ed. Bruce Gillespie (Melbourne: Norstrilia Press, 1975).

telgeuse, but what we are as we make our pilgrimages there. Our natures will be going there, too. *Ad astra*—but *per hominum*. And we must never lose sight of that." In *Palmer Eldritch* Dick takes us on a pilgrimage where we discover the nature of the human heart. It is filled with the potential to create and the potential to destroy. Only by fighting the evil and nurturing the creative can we evolve to become fully human.

What is it about this novel that so fascinates? No pat answers here, but a few comments. A terrible power propels the work—a schizophrenic power. Pattern and chaos dance together, first one leading and then the other. The Form Destroyer, when he succeeds, pulls the narrative down into the isolation of subjective awareness where the reader can no longer understand it. The Form Creator, when she succeeds, pulls the narrative thread back to the world of the shared reality we understand together—and even lifts us momentarily to the upper realms of the mystical vision. In this novel, surely Dick's most dazzling work imaginatively, he manages to create near chaos without falling into it. His brooding intelligence stands above the little world of the novel, watching the two forces struggle but never letting chaos win for very long. Author and fictional creation thus become a metaphor for the cosmos as Dick will in later works explain it. Some Power beyond good and evil has created a universe where the Form Destroyer struggles to overcome the Form Creator—but does not win. As that Power "makes up" reality, so the author in making up fictional reality mimics his Creator.

The presence of evil in the world would continue to haunt Dick over the years even after he had written *Palmer Eldritch* as a means of exorcising from his consciousness that satanic face in the sky with its metal leer. He would struggle with the question of how the omnipotent, omnipresent, loving God of the Christian religion can allow evil to exist. The motif reappears in much of the fiction that follows. Two short stories are particularly interesting to us as we complete our exploration of *Palmer Eldritch*.

First is "Faith of Our Fathers." It was published in 1967, three years after *Palmer Eldritch* and it serves as a little commentary on the novel. Dick wrote the story for Harlan Ellison's *Dangerous Visions*, a collection of stories hailed as experimental New Wave science fiction. Dick uses no new material here but instead draws once again on the theme of illusions, drugs, and evil—this time doing a flipflop to reverse one of the major ideas of *Palmer Eldritch*. The story provides another example of the dialectal process propelling Dick's imagination. In *Palmer Eldritch* he created a world where the God of evil uses a drug to trap each individual in a private hallucination that isolates him from his fellowmen. In "Faith of Our Fathers" just the opposite happens. All the population is trapped in a shared hallucination achieved when the Ministry puts a drug in the water supply. A small group of rebels become suspicious and take a drug to counter the hallucinatory drug and allow them to experience true reality. But to their surprise, reality comes in twelve different versions. As one character puzzles, "That makes no sense, rationally. It's the hallucination which should differ from person to person, and the reality experience which should be ubiquitous—it's all turned around."

The story is set in Communist-dominated Hanoi where Tung Chien, a middle-level functionary, lives. A coalition of Asiatic Communist nations has won the war and established control over the United States. The totalitarian regime is headed by the Benefactor, a mysterious, all-powerful, messianic leader whom Tung sees only on television. He advances in the party and is finally invited to a social event where he will actually meet the Benefactor. Tanya Lee, the representative of the rebels, gives him some of the anti-hallucinatory drug to take to the party with him so that he will be able to see what the Benefactor is really like. She hopes Tung can give them some idea of whether the Benefactor is non-Terran, their worst fear.

The Benefactor possesses all Palmer Eldritch's evil characteristics, but now they are magnified. It is a mere blob, without any redeeming human qualities at all. And it is filled with hate. "As it moved it drained the life from each person in turn; it ate the people who had assembled, passed on, ate again, ate more with an endless appetite." Tung watches in horror, realizing that it is "a globe hung in the room, with fifty thousand eyes, a million eyes—billions: an eye for each living thing as it waited for each thing to fall, and then stepped on the living thing as it lay in a broken state."

When Tung tries to leave, the evil power follows him. Desperately he attempts to escape into death by throwing himself off a balcony but it restrains him by laying its extension on his shoulder and it tells him he may not die until it is ready to kill him. Tung finally strikes out at it in desperation and then falls into blackness. When he awakens it has vanished and he has returned to the shared hallucinatory world. But he carries with him on the shoulder where it had restrained him a mark, a stigmata, from which blood oozes.

The idea of alien power among the stars stays with Dick. He next flips the evil Palmer into his opposite to create Thors Provoni in *Our Friends from Frolix 8* (1970). While the novel is not successful, it does contain passages rich with interesting ideas and characters that allow us better to understand Dick's methods of creativity. Provoni is one such character. Because the masses on Earth are held in bondage by a totalitarian government, Provoni sets out in space to seek help from aliens. Ten years later he returns, just as Palmer did. But Provoni brings with him an alien motivated by love and empathy who uses his mysterious and awesome powers to free the masses and vitiate the ruthless bureaucrats. This alien, called Morgo, has the power to engulf men in his body, just as the evil force encountered in space for the industrialist Palmer Eldritch consumed him. But Morgo uses his power only against totalitarian bureaucrats.

The idea of a cannibal god who eats men remains in Dick's mind. Years later he returns to explore it once again in "Rautavaara's Case" (1980). Now he strips away all the supernatural qualities from the extraterrestrials. They are merely three technicians from Proxima Centauri, where life has evolved as a plasma rather than the somatic form of life on Earth. Their religion has developed so differently from Earth's that it is the exact opposite. Their parallel to our Christ is called the Afterlife Guide of the Soul, and their concept of their basic relationship to God is diametrically opposite ours. The Proxima technicians attempt to rescue three Earthpersons when their survey ship is destroyed. They can resuscitate just one, Rautavaara, and they restore only her brain since, without bodies themselves, they count the brain as the vital site of life where the psyche is located.

The story flips between the Proxima point of view and Rautavaara's point of view. Thus Dick can powerfully dramatize for his reader what it means to encounter a totally alien mindset. For when Christ (now appearing as the Proxima Guide to the Soul) comes to take the souls of the two dead Earthmen, he calmly eats them. As the Proxima technicians explain later to an Earth Board of Inquiry, "the Earth race drinks the blood of their God in the Eucharist; they eat his flesh; that way they become immortal. To them, there is no scandal to this. They find it perfectly natural. Yet to us it is dreadful. That the worshiper should eat and drink its God. Awful to us; awful indeed. A disgrace and a shame—an abomination. The higher should always prey on the lower. The God should consume the worshiper."

"Rautavaara's Case" is a small bright diamond, sparkling with the essence of Dick. It is open in exploring religious possibilities, a contrast to *Palmer Eldritch*, which was written seventeen years earlier, and a work in which he hides his religious interest. When he wrote the short story he had been meditating for a number of years about the meaning of his 1974 mystical encounter with the light beam. In contrast, when he earlier wrote *Palmer Eldritch* his only mystical experience was the leering satanic face in the sky. As a close reading of the novel demonstrates and as Dick later tells us, he was attempting through his writing to exorcize that devil from his consciousness. During this period he had joined the Episcopal church in Point Reyes, partly at least because his wife Anne urged him to do so in the hope that it might benefit their deteriorating marriage. Outwardly he gave no indication to her that religious questions were of much importance to him. The novel suggests otherwise; that subconscious world from which he drew the images for his fiction was bubbling with tormented activity.

Eventually he would find answers to assuage the guilt and alienation distressing him during this period. But not for a long, desolate stretch of time, not until he had been totally sucked down into the entropic tomb world that Barney manages to escape in *Palmer Eldritch*.

6
Mechanical Mirrors, the Double, and
Do Androids Dream of Electric Sheep?

Do Androids Dream of Electric Sheep? was written during the first half of 1966. Based on this date, it belongs in Dick's third Entropic Period, when both the form and the subject matter of his fiction began to change from what they had been in the previous period. As noted earlier, the novel is a revision of *We Can Build You* (written in 1962 but not published until 1969), and it uses some structural patterns more common to the second than to the third period of his fiction. Thus the novel is difficult to categorize. It is concerned with entropy and death, as are most of the novels of the third period, but it is much less pessimistic than the other novels written between 1965 and 1972. Nor does it have the runaway plot usually present in the fiction of this period.

Do Androids Dream is one of Dick's most important novels, not only because it is so intricately and beautifully patterned but also because it explores a question of great importance to Dick: How do we tell the authentic human from that which only masquerades as a human? The titles of two of Dick's major essays emphasize the significance of the theme. "The Android and the Human" was the first delivered as a speech at the Vancouver SF Convention in 1972. "Man, Android, and Machine" was written to be delivered at a convention in London in 1976. Ill health prevented Dick from going to England, but the speech was read in his absence.

In the Vancouver essay, Dick expresses his concern:

> I would like then to ask this: what is it, in our behavior, that we can call specifically human? That is special to us as a living species? And what is it that, at least up to now, we can consign as merely machine behavior, or by extension, insect behavior, or reflex behavior? And I would include, in this, the kind of pseudo-human behavior exhibited by

what were once living men—creatures who have, in ways I wish to discuss next, become instruments, means, rather than ends, and hence to me analogues of machines in the *bad* sense, in the sense that although biological life continues, metabolism goes on, the soul—for lack of a better term—is no longer there or at least no longer active. And such does exist in our world—it always did, but the production of such inauthentic human activity has become a science of government and like agencies now. The reduction of humans to mere use—men made into machines, serving a purpose which although "good" in the abstract sense has, for its accomplishment, employed what I regard as the greatest evil imaginable: the placing of what was a free man who laughed and cried and made mistakes and wandered off into foolishness and play a restriction that limits him, despite what he may imagine or think, to the fulfilling of an aim outside of his own personal—however puny—destiny.

Robots and androids (Dick uses the terms interchangeably) appear in the earliest short stories, for example, "Imposter," "Second Variety," and "The Defenders." In these stories, robots are usually controlled by alien forces and used to attack men. They and a variety of other electronic constructs are everpresent in his fiction, but perhaps most prolific in his first two periods. Here the robots work as straightforward metaphors, but by the time of *Do Androids Dream* Dick's metaphors become more complex, and he regularly uses doubles or twins. The metaphor evolves to the four-chambered structure discussed in chapter 1—a double ironic metaphor built of opposites facing each other. Comprehension requires a flip-flop, or reversal, in which awareness slips simultaneously in both directions through the mirror, viewing the polarities of possibility from each direction in the same instant—a complementary perception. At the same time the negative and positive aspects of each polarity must be seen.

During the last half of the 1960s, when Dick writes most of the fiction of his third period, he turns from political fiction exploring capitalist-fascist-bureaucratic structures to epistemological and ontological questions. His interest now is in exploring inner rather than outer space because he has become aware, he tells us, that "the greatest pain does not come down from a distant planet, but up from the depth of the human heart." The richest meanings derive from reading *Do Androids Dream* as a dramatization of the mind, or inner world, of the protagonist, Rick Deckard. Given this task, the novel discards the multiple-foci narrative technique of his previous novels and uses a single point of view. It also makes heavy use of doubles, since Dick sees man's nature as divided (although at the time he wrote the novel Dick was not aware of the research, first published by Robert E. Ornstein at Stanford University in 1973, describing the bimodal nature of the prefrontal brain).

The double first appeared in German literature. Jean Paul Richter coined the term *Doppelgänger* and used it in his novel *Siebenkäs* (1796), where a pair of close friends, each dependent on the other, stand before a mirror dressed alike, thus making four doubles. Doubles soon became frequent in German Romantic literature. Knowing Dick's fascination with all things German and also his love of classical music, one is not surprised to find that he first encountered the word *Doppelgänger* as the title of a song. It was a Heinrich Heine poem written early in the nineteenth century and set to music by Franz Schubert. Dick said that another source which influenced his use of the double was Offenbach's *Tales of Hoffman*. The life-size windup doll in that opera first gave him the idea for a female robot. He was intrigued by the tale when he encountered it in the opera in the 1940s and as a result began to read the short stories of the German writer, E. T. A. Hoffman, including "The Sandman" (1814), the source for the mechanical woman in Offenbach's opera.[1] In the story a student named Nathaniel is tormented by an obsessive love for Olympia, an automaton doll. The story also involves doubles—an itinerant optician named Coppola and a lawyer called Coppelius who resemble each other. Nathaniel eventually realizes that Coppola and Coppelius exist only in his mind, phantoms of his own consciousness.

Dick's first use of the double occurs in a very early short story, "The Skull" (1952), in which Conger, the protagonist, is sent by the authorities back in time to kill a man who established a religious movement they wish to eliminate. His only clue to the man's identity is his skeleton. Returning to the time when the man was last seen, Conger looks closely at the skull and recognizes it as his own. Other early stories containing doubles are "Upon the Dull Earth," "Second Variety," and "Paycheck." *The Cosmic Puppets* (1957) portrays a

---

1. Dick provided this information to me in telephone conversations.

cosmic struggle between the twin gods, Ahriman and Ormazd. The novel also describes a young girl who makes a miniature golem, a duplicate of herself, and thus she is able to act as two.

Sigmund Freud warned of man's irrational nature, claiming that, unbridled, it would become a destroyer. Half a century earlier, Dostoevski had known better. He warned instead in *Notes from the Underground* that the danger of man's self-destruction lay not in his failure to control the irrational but in his denial of its existence and his adulation of the rational. Dick, writing in the Dostoevskian tradition, creates a world where Dostoevski's fears have come true. Man's rational nature, metaphored by a host of robots who are highly intelligent and free from emotions, predominates. *Do Androids Dream,* shaped with the poetic economy that is a hallmark of Dick's finest fiction, dramatizes the painful awakening of the protagonist to the realization that as he struggles to survive in a modern mechanized wasteland, he himself is turning into a machine.

Is a rational world a better world? Can problems best be solved by using logic and denying emotions? To dramatize his answer, Dick relies heavily on doubles. He uses a double narrative line and numerous sets of character doubles, both human and robot.

At first reading the novel appears to be a conventional cops and killers tale, with the future setting and the robot killers giving the required science fiction twist. It is tightly knit and, except for the double plot, even observes the classical unities. The action occurs in a single day in a single setting—the postholocaust, nearly lifeless, wasteland of San Francisco. Rick Deckard, the tough bounty hunter, wants to make money—to make a killing—so that he can buy a big live animal. Such an animal is a status symbol because big live animals are rare. He is chagrined because he now owns only a fake electronic sheep. He earns $1,000 for every outlaw android he kills, and he proposes to kill six in one day. *Do Androids Dream* can be read as a fast-paced adventure tale. And yet, even on first reading it seems to be something more—a story strangely haunted by the gentle, lonely idiot, John R. Isidore, who falls in love with a robot and weeps when she is killed. What has John Isidore to do with Rick Deckard? They never even meet until the final chapters of the novel.

The answer to that question provides the necessary key to unlock the novel's meaning. *Do Androids Dream* is not really concerned with the outer events in a policeman's day. The novel creates a complex metaphor mirroring the inward action which transforms Rick's mind. Isidore is Rick's second self, his alienated self—the complementary opposite of the Rick who kills for money. Only at the end of the novel, as the two men weep and mourn together over the dead body of the mechanical woman they loved, are the two selves united. The novel is best read as the inner journey of a divided, restless mind seeking wholeness. The function of the many doubles in the novel becomes clear. They represent all the alternatives the individual encounters as he struggles to make those choices and take those actions that will give authenticity and moral dignity to his existence. At the end the reader discovers no pat answer. According to Dick none is available. But as one character asks, "Isn't that the revelation?"

The structure of the novel follows the mode of polyphonic music, with various voices singing once again the ideas that haunt Dick's mind. One is the transformation of our landscape, both mental and physical, by the fall of the atomic bomb and by the development of sophisticated electronics that gives us such technologies as TV and high level artificial intelligence. Isidore is a victim of atomic fallout. Once a bright youth, he is now "hairy, ugly, dirty, stooped, snaggle-toothed and gray," although he is still young. As he is painfully aware, his intelligence has devolved.

A second theme explores the cosmic dimension of man's existence. He lives in a universe where entropy constantly increases and he must contemplate not only his own death but the death of the universe. Everything runs down. J. R. Idisore has his own term for it—*kipple*. He says, "No one can win against kipple, except temporarily and maybe in one spot, like in my apartment I've sort of created a stasis between the pressure of kipple and nonkipple, for the time being. But eventually I'll die or go away, and then the kipple will again take over. It's a universal principle operating throughout the universe; the entire universe is moving toward a final state of total, absolute kipple-ization."[2]

The third theme once again explores the question of evil. How are we to account for a universe where the destruction of forms seems to proceed at a faster rate than their creation? How can we believe in

2. *Do Androids Dream of Electric Sheep?* (New York: Doubleday, 1968), p. 49.

good when evil predominates? How can we justify killing, even when
it is done with the approval of the law, as in the case of Rick Deckard?
The creative good that opposes the destructive is metaphored by the
repairman or the artist—a single individual struggling alone and
achieving small successes. Isidore works for a little firm that repairs
electronic animals. Luba Luft, the opera singer who admires the
paintings of Expressionist Edvard Munch, is the inciting agent causing Rick Deckard to first question the morality of destroying robots.

The fourth theme, and the predominant one in *Do Androids
Dream*, explores the response of the individual to the contemporary
wasteland universe where he must live. Unable to remain whole, he
splits and occupies either the schizoid or the schizophrenic half of his
divided self. The schizoid individual is dominated by left brain functions. He denies his emotions and operates as an intelligent, logical
machine. The robot, or android, metaphors this schizoid personality.
In contrast, the schizophrenic personality is analogous to the right
brain function. He still responds emotionally to the world around
him, but in doing so, he experiences anxiety and cosmic angst so great
that he is driven to madness. In his madness he may descend into the
tomb world of death, as did Manfred in *Martian Time-Slip,* or ascend
into a momentary vision of light where he feels he experiences the
true nature of reality. Isidore's life is lived in cycles that lift him up
and then plunge him down. As a youth before the holocaust, he had
been able to restore animals to life. Then the creative power reversed
itself and he descended into the tomb world, from which he later
ascended. Another descent and reversal occur during the day portrayed in the novel.

The final theme is the possibility of a messiah, a theme to which
Dick has devoted little attention before *Do Androids Dream.* Will
someone come to save man from destruction in the entropic wasteland where he finds himself? Traditional religions say yes. Dick
discards that answer and explores the question anew. He uses the
device of Mercerism and the black empathy box to metaphor
metaphysical possibility. His answer to the question of a messiah
reminds the reader of that found by French existentialists Camus and
Sartre, and makes readily understandable the great popularity Dick's
fiction enjoys in France. Like Sisyphus, we must daily push our
boulder up the hill of uncertainty, hoping for an answer if the summit
is ever achieved.

The messiah in the novel also has a double. Both arrive via electronic media—the screens of the two TV sets. Buster Friendly on the conventional TV set and Wilbur Mercer on the fusion box are complementary opposites who both deal in image making. One acts; one talks. One creates faith; one destroys it. Buster Friendly, the ubiquitous TV commentator, chats endlessly and vacuously with glamorous stars, while Wilbur Mercer eternally toils up his barren hill, dodging rocks. They both turn out to be doubly inauthentic. First, we never encounter them in physical reality but know them only by their images on the screen. In the end, Buster is revealed to be an android, not a man. Mercer turns out to be a drunk from Gary, Indiana, not a savior. And yet—for those who believe in them, their images become reality. However, one cannot believe in both since Buster reveals Mercer as a fraud. Or can one? Can a man's actions or his words be true, even though he himself is a fraud? The double-edged contradiction in the Buster Friendly/Wilbur Mercer image is an excellent example of Dick's ability to embody a complex paradox in a dynamic metaphor.

A comparison of Rick's day with Isidore's reveals the parallels between the two narratives. Each man's mind is in motion, but because their starting points are at opposite poles, their motions counter each other. As the novel opens, Isidore is an innocent who accepts and loves all forms, living and electronic. He makes no distinction between authentic and false, android and human. In contrast, Rick is a killer of androids. He dislikes them even though he has difficulty differentiating them from humans. Isidore merges with Mercer through the black empathy box before he sets off to work. Rick has not merged for a long time.

Each man returns home in the evening a changed man. Rick, the killer, is transformed by love; Isidore, who loves and nurtures, is altered by violence. Each, prodded by anguish, discovers the answer to the question of how a human is different from an intelligent machine that resembles a human.

The Isidore chapters are interwoven with the Deckard chapters, the action in one echoing the other but reversing it. Deckard destroys; Isidore heals. And although their actions occur simultaneously, in order to understand how they function in the novel, I shall examine each separately.

Analysis is made even more difficult by the fact that each narra-

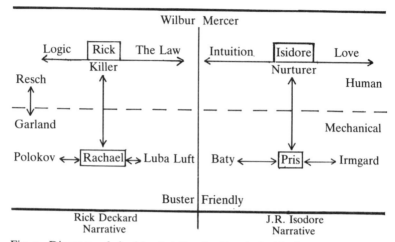

Fig. 3. Diagram of double-plot line in *Do Androids Dream of Electric Sheep?*

tive contains sets of Janus-faced metaphors comprised of opposites constantly reversing themselves. Thus each pole of the paradoxical metaphor is both true and not true at the same time. The power comes from their dynamic interaction. One needs to examine the opposites simultaneously, a task easy enough for the mind but not for the printed page. Figure 3 presents a diagram of the intricate structure of the machine-human metaphor used in the novel.

Rick and Isidore each encounter three androids that are mirrors of but not identical to each other. The only exact duplicates are Rachael, whom Rick loves; and Pris, whom Isidore loves. Rachael, however, is a legal android since she is a model that the Rosen Corporation has kept for experimentation rather than exporting it to Mars. Pris, her double, is an outlaw—one of the eight androids who have killed Martian settlers and escaped to Terra. Android Max Polokov is an aggressive killer; Luba Luft is an artist. In the other plot, Roy Baty is the aggressor; Irmgard the warm, responsive female. Another set of doubles exists in Rick's world: the bounty hunter Phil Resch seems to be an android but turns out to be a man; the police chief Garland poses as a human but turns out to be an android.

Rick metaphors law. He is free from ambiguity. As he begins his day of killing, he is certain of his ability to distinguish android from human. It is not superficial appearance (they look like humans); it is not intelligence (they are as intelligent as humans). It is their lack of emotional response and empathy. They are cold, solitary, indifferent to anyone's survival but their own. They are unable to fuse with others on the empathy box. True, some schizoid humans demonstrate these same symptoms, but the Voight Empathy Test differentiates the androids in those instances. Rick is certain he has never killed a human and that he is justified in killing androids. After all, they are escaped killers from Mars. But by day's end his encounters with androids have reversed his view about killing and moved it to a kind of anguished and instructed innocence that holds killing to be wrong but an inescapable evil in the world.

In contrast to Rick, Isidore metaphors love.[3] He does not differentiate between good and evil. By nightfall he has lost his naïve innocence, schooled by the ruthless android Pris, who holds life valueless and sadistically tears the legs from what may be Earth's last living spider. He learns that Mercer, in whom he believed, is a fraud. And yet, his descent again into the tomb world of death brings about a reversal and the return of his faith even in the face of his shattered illusions. As the novel ends, Mercer appears to him in a vision and the spider comes back to life with its legs restored. Isidore joins Rick—to whom Mercer also appears—in a regained and wise innocence, aware of the existence of death, destruction, and evil, but still able to keep faith with life.

The major narrative dramatizes Rick's encounters with seven mechanical humanoids. As the day begins he is a man of conventional convictions. During the day he completes the assignment his police chief has given him to destroy six escaped killer androids from Mars. Each encounter with an android disorients him further from

3. John Isidore is reminiscent of Jack Isidore in *Confessions of a Crap Artist*. Comments Dick made during the last years of his life suggest he regarded them as the same character, a character of whom he was very fond. John Isidore is one of Dick's divine fools, one we can easily admire. I find Jack Isidore of *Crap Artist* somewhat less admirable, and wonder if Dick's memory of Jack had not been colored by time. When *Crap Artist* was submitted to publishers after it was written (probably in 1958), Dick used the pseudonym Jack Isidore. When in 1977 he sent me an autographed copy, he signed it with both names, Philip K. Dick and Jack Isidore.

his certainty that his conventional view of reality and morality is the correct one.

The secondary narrative pictures J. R. Isidore's encounter during the same day with three of the androids that Rick has been assigned to kill. Isidore is unable to recognize the androids as anything but lonely, frightened humans, so he shelters them and feeds them. His later discovery that they are androids does not change his behavior because he loves all creatures regardless of their form and he opposes all destruction.

Outer mirrors inner in the novel. The episodes of the major narrative are carefully structured to represent the inner changes that alter Rick from a killer to a man who abhors violence and finally unite him with his lost second self, Isidore. The most interesting reading of the novel examines the change in Rick's awareness resulting from each of his encounters with an android.

His first encounter with Rachael makes him vividly aware of how difficult it has become to distinguish between a human and an android. He is uncertain whether she is truly an android or merely a schizoid human—one who is cold and unable to respond emotionally. The essential element of an authentic human, Rick believes, is empathy—the ability to respond to the needs of other humans. Rachael's android nature can only be established by the delicate Voigt Empathy Test. Uncertainty and the possibility of error are introduced into Rick's awareness.

Rick's second encounter leads him to realize he cannot trust his perceptions of reality. The android Polokov has so successfully disguised himself as a Russian law officer named Kadalyi that he is almost able to kill Rick before Rick discovers the disguise. When Rick exclaims in surprise, "You're not Polokov, you're Kadalyi," the android replies, "Don't you mean that the other way around? You're a bit confused" (65). Thus early in the novel Dick gives the reader a clue about the reversals and disguises that are to follow. After killing the android, Rick muses that "the encounter with Kadalyi-Polokov had changed his ideas rather massively" (p. 67). Now he knows that things may not actually be as they first appear.

His third encounter is with Luba Luft, who performs with the San Francisco Opera. She mirrors to him the feminine, creative part of his nature which he has so totally suppressed. She sings with great beauty an aria from his favorite opera, Mozart's *The Magic Flute*.

Thinking of Mozart, who was also young and who died so soon after creating such beautiful music, Rick notes the parallel with Luba. Her fate will be the same as Mozart's when she finishes singing. He is shocked when Luba points out how cold and indifferent he is and suggests he take the Empathy Test to determine if he too is an android.

The fourth encounter is with an android police chief named Garland in a fake police station rigged by the androids to look real. Rick soon discovers that the apparent reality of the police station is merely illusion. This recognition leads to his awareness that any supposed reality is probably only an illusion one's head has been programmed to accept as real.

The episode that follows is a classical recognition scene. Rick looks into the mirror of a character who is his double and discovers his own reflection. In the fake police station he is joined by Phil Resch, the bounty killer who is his twin in inner appearance. They are both men who hunt androids. Or can it be that Phil Resch is really an android who has been programmed to believe he is a man? His cold-blooded killing of Luba Luft makes Rick believe it possible. As he looks at his killer double, Rick recognizes that he may have become what he abhors in Phil Resch. Resch is a man unable to feel empathy. This insight about himself is so shattering that Rick can hardly go on with his assignment of killing androids. Appropriate to this awareness that he has quite wrongly suppressed his feeling self, Rick goes to an animal store and purchases a female goat.

He also impulsively merges with the Mercer box, begging for help as he realizes that he will violate his newly discovered identity if he continues to kill. And yet . . . the androids are killers and must be destroyed. Mercer tells him to carry out his task, saying, "You will be required to do wrong no matter where you go. It is the basic condition of life, to be required to violate your own identity. At some time, every creature which lives must do so. It is the ultimate shadow, the defeat of creation; this is the curse at work, the curse that feeds on all life. Everywhere in the universe" (119). The view expressed by Mercer is essential Philip Dick philosophy, and we find it in novel after novel. Nothing is easy; nothing is comprehensible. Still, we must go on.

The pair of scenes that next occur are the most powerful in the novel. The two men learn the wrenching pain of loving someone who is unable to respond. Rick makes love to Rachael while at the same moment Isidore has an encounter with Pris, her twin. The scenes are mirror opposites of each other. Each catches the tragic essence of creative power when it has become perverted to destruction. The sexual union of Rick and Rachael is the summa of falsity and mechanical motions. They both yearn for something more than the barren act can possibly produce. She longs to be human and bear a child. She knows she never will. She wonders, "Is it a loss? I don't really know; I have no way to tell. How does it feel to have a child? How does it feel to be born for that matter? We're not born; we don't grow up; instead of dying from old age we wear out like ants. Ants again; that's what we are. Not you; I mean me. Chitinous reflex-machines who aren't really alive . . . . I'm not alive!" (128).

Rick hopes his lovemaking will lead her to be willing to help him destroy her twin, Pris. She promises. But after the act, her promise turns out to have been a mere maneuver to get him in bed so she could vitiate his will to kill, a performance she has successfully carried out with other men on at least nine occasions. She tells him afterward, "Anyway, you know the truth, the brick-hard, irregular, slithery surface of truth. I'm just an observer and I won't intervene to save you; I don't care if Roy Baty nails you or not. I care whether I get nailed" (126).

At the same time Rachael is making love to Rick, we see her double, Pris, mutilating the living spider Isidore has just found with such delight. This is a brilliant metaphorical yoking of meaningless love and death if the reader envisions the scenes simultaneously, as Dick intends he should. The words of Rachael in one scene are echoed by Pris in the parallel scene.

The three brief concluding chapters of the novel bring Isidore and Rick together after each has undergone his destructive experience with a female robot. Again, parallels echo throughout the scene and contradictions abound. The action opens with Isidore's vision of Mercer after Pris has destroyed his spider, and the TV revelation has shattered his faith in Mercer's authenticity. The action closes with Rick's hallucination in the desert where he, too, sees Mercer.

Each man has been schooled by suffering and made ready for an epiphany. Isidore's occurs after he drowns his multilated spider. Driven by despair, he descends again into the tomb world of death that forever haunts him. Frightened, he calls for help and Mercer seems to answer. Miraculously, the spider returns, alive and with its legs restored. Mercer appears in a vision and tells Isidore that he really is a fraud. The paradox of the imagery is followed immediately by another contradiction. Rick and Isidore meet at last. To Rick's request for help so he can find the androids he must kill, Isidore says no. But Mercer suddenly appears to warn Rick. Just in time Rick saves himself by shooting Pris, who awaits him, gun in hand, on the stairs.

Afterward, when Rick has killed the last two androids, Isidore joins him and the two men mourn over the dead bodies. The contraries of life are united—the logical and the emotional, the masculine and the feminine, the left- and the right-brain lobes. The two halves seem contradictory. Rick destroys; Isidore nurtures. And yet they both exist. Rick, finally arriving at a wisdom beyond definition, says, "Everything is true."

The novel appropriately concludes with a final scene containing a contradiction. Rick flees alone into the desert, in anguish because he has been forced to kill. As he plods along, hungry in the desert heat, a "vague and almost hallucinatory pall hazed over his mind." He experiences a vision. Afterward, musing on the experience, he tries to describe it. "It's strange. I had the absolute, utter, completely real illusion that I had become Mercer and people were lobbing rocks at me. But not the way you experience it when you hold the handles of an empathy box. When you use an empathy box you feel you're with Mercer. The difference is that I wasn't with anyone: I was alone" (153).

Maybe reality is a fake. The living toad Rick stumbles upon in the dust after his visions is, he concludes, like life—"Life carefully buried up to its forehead in the carcass of a dead world." He believes his finding of the toad, Mercer's favorite animal, is an omen of regeneration. But upon taking it home, he discovers it is only an electronic construct.

What are we to believe? What is false appearance and what is true reality? How can we differentiate illusion from reality? Finally, this is the question which subsumes every other question for Dick in all his fiction. In *Do Androids Dream* the reader is spiraled through so many assertions and negations and negations of negations that at the end of the novel he is uncertain of what Dick would have him believe. Dick consistently refuses to provide straightforward answers because language limits; a statement can encompass only one view at a time, and he holds truth to be comprised of complementary statements and also to be very tentative. He must often resort to irony, which contains a negative of the assertion, and to paradox, which embodies an apparent contradiction because both modes allow him to express his double vision.

The novel does provide clues to its meanings for the reader who is willing to track down all the allusions to music and art and literature. There are two paintings of Edvard Munch at the museum, *Puberty* and *The Shriek*. Munch was a Norwegian artist who painted the themes of death, fear, and anxiety, claiming he "heard the screams of nature." Dick uses these allusions in the novel to suggest that, like the girl in the painting, we are adolescents awakening into a new age, an age when human life will set out into the lifeless cosmos with electronic constructs as companions. The allusions to Mozart suggest the same antithetical condition: creativity in the face of death. Certainly the most revealing clue of all is the allusion to Alfred Jary, the French writer who held that hallucinations are superior to rational intelligence.

Perhaps Wilbur Mercer, toiling up his endless hill, is *not* a fraud. Perhaps we are to believe in him after all. Perhaps he still lives. Dick plants fascinating little clues for us. Mercer until his sixteenth year could bring things back to life, just as could his double, J. R. Isidore, who was found, Moses-like, floating in the water on a rubber rescue raft and raised by foster parents Frank and Cora Mercer. J. R. Isidore is certainly very much alive as long as people read Dick's fiction. He is the writer's most enduring wise fool and a character of whom Dick was especially fond.

It is difficult to reach a final conclusion about a novel like *Do Androids Dream,* which is certainly one of Dick's most complex and condensed works. Each reading reveals fascinating and strange details one had not noticed before. The revelation in turn requires a revision of the flash of insight one first experienced. It is a strange, haunting novel, and the last word about it has not been said. What can be said is that in Dick's use of the mechanical double to mirror man's fragmentation as he adulates reason and ignores the intuitive self, he has made a major contribution to the literature of the *Doppelgänger.*

Refusing to preach and relying totally on the power of the

metaphor, Dick gives powerful testimony to what happens when humans fall in love with machines; when they glorify reason and aggression—all those characteristics associated with the masculine polarity—and ignore the feminine qualities of creativity, nurture, and love. Survival requires not dominancy of one or the other but the union of opposites and, beyond that, the fusing of all individuals through an empathetic concern that creates human solidarity. The concept of empathy, so vividly expressed in the novel with the metaphor of the empathy box, becomes for Dick the critical characteristic that identifies a human.

Beyond empathy, our age must also continually seek out the feminine if life—that toad sunk up to his eyes in cosmic dust—is to survive. The search for the lost feminine half of oneself is not a new theme for Dick, who seems forever tormented by the loss of that twin sister who died in infancy. He first captured the image of this ghost buried in his psyche in a very early story, "Upon the Dull Earth" (1954). It tells of a young man named Rick whose bride Sylvia dies soon after they are married. She haunts him after her death, yearning for life but unable to return. Rick keeps seeking for ways to recover her. Finally in the conclusion of this strange, moving story he comes back home, defeated, alone, and desolate. He looks into the mirror and watches his face turn into Sylvia, begging for help. Sylvia is buried within, crying for release.

Almost thirty years later Dick finally becomes conscious of the melancholy theme of the loss of a female that haunts the pages of so many novels. In 1982 he noted, "If there can be said to be a tragic theme running through my life, it's the death of my twin sister . . . . My psychological problems are traceable to the loss of my sister."[4]

In closing our discussion of the mechanical double in Dick's fiction, one particularly powerful short story deserves mention. It is "The Electric Ant," written at about the same time as *Do Androids Dream*. In the novel Dick portrays androids as cold and indifferent to human pain, unable to empathize. In the short story he flips to the opposite point of view and imagines what it must be like to be an android. Garson Poole awakes in his hospital bed after an accident that amputated his right hand and discovers that he is not a man but a

---

4. Gregg Rickman, *The Last Testament*, (Long Beach: Fragments West/The Valentine Press, 1985), p. 93.

robot. His skin covers not flesh and blood but wires, circuits, and miniature components. Poole is shocked. "Christ, he thought, it undermines you, knowing this. I'm a freak, he realized. An inanimate object mimicking an animate one. But—he felt alive. Yet . . . he felt differently, now. About himself. Programmed. In me somewhere, he thought, there is a matrix fitted in place, a grid screen that cuts me off from certain thoughts, certain actions. And forces me into others. I am not free. I never was, but now I know it. That makes it different."

Having discovered that he is a machine with a programmed "reality" tape, Poole next realizes that this insight gives him the option of altering his tape. He thinks, "If I control my reality tape, I control reality. At least so far as I am concerned. My subjective reality . . . but that's all there is. Objective reality is a synthetic construct, dealing with a hypothetical universalization of a multitude of subjective realities."

This story is one of my favorites because it is quintessential Dick. It addresses the questions of illusion and reality, of machines masquerading as humans, and of human freedom—those questions so important to Dick that he answers them again and again in his writing, never satisfied with the answers he finds, constantly tossing them aside to look for new answers.

In his "Man, Android, and Machine" (1976) he speculates once again on the subject:

> We humans, the warm-faced and tender, with thoughtful eyes—we are perhaps the true machines. And those objective constructs, the natural objects around us and especially the electronic hardware we build, the transmitters and microwave relay stations, the satellites, they may be cloaks for authentic living reality inasmuch as they may participate more fully and in a way obscured to us in the ultimate Mind. Perhaps we see not only a deforming veil, but backwards. Perhaps the closest approximation to truth would be to say: "Everything is equally alive, equally free, equally sentient, because everything is not alive or half-alive or dead, but rather *lived through.*

Here we see the germ of the idea that Dick will develop into his Vast Active Living Intelligence System in *Valis*. But not before he himself has fallen into the tomb world of despair that haunts Jack Bohlen, J. R. Isidore, and various other characters in his fictional worlds.

7
Entropy, Death, and *Ubik*

For years depression had occasionally cast a dark glance in Dick's direction, but as the 1960s advanced, it began stalking him in earnest. Every place he turned, things fell apart. He was deeply troubled by the involvement of the United States in the Vietnam War and by the arms race between Russia and the United States. In 1966 the son of his friend Bishop James Pike committed suicide. Death seemed ubiquitous. The chaotic end of his marriage to Anne left him resentful and bitter. His depression led him to toy with the possibility of suicide. Entropy seemed to have caught him in a trap so strong that he could see no way to escape. As a temporary solution, he turned more and more to drugs.

From the beginning of his writing career Dick had regularly written about a nearly collapsed world where people were struggling to survive. But it was usually a postholocaust world where the worst was past, where people worked to rebuild the wasteland. Now as the decade of the sixties passed its midpoint, the theme of entropy and death shrouded his writing, shutting away the sparkle of humor and optimism often brightening his earlier novels. But his output did not diminish. He was driven by a demon of creation that would not let him rest. The number of books he produced from the time he finally divorced Anne in 1965 until his near fatal suicide attack in 1972 is impressive—at least ten novels and fifteen short stories although not all of the novels were new work. Some were either expansions of stories written in earlier periods or were old works just now being published. We need to remind ourselves that the order of publication is often not the order of writing. The critic who thinks he discovers developments and trends in the novels based on their order of publication has engaged in an act of the imagination, not scholarship.

Many of the novels written in this third or Entropic Period are of lesser quality than those of the preceding period. Some of them are near failures, but even these have their bright moments. Dick collaborated with Ray Nelson during this period, and the result was *The Ganymede Takeover,* one of the most dreadful novels to bear Dick's name. Dick did not work well with another writer. His later collaborative attempt with Roger Zelazny, *Deus Irae* (1976), was scarcely more successful and took years to complete.

Almost all the Dick novels written during this period call up once again character types, conflicts, settings, and electronic gadgets that had served Dick in earlier writings. He searches once more through his old short stories for material he can lift and use as part of a new novel. But a few works gleam amongst this heap of uneven writing pouring out from an author stalked by drugs, depression, and failing personal relationships, while simultaneously being driven by the need to write in order to survive economically.

As always with his incisive intelligence and acute sensitivity, Dick noted significant cultural and technological developments and used them in his fiction. The counterculture movement of the 1960s particularly attracted him. He agreed with their opposition to military involvement in foreign countries, suppression of minority groups, and totalitarian government. He applauded their reaction against materialistic values. He shared their fascination with drugs and music. He used amphetamines to aid him in turning out the prodigious amount of fiction he wrote during this decade. He also received prescription drugs for various physical problems he began to develop, including arrhythmic tachycardia. Sometime during the middle of the decade he took LSD on at least several occasions.

In 1964 after he left his wife Anne, he moved to Oakland where he lived with his mother for a short time. He had a brief affair with Grania Davidson, and then another with Nancy Hackett, whom he married in July of 1966. She was a beautiful, dark-haired girl about half his age who suffered from schizophrenia. He was now almost forty. During this period Dick met and had lengthy theological discussions with Bishop James Pike, a good friend of Nancy's stepmother, Marion Hackett. In March of 1967 a daughter was born to Nancy and Phil and they named her Isolde. In 1968 they moved into a house in San Raphael, where they lived until Nancy left him in 1970. According to letters he wrote at the time, she ran off with a member of the Black Panthers who lived next door. Now Phil's house became a hangout for teenagers who were part of the street drug scene. They listened to The Grateful Dead and played their guitars through his huge amplification system.

In 1971 Dick's house in San Raphael was burglarized, a puzzling event which was never explained either by Dick or the police who investigated. In a letter Dick wrote a few months after the burglary (included in an interview with Paul Williams in 1975 and published in *Rolling Stone*), he maintains that he was terrorized by a neo-Nazi group, who not only destroyed the contents of his house but threatened his life. Later he developed several different theories about who hit the house, none of which was ever proved or disproved. By now his writing had ceased, his financial condition was precarious, and he was heavily depressed.

In February 1972 he went to Vancouver, British Columbia, to deliver the Guest of Honor speech at the Science Fiction Convention there. He insisted his life was in danger if he remained in the San Francisco area. After the speech, he stayed in Vancouver, still so depressed that in a suicide attempt, he swallowed 700 milligrams of potassium bromide. But he also wrote the telephone number of a suicide center in large letters on a piece of cardboard—so he could dial it if he changed his mind. He did. He was admitted to X-Kalay, a drug treatment center, where he spent a number of weeks before he recovered enough to be released.

Although Dick does not fixate on the subject of entropy and death until this third period of his writing, it is by no means a new theme for him. As with all his themes, it is sprinkled in seed form throughout his short stories. In a very early story, "The Cookie Lady" (1953), he describes a small boy whose youth is mysteriously drained away by an older woman. At story's end, the little boy has become no more than a scrap of rubble, "something grey, something grey and dry . . . blowing up against the porch, carried by the wind." In "The Father-thing," written the following year, a little boy discovers that the father-thing has eaten his real father, leaving only his empty skin, brittle and cracking. And "Pay for the Printer" (1956) pictures a town nearly destroyed by war. The Biltong, an alien life form, has come to rescue these people by using its reprinting ability. It can duplicate artifacts as they wear out. But at the story's end, the Biltong himself begins to wear out and his reprints are full of errors as he approaches death.

Characters in a number of novels from Dick's second period are concerned about if not obsessed with death. Jones in *The World Jones Made* must remain conscious while he undergoes his own devolvement after death since he experiences time a year in the future. Manfred Steiner in *Martian Time-Slip* has terrifying visions of aging and death, and Hoppy Harrigan in *Dr. Bloodmoney* is afraid of the dead. J. R. Isidore in *Do Androids Dream* sees the kipplization, or decay, of the universe. Various characters also experience depression and consider or use suicide as an escape—Pete Gardner in *The Game Players of Titan,* Lydia Dangerfield in *Dr. Bloodmoney,* Barney Mayerson in *The Three Stigmata of Palmer Eldritch.*

In this third period Dick writes incessantly of death and entropy—or the Form Destroyer as he often calls it. In *Counter-Clock World* time runs backward, and people return from the grave. In *Ubik* half-lifers exist in a frozen limbo somewhere between life and death. In *A Maze of Death* many of the members of a colonizing party on an uninhabited planet are claimed by death.

The male characters of the novels of the late sixties are often aging, and they have young wives or mistresses, mirrors of Dick's personal life at this time. Gino Molinari (*Now Wait for Last Year*) is an aging secretary general kept alive by organ transplants and the wheedling tirades of his eighteen-year-old mistress. In *Counter-Clock World* Sebastian Hermes, the elderly owner of vitarium that assists dead persons in returning to life, has a beautiful wife who is twenty-two years younger than he.

The Zap Gun is perhaps as closely autobiographical of Dick's emotional life as any of his novels, although as noted previously, he draws freely on persons, places, and events in his life for material in all his novels. Here Lars Powderdry has a domineering mistress, Maren Faine, whom he discards when he meets a younger woman, Lilo Topchev. In trance states Lars has visions of new weapons which he then sketches and supplies to the government. This is his means of earning a living, and he fears the day he will lose his talent and be unable to produce sketches of new weapons. He is so weary and overworked that he constantly takes a variety of pills to keep going.

Ubik (1969), of all Dick's novels on the subject, most successfully embodies the essence of entropy and death. It is a strange novel, almost a half-life novel, neither dead nor alive. From its opening page *Ubik* struggles to overcome the entropic process. Its author is tired, he needs to write to stay alive but he has nothing new to say, his creative powers have been nearly devoured by emotional stress. Still he must try. As a starting point, his mind seems to gather up scraps of material for the novel in almost a random fashion. He assembles the usual SF conventions—time travel, space travel, psionic powers.

For characters he goes to the huge palette he has accumulated over the years and dips in his brush. There's the disturbed child Jory fallen into the tomb world like Manfred from *Martian Time-Slip*. Pat, the destructive female, lacks the robot qualities of Pris in *Do Androids Dream* but she is just as vicious. The character traits of the two protagonists, Glen Runciter and Joe Chip, remind us of Leo Bulero and Barney Mayerson in *Palmer Eldritch*. Both Glen and Leo are businessmen who in a crisis set aside economic concerns to attempt to rescue a fellow man. The mainstream novel *The Man Whose Teeth Were All Exactly Alike*, written about 1961 but not published until 1984, has as its protagonist Leo Runcible, who at great financial cost performs a service to the citizens of a small California community. He reminds us of Glen Runciter in *Ubik*. Joe Chip struggles to rise out of passivity and despair as did Barney in the earlier novel. Negro Al Hammond echoes Stuart McConchie in *Dr. Bloodmoney*. No new character inventions here.

Nor does Dick begin with any new ideas. Once again he asks, What is reality? What signs tell us we can trust commonplace reality? How do we explain a material reality that keeps changing as it moves through time? What universal forces are responsible for the evolving forms we observe around us? What powers have taken over when these forms begin to devolve and decay? Now he pushes decay to its ultimate and imagines what might lie on the other side of death.

In the 1960s the legal definition of death had been altered. The new definition stated that death occurs not when the heart stops beating but when brain activity ceases. During this period R. C. W. Ettinger wrote *The Prospect of Immortality*, a book popularizing the idea of freezing newly dead bodies until a cure for their disease could be found, and soon the Cryonics Society of California actually began freezing dead bodies. Probably Dick fertilized this event with his tireless imagination, and the fascinating idea of "half life" was born. The question Dick addressed to the possibilities of half life was brilliant. What would go on in the subconscious minds of those frozen persons? Certainly some activity, since the brain waves would not have ceased at the time they were frozen. Add the possibility of a technology allowing communication between their brains and those of the living. And lo, Herbert von Vogelsang's Beloved Brethern Moratorium in Zurich, Switzerland, appears.

Now Dick has assembled the pieces for *Ubik,* and he begins to write, but with ennui. The first third of the novel nearly succumbs to the entropic process. Critics who belittle *Ubik* find ample evidence for their condemnation in the first six chapters. The plot is tired— once again two corporations engage in a business war. The characters have no more existence than a name and a garrish costume. Joe Chip dresses in "a sporty maroon wrapper, twinkle-toes turned-up shoes and a felt cap with a tassle." The eleven psionics assembling in Glen Runciter's office might well have dressed for a crazy costume party. Edie Dorn wears a cowboy hat, black lace mantilla, and bermuda shorts; Tippy Jackson, ersatz vicuña trousers and a gray sweat shirt printed with a full-face portrait of Bertrand Lord Russell, Fred Zafsky, a shift dress the color of a baboon's ass. The name of the spaceship carrying them to the moon is Pratfall II, a further signal of Dick's mood as he forces himself once more to write even though he is too tired and depressed to undertake the task. Dick has begun to use an occasional garrish detail of dress a few years earlier. For example, in *Now Wait for Last Year* (1966) Kathy's nipples are gilded with Martian living matter. But now in *Ubik* its use becomes excessive. Only Pat Conley escapes with normal dress, and this is because Dick lifts her description from the early short story "A World of Talent" and does not bother to rewrite to make her costume match those of the other characters.

The opening third of *Ubik* describes the world of 1992 where Runciter Associates, a "prudence organization," provides "inertials," people with the ability to block psionic powers. Their services counter those of the agents working for Hollis Talents, who use their psionic talents for industrial spying. Glen Runciter begins to worry about the future of his business when a number of Hollis's telepaths vanish. He goes to Zurich to consult his wife and former partner, Ella, who died a decade earlier at the age of twenty and was placed in cold pack in a Zurich moratorium. His conversation with her is terminated by the intrusion of Jory, a boy who died at fifteen and lies near Ella.

Back in New York, Runciter receives an order for eleven inertials to nullify a powerful psi field at industrialist Stanton Mick's research facility on Luna. He assembles a variety of anti-psis, including Joe Chip, his chief tester, and a new employee whom Joe has recently discovered. Her name is Pat Conley, and Joe recognizes her as potentially dangerous because she is able to change parts of the past and thus determine the future. Although Runciter is suspicious about several details of the job offer, he cannot resist the chance to charge a high fee for his services. Against his better judgment, he sets out for Luna with his eleven inertials in the newly built space ship Pratfall II.

At the Luna research lab he soon discovers he has walked into a trap. Testing reveals no psionic fields exist to be neutralized. Stanton Mick appears, dressed in fuscia pedal pushers, pink yak-fur slippers, and a snakeskin sleeveless blouse. Just as Runciter orders his inertials to collect their possessions and return to the Pratfall II, Stanton Mick floats to the ceiling like a balloon—and explodes!

The novel begins to come to life at this point. What had been for Dick a writing task required by his poverty and executed with wry weariness now turns into a tale whose telling interests him. The bomb explosion kills Glen Runciter and his employees rush him aboard the ship and into cold pack. They are carrying out his wish that at his death he be united with Ella in the Zurich moratorium. As they begin the return journey, Joe reaches for a cigarette. He discovers it is old and stale when it falls apart in his fingers. The deteriorating cigarette is the first of many entropic events that engulf the inertials first in decay and then death.

The middle third of the novel becomes a mystery-suspense story. Will Runciter's brain activity be revived at the moratorium? What causes a vending machine to offer clotted cream? Obsolete money to appear? A puzzling message from Runciter on a matchfolder? Who will be the next inertial trapped by the entropic forces? What frightening process of deterioration is occurring, and who is responsible?

Joe Chip and his fellow inertials struggle to understand the cryptic messages they continue to receive from Runciter. Manifestations of Runciter, they call them, and they finally conclude they must somehow contact Runciter if they are to live. They realize Runciter represents a process of "coming-into-existence" while the other process is just the opposite, a "going-out-of-existence." It is decay vs. Runciter.

First Wendy dies. Joe Chip finds a "huddled heap, dehydrated, almost mummified, curled up," and identifies her. Next, Al Hammond feels himself engulfed in the cold and realizes he is dying. He sees a desert of ice and feels a wind sweep across the plain, bringing darkness with it. He thinks:

> But this is a projection on my part. It isn't the universe which is being entombed by layers of wind, cold, darkness and ice; all this is going on within me, and yet I seem to see it outside. Strange. Is the whole world inside me? Engulfed by my body? When did that happen? It must be a manifestation of dying, he said to himself. The uncertainty which I feel, the slowing down into entropy—that's the process, and the ice which I see is the result of the process. When I blink out, he thought, the whole universe will disappear. But what about the various lights I can see, the entrances to new wombs? Where in particular is the red smoky light of fornicating couples? And the dull dark light signifying animal greed? All I can make out, he thought, is encroaching darkness and utter loss of heat, a plain which is cooling off, abandoned by its sun.[1]

Just before he dies Al finds a cryptic message from Runciter written, like graffiti, on the wall of the men's urinal: "JUMP IN THE URINAL AND STAND ON YOUR HEAD. / I'M THE ONE THAT'S ALIVE. YOU'RE ALL DEAD" (118). Another puzzle is added to the mountain of uncertainty. Is it possible that all the inertials are in half life and Runciter is the single person who has survived the explosion? Also added is another metaphor yoking the profound and the trivial—a technique that becomes the trademark of this most bizarre of Dick novels. If Runciter is a manifestation of the creative force in the universe, and the final chapter overwhelmingly confirms all the speculations of Joe Chip and his fellow inertials that this is Runciter's true identity, why does he send messages in hackneyed rhymed couplets in such places as men's urinals? What kind of game is Dick playing with his reader? Does he even know what he's doing?

My own theory holds that Dick here writes with no more intent than to keep the plot moving forward. His unconscious dictates the ideas about entropy and death, his conscious mind thinks of the most unlikely possibilities, and he uses metaphors from the trivial to convey them. Only years later will the reasoning power of his left

1. *Ubik* (New York: Bantam, 1977), p. 117.

brain go back and probe the meaning of the metaphors his right brain creates in *Ubik*. (Citations from his Metz speech of 1979 and letters written in 1982, which I will discuss later in this chapter, provide convincing evidence for my theory.)

Chapter 10 is a critical chapter in the novel and it lies precisely at the heart of the middle third of *Ubik*. Now Ubik appears in the text of the novel for the first time when Runciter advertises the product in a television commercial. Until this point the reader has encountered Ubik only in advertisements that serve as the epigrams for each chapter. Runciter's TV commercial claims Ubik can prevent the reversion of matter to earlier forms. This is very confusing, Joe Chip decides as he considers a number of possibilities—Plato's ideal forms, for example. But Plato does not adequately explain the procession of forms on earth. Is the earlier form latent in the present form? What happens to the form when its manifestation dies? Joe asks:

> Didn't Plato think that something survived the decline, something inner not able to decay? The ancient dualism: body separated from soul. The body ending as Wendy did, and the soul—out of its nest the bird, flown elsewhere. Maybe so, he thought. To be reborn again, as the *Tibetan Book of the Dead* says. It really is true. Christ, I hope so. Because in that case we all can meet again. In, as in *Winnie-the-Pooh,* another part of the forest, where a boy and his bear will always be playing . . . a category, he thought, imperishable. Like all of us. We will all wind up with Pooh, in a clearer, more durable new place. (129)

Again, an almost careless yoking of opposites—in the extreme. Plato and Winnie-the-Pooh! Never has Dick seemed to care less about metaphysical speculations on the nature of reality. As Dick himself seemed to be without answers and direction at this stage in his life, so he allows Joe Chip none in his uncertain existence within the fictional world his author had made for him. How comforting, Joe first thinks when Runciter tells him about the spray can of Ubik. But when, following instructions, he goes to his apartment to get the Ubik, he finds that both apartment and Ubik have regressed. He glumly concludes, "An irony that is just plain too much: The substance created to reverse the regressive change process has itself regressed." He continues on to Runciter's funeral in Des Moines with no clue about whether it is he or Runciter who lives. Forms continue to devolve around him, and he senses that he will soon become a decaying, inert heap. He considers suicide, but almost immediately receives another cryptic message from Runciter: "Don't do it, Joe. There's another way. Keep trying. You'll find it. Lots of luck" (139).

Joe decides to continue his race to contact Runciter and find the answer before death destroys him. Back at the hotel in Zurich after the funeral, he begins to suspect that Pat Conley may possess the destructive powers that are destroying the inertials one by one. When he accuses her, the hotel lobby blows up in his face. The central third of the novel is now complete.

In the final part, Joe must confront the entropic powers and attempt to survive them. Chapter 13 portrays Joe's climb up the stairs as Pat stands by taunting him and refusing to help him. It is a critical chapter, and brilliant in its power. It creates a metaphor central to Dick's moral vision. Yet in its essence it is not new. Wilbur Mercer made the same climb in *Do Androids Dream* tormented by stones as he struggled upward.

As Joe labors up the stairs, he feels cold overtaking him and realizes that

> they must be wrong about hell . . . . Hell is cold; everything there is cold. The body means weight and heat; now weight is a force which I am succumbing to, and heat, my heat, is slipping away. And, unless I become reborn, it will never return. This is the destiny of the universe. So at least I won't be alone.
>
> But he felt alone. It's overtaking me too soon, he realized. The proper time hasn't come; something has hurried this up—some conniving thing has accelerated it, out of malice and curiosity: a polymorphic, perverse agency which likes to watch. An infantile, retarded entity which enjoys what's happening. It has crushed me like a bent-legged insect, he said to himself. A simple bug which does nothing but hug the earth. Which can never fly or escape. Can only descend step by step into what is deranged and foul. Into the world of the tomb which a perverse entity surrounded by its own filth inhabits. (175)

But Joe painfully continues his struggle upward. Near death, he finally crawls down the hall to his room. There Runciter waits for him with a can of Ubik.

The next chapter offers a respite in Joe's fight with the destructive forces of the universe. He and Runciter talk, but Runciter is not able to tell Joe everything he wants to know. He attempts to explain:

"This situation is very complex, Joe. It doesn't admit to simple answers" (p. 184). But Runciter does confirm that Joe is in coldpack and that he, Runciter, is alive in the moratorium talking to Joe. And Runciter agrees with Joe's conclusion that two forces are at work, one helping them and one destroying them.

As the novel nears its end, Joe finally meets that destructive force, and it is the misshapen boy Jory, with chitinous eyes and a thwarted smile that has become a jeering leer. Jory claims himself as creator of the regressed world the inertials have occupied since the bomb exploded on Luna. Having eaten the others, he is now ready to kill and eat Joe. He fastens his great shovel teeth into Joe's right hand and begins grinding away. Joe escapes by kicking Jory, and he heals his wound by spraying it with the last of his can of Ubik.

Still trapped in the world of 1939 to which he has regressed, he goes to look for more Ubik. This time he encounters a lovely young girl who identifies herself as Ella Runciter. She admits she is the creative power in half life who struggles against Jory's destructive powers. She explains, "There are Jorys in every moratorium. This battle goes on wherever you have half-lifers; it's a verity, a rule, of our kind of existence" (p.204). She leaves Joe at the drugstore where he can purchase more Ubik.

There he once more encounters Jory who has devolved all the Ubik. Joe takes a square pasteboard container and calls up all his mental energy to evolve it into the real thing. He apparently fails. He leaves the store and boards a streetcar, where another young woman gives him a can of Ubik. She says his mental efforts in the store brought her from the future and that if he could do it once, he can do it again. After she leaves, Joe muses, "We are served by organic ghosts who, speaking and writing, pass through this our new environment. Watching, wise, physical ghosts from the full-life world, elements of which have become for us invading but agreeable splinters of a substance that pulsates like a former heart. And of all of them, he thought, thanks to Glen Runciter. In particular. The writer of instructions, labels, and notes. Valuable notes" (210).

So the plot ends. But our questions do not. What is Ubik? Who is Runciter? The concluding chapter, only two pages long, provides one more clue. The trivial epigrams harranging the public to buy Ubik for bad breath, perspiration odors, and better coffee now change. The final one declares, "I am Ubik. Before the universe was,

I am. I made the suns. I made the worlds. I created the lives and the places they inhabit; I move them here, I put them there. They go as I say, they do as I tell them. I am the word and my name is never spoken, the name which no one knows. I am called Ubik, but that is not my name. I am. I shall always be" (211).

But the text of the last chapter still refuses to connect itself with the epigram. Runciter returns to the moratorium to talk again with Ella. The coins which he offers as a tip draw a question from the attendant. "What kind of money is this?" he asks, for the coins bear a profile of Joe Chip. Runciter can offer no explanation. He has an intuition that the Joe Chip money is only a beginning.

This plot summary should more honestly be called a plot interpretation. It ignores as much of the action as it discusses, selecting only those events and speeches that support my view of the novel's meaning. Other critics give quite different readings to *Ubik*. No consensus exists about whether Joe or Runciter is killed in the explosion, although I think a very careful reading makes clear that Joe Chip and the other inertials, not Runciter, are in half life. Runciter is present with them because they live "as in a dream," not realizing they lack full life, and in that dream world they take to be the real world, there is a Runciter.

The reality pictured in the opening third of the novel is the same middle level or commonsense reality Jack Bohlen saw in *Martian Time-Slip*. The first explosion shatters that reality for Joe Chip. In the middle third of the novel, he climbs up to a creative reality metaphored by the Runciters, after narrowly escaping the tomb world where Pat wishes to drag him. In the final third, he once again encounters the powers of the lower world and once again escapes. The encounter with death and nothingness seems never to end.

Who is Runciter? What is Ubik? The novel provides no key to unlock the answer, just as no key is given to man when he asks, What is death? What lies beyond? Dick himself does not know. He can speculate, as he does in the novel, but here he refuses to provide an answer for anyone else. Each man must make the intuitive leap to his own answer.

Is there help as one goes on a quest for the answer? Only a few clues. They may come in cryptic messages, according to the complex metaphor Dick creates in *Ubik*. Joe notes that "nothing can come in from the outside except words" (194), and as the final epigram states,

Ubik is the word, but his name is never spoken. He is the "I am," and Ubik's messages to humanity are carried by ordinary men like Glen Runciter who in a time of crisis rise up to become brief heroes.

Help may also come in dreams. Several women break through to another reality in their dreams. Tippy Jackson dreams of feral twins named Bill and Matt, who threaten to "get her." Ella dreams of a smoky red light that signals she is heading for a new womb to be born again. The *Tibetan Book of the Dead* tells about this rebirth. She feels she may be dreaming constantly while she lies in half life. Often she seems to share the dreams of those around her. Finally in the dream of Francesca Spanish, "a great hand came down from the sky, like the arm and hand of God." When the closed hand opened, it contained a great spray can. Golden fire spelled out a single word—UBIK.

The reader of *Ubik,* trying to puzzle out its meaning, shares the task with the author. Very often Dick created a complex metaphor in a work of fiction and then afterward attempted to understand with his logical powers what meaning his intuitive powers could have intended in the metaphor. Truth always came first in metaphor for Dick. Comprehension followed. No novel fascinated him more than *Ubik*. In the speech he wrote to be delivered at a science fiction festival in London in 1975, he made several extensive references to it, noting that the material for the novel came primarily from a series of dreams. "In my opinion," he says, "it contains strong themes of pre-Socratic philosophical views of the world, unfamiliar to me when I wrote it (to name just one, the views of Empedocles)." Dick by the time of the speech had decided on his interpretation of *Ubik*. "Each of us, then partakes of the cosmos—if he is willing to listen to his dreams. And it is his dreams which will transform him from a mere machine into an authentic human. He will no longer strut about and clank with majestic iron, no longer rule his little kingdom here; he will soar upwards, flying like a field of negative ions, like the entity Ubik in my novel of that name: being life and giving life, but never defining himself because no clearcut name to him—to us—can be given."[2]

Again in 1977 he cites *Ubik* in his meandering, interminable Metz speech which was first titled "Lateral Time Tracks and Other

2. "Man, Android, and Machine," in *Science Fiction at Large*, ed. Peter Nicholls (New York: Harper, 1976), p. 215.

Realities." Here he points out, "In my novel *Ubik,* I present a motion along a retrograde entropic axis, in terms of Platonic forms rather than any decay or reversion we normally conceive. Perhaps the normal forward-motion along this axis, away from entropy, accruing rather than divesting, is identical with the axis-line which I characterize as lateral, which is to say, in orthogonal rather than linear time. If this is so, the novel *Ubik* inadvertently contains what could be called a scientific rather than a philosophical idea. But here I am only guessing. Still, the fiction writer may have written more than he consciously knew."

Why does *Ubik* succeed as a work of fiction when it is so pockmarked by hackneyed writing, clichés, and carnival characterization? First and most obviously, its narrative suspense. The reader wants to know whether entropy will shrivel Joe into a decaying heap of cloth and flesh, whether he will be able to contact Runciter, whether Joe is alive or in half life. The reader's appetite for unraveling the mysterious is whetted by those odd epigrams, and the puzzle of Ubik. What is it? Second, The characters, too, contribute to the power of the novel. Joe Chip, Glen Runciter, Jory, Ella, and even a minor character like Al Hammond, remain alive for the reader long after he has finished the novel.

Further, the concept of half life is one of the best of Dick's myriad brilliant inventions, and having once conceived it, he uses its possibilities to the fullest. Beyond its use on a literal level in *Ubik,* half life serves as a metaphor of possibility for the human condition. Perhaps we all now live in half life, in a frozen dream world which we falsely imagine to be true reality. Occasional messages come to us giving clues of our condition, but we too are inertials like Runciter's group—better at negating psionic powers than anything else.

The power of *Ubik,* in the last analysis, lies in Dick's perfect yoking of content and form. He is writing of entropy, of a time when things fall apart, when death begins to eat at social structures and at the individuals who live in society, and he uses a form that is itself decayed and nearly worn out. He writes of the struggle between order and entropy, and the form becomes the content. *Ubik* often lumbers along toward its end as painfully as Joe Chip climbing the stairs to the haven of rest in his bedroom. He does succeed in his climb, just as later, with great mental exertion, he manages to evolve the pasteboard container of Ubik into a spray can of the real thing.

Analogous to Joe Chip and his physical struggle, Dick at this period in his life must have driven himself to strenuous mental exertion to hold back the entropic powers and to complete the novel—an effort so exhausting that, in the early seventies, he would give up writing entirely.

Counter-Clock World, published two years before *Ubik,* is in many ways its reversed double. Looking at the earlier novel, we are better able to understand the ideas yoking the images in *Ubik. Counter-Clock World* also uses epigrams, but they come from classical and medieval philosophers—Lucretius, Saint Augustine, Erigena, Boethius, Thomas Aquinas. Dick seems to suggest that as the trivial commercials of the contemporary world create reality for modern man, so the words of the metaphysicians and theologians defined the nature of reality in earlier periods. In this novel time runs backward, carrying man from death to life. In the Bible Saint Paul asked, "Grave, where is thy victory?" "Behold! I will unfold a mystery: we shall not all die, but we shall be changed in a flash, in the twinkling of an eye, at the last trumpet call." Now, almost two thousand years later, Paul's words have come true. A great reversal of time is occurring, in which time continues to move backwards, "continually sweeping out a greater span; earlier and still earlier deaths would be reversed . . . and, in two thousand years from now, Paul himself would no longer "sleep," as he himself had put it."[3] This reversal is a vast sidereal process, occurring every few billion years.

Anarch Peak, the founder of a religious cult and one of the central characters, is patterned on Bishop James Pike. A substantial reference to Pike early in the novel points out that Pike after a heresy trial was booted out of the Episcopal church. As noted earlier, Dick at this time was friends with Pike, whose son had committed suicide, and he attended seances where Pike attempted to contact his son. In the author's foreword to *A Maze of Death* Dick gives credit to Pike who, he says, "in discussions with me brought forth a wealth of theological materials for inspection, none of which I was previously acquainted with."

Anarch Peak at novel's end reveals what he has learned when he was in the grave. "There's no death; it's an illusion. Time is an illusion. Every instant that comes into being never passes away. . . . it

3. *Counter-Clock World* (New York: Berkley Medallion, 1967), p. 15.

doesn't really even come into being; it was always there. The universe consists of concentric rings of reality; the greater the ring the more it partakes of absolute reality. These concentric rings finally wind up as God; He's the source" (146).

Peak continues his explanation of reality, "Eidos is form. Like Plato's category—the absolute reality. It exists; Plato was right. Eidos is imprinted on passive matter; matter isn't evil, it's just inert, like clay. There's an anti-eidos, too; a form-destroying factor. This is what people experience as evil, the decay of form" (146).

Sebastian Hermes, the favored narrator, has been dug up only ten years earlier, and he still feels "about him, in the dreary part of the night, the coldness of the grave." He is aware that his young wife has the optimism of youth while he still has the despair of old age. In Sebastian's explanation of what it is like to awaken in the coffin, waiting for the body to return to life, we find the seed of the idea that, once born, will become half life in *Ubik*. Sebastian tells his wife how frightening it is: "The thing about lying there in your coffin like that, the part that makes it so bad, is that your mind is alive but your body isn't, and you feel the duality . . . . A living mind tied to a corpse. Lodged inside it" (135). *Ubik* reverses the backward direction of time Dick uses in this novel. There people are taken not to a vitarium but to a moratorium, and they await rebirth into a new womb, not regression into the womb from which they came, as in *Counter-Clock World*.

In both these novels Dick uses the multiple point of view. A character in *Counter-Clock World* comments about a religious sacrament in which people are unified into one entity that possesses absolute knowledge because it has no single, limiting point of view. Dick's novels of the sixties aspire to this goal, refusing as they do to present their tales through the perceptions of any single narrator.

A Maze of Death, written in 1968 and published in 1971, pushes to the limit the use of multiple points of view. It tells the story of fourteen individuals who, following instructions, assemble on the planet Delmak-O. They await word that never comes. In the meantime they try to figure out answers to questions like, Where are we? Why are we here? What will become of us? In the end, they discover, as Dick's characters learn again and again, that reality turns out to be much different from first appearances. The author's foreword notes that the approach of the novel is highly subjective—that at any given time reality is seen through the mind of one of the characters. The point of view differs from section to section, with Seth Morley as the favored narrator.

Once again, death and entropy are the subject. One by one, the fourteen men and women on Delmak-O begin to meet death through murder or suicide, and the survivors recognize that they are apparently mere "rats in a maze with death; rodents confined with the ultimate adversary, to die one by one until none are left."[4] Most of the colonists read regularly from The Book, which is written by A. J. Specktowsky and titled *How I Rose from the Dead in My Spare Time and So Can You.* The Book explains that God is the Creator, forever struggling against the Form Destroyer. The basic condition of life for man is to be part of this struggle—the "dialectic of the universe," order against chaos. Occasionally a mysterious stranger called the Intercessor, or the Walker-on-Earth, appears to aid the colonists.

The answer to the puzzle of the colonists and their purpose on the planet is more grim than any answer Dick has ever offered to his innumerable puzzles. The final two chapters of the novel reveal that the fourteen individuals are the crew of a spaceship that will never reach its destination. Because of an accident, it has been in endless orbit around a dead sun for fifteen years. A polyencephalic device had originally been provided the crew as an escape toy to amuse them on their twenty-year voyage. Aided by a computer, they could simulate and experience various worlds. Now they must use it to pass the time until, one by one, they die.

Awakened to the reality of their doomed spaceship, the crew long to return to the imaginary world of Delmak-O, even though their behavior to each other there was shockingly hostile and violent. At least there the religious system of Specktowsky, with its Intercessor, gave them hope. But here on the ship they have no hope. Nothing awaits them but death. They plot out another polyencephalic world where they can go to pass the time.

Seth Morley is so depressed that he excuses himself, going into the passage way where he considers opening the ship's vents, causing all the crew to die almost instantly. "I wish to God there really was an Intercessor," he thinks.

4. *A Maze of Death* (New York: Warner Paperback, 1971), p. 98.

Suddenly a figure in flowing, pale robes appears, a man with a pure shining face. He says he has come to take Seth away. He holds out his hand to Seth, and guides him away from the ship into the stars.

In the final scene the crew have put on the polyencephalic cylinders that wire them together and have gone into their next illusory world. Seth is missing.

The Maze of Death is a bitter, gloomy novel if we interpret the meaning of its metaphor in the way the author seems to have intended it. The Earth is our doomed spaceship, and we the crew, while we await death, escape to illusory worlds. There as we make up religious systems to comfort us, we hate and kill each other. Still— what about that one small detail at the end—the missing Seth? Seth, who wanted so desperately to believe in the theology they invented.

This third period of Dick's writing drew to an end soon after *A Maze of Death*. The three novels appearing early in the decade of the seventies—*Our Friends from Frolix-8, We Can Build You*, and *Flow My Tears*—were works written at an earlier time for which a publisher had not previously been found. They are not among his strongest works. His wife Nancy left him in 1970, reportedly because he was so heavily depressed. Dick wrote a letter to *SF Commentary* in November 1970 in which he noted that on a number of occasions in his life he had become suicidal. He continued that he often wrote about a universe of cynicism and chaos, where belief, faith, and trust were lacking; that in each successive novel the doubt grew deeper and the universe disintegrated further and further.

For Dick *Ubik* was an important novel. The images, he said, originally appeared to him in a series of dreams. He recorded those images and then kept returning to them, attempting to understand their meaning. In "Man, Android, and Machine" (1976), he offers a commentary on *Ubik*. He is discussing time and his theory of why we humans do not experience time as it really is and why true reality is so often veiled. He says:

> Within a system which must generate an enormous amount of veiling, it would be vainglorious to expostulate on what actually is, when my premise declares that were we to penetrate to it for any reason this strange veil-like dream would reinstate itself retroactively, in terms of our perceptions and in terms of our memories. The mutually dreaming would resume as before, because, I think, we are like the characters in my novel *Ubik;* we are in a state of half-life. We are neither dead nor

alive, but preserved in cold storage, waiting to be thawed out. Expressed in the perhaps startlingly familiar terms of the procession of the seasons, this is winter of which I speak; it is winter for our race, and it is winter in *Ubik* for those in half-life. Ice and snow cover them; ice and snow cover our world in layers of accretions, which we can *dokos* or Maya. What melts away the rind or layer of frozen ice over the world each year is of course the reappearance of the sun. What melts the ice and snow covering the characters in *Ubik,* and which halts the cooling-off of the lives, the entropy which they feel is the voice of Mr. Runciter, their former employer, calling to them. The voice of Mr. Runciter is none other than that same voice which each bulb and seed and root in the ground, our ground, hears. It hears: "Wake up! Sleepers awake!" Now I have told you who Runciter is and I have told you our condition and what *Ubik* is really about.

8
Drugs, Hallucinations, and
A Scanner Darkly

"Mors ontologica. Death of the spirit. The identity. The essential nature." These words in a final chapter of *A Scanner Darkly* succinctly summarize the novel. It is about "the winter of the spirit . . . . When the spirit is dead." The destruction of the mind and spirit of the protagonist results from drug addiction.

The novels Dick wrote late in the 1960s, as we have noted, were about death—physical death. In 1973 he wrote a novel about the death of the spirit—a coda to the long movement of entropic fiction he had poured out for a number of years. Before this novel, he had portrayed drugs as a device for exploring, expanding, and manipulating reality. Now his view of drugs changed radically and he wrote in *A Scanner Darkly* about drugs as the destroyer of reality. Drug-induced hallucinations were not doors to ultimate reality but prison houses of isolation where the mind suffered and finally died.

Dick wrote very little fiction in the fourth period of his career, the period from 1970 to 1980. Just two new novels were published—*Flow My Tears, the Policeman Said* (1974) and *A Scanner Darkly* (1977). Even so, I have chosen to call this the Regenerative Period because his efforts and experiences during the decade did lead to the creative outpouring of the metaphysical novels in his fifth and final period. Now he began to recover from the entropic forces that had dragged him down to suicidal depression.

When his wife Nancy left him in August 1970, taking their daughter Isa with her, he was at the midpoint of *Flow My Tears*. After her departure he ceased writing entirely, except for his Vancouver speech, "The Android and the Human." In April 1972, two months after his suicide attempt, he was released from X-Kalay and went to Fullerton, California, where he was befriended by Professor Willis McNelly of California State University—Fullerton. Because

Dick was totally without funds, he sold his papers to the Special Collections of the university library.

The period leading to his suicide attempt had been the darkest of his entire life. He became totally exhausted emotionally and physically, and he had no will to write. It was a dreadful world, he later recalled to John Sladek in a letter published in *SF Commentary* in 1973. At the time he was so deeply involved in the drug culture, he had thought he was merely turning on with his friends. But in reality he had "plunged into something farther down than hell ever could be." Toward the end of 1971, he continued, "I woke up one day and noticed that all either were dead, had burned-out brains, were psychotic, or all of the above." Many of the episodes in *A Scanner Darkly* are literal transcriptions of his experiences during this period.

In the new environment of Fullerton the regenerative process began. He felt a deep attachment to Professor McNelly because they shared the same birthday, December 16. He visited McNelly's university classes and made new friends. He fell in love and formed a liaison with Tessa Busby, an eighteen-year-old student at the university. His love affair with Tessa, he believed, offered the way up out of the dark, destructive world of drugs where he had lived for the past two years, and his immediate burst of productivity seemed to confirm his hopes. He began writing again early in 1973, and finally finished *Flow My Tears*. Within the next two months he produced the first draft of *A Scanner Darkly*. In April, just a few days after the novel was completed, he married Tessa, and a son, Christopher, was born in July 1973.

Unfortunately, his reborn creativity did not survive. Two events seem to have interrupted it. First, the mystical visions that began in February and climaxed with his eight-hour epiphany in March 1974 continued intermittently. These visions were to have an effect on him so profound that it became almost obsessive. The second event was the collapse of his marriage with Tessa, who separated from him and obtained a divorce in 1976, taking their small son with her. After her departure he again made a suicide attempt that required hospitalization. When he recovered he moved to Santa Ana. For the remainder of the decade, he wrote almost no fiction.

Dick now said his writing career was finished—he would never write another novel. Instead, he spent his time working on his Exegesis. This nonfiction text began as an attempt to erect a rational explanation for the mystical experiences that occurred in 1974. As he continued this quest, his goal changed and he became obsessed with developing his own cosmogony. He wrote hundreds of pages as he developed, then discarded theory after theory.

During this fourth period he began to receive substantial critical recognition, highlighted when *Science-Fiction Studies* devoted a special issue to his fiction in 1975. As his reputation continued to grow, sales of his already published books improved and reprints of his best novels were published in hardcover by Gregg Press. As a result his financial condition became much more comfortable. He no longer had to write and sell new fiction to survive, and so he began to write only what interested him.

The dark, destructive world of drugs pictured in *A Scanner Darkly* marks it as one of the great antidrug novels. It is a tragic novel, which, Dick commented, was the most nonfiction novel he had ever written. In 1971 he had unknowingly done research for the novel after his wife Nancy left him and his house in San Raphael became a center for the activities he describes in the novel. However difficult one finds it to accept a brilliant Philip K. Dick who has ceased to write and chosen instead to play with the young people of the drug culture, the task must be done because it is true. As he says in his author's note to the novel, "For a time I myself was one of these children playing in the street . . . I was, like the rest of them, trying to play instead of being grown up, and I was punished."

A history of Dick's use of drugs over the years is a miniature of the history of drugs in the United States since World War II. The pharmaceutical industry grew rapidly in the 1950s as new drugs were developed and promoted. The medical profession began to prescribe more and more drugs for their patients. In the mid-sixties, an LSD cult appeared, with Timothy Leary as its guru—a response to the ban on the sale of the drug. LSD had first been studied by the government during the war as a drug to facilitate brainwashing or for disorientation of enemy troops in the field. When the military lost interest, psychiatrists briefly experimented with it as a treatment for schizophrenia, but soon discarded it. Renewed interest in the vision-producing drug occurred with the publication of Aldous Huxley's *New Doors of Perception* in 1954 (a book which Dick later read). It describes Huxley's hullucinatory experiences after taking mescaline.

However, marijuana, not LSD, was the drug most commonly used in the 1960s. Because its effects appeared to be less harmful than those of LSD, cocaine, or heroin, it was widely used. It seemed to offer no possibility of a bad trip, as did LSD.

Dick's personal drug history echoes that of the drug culture in the United States. His mother used prescription drugs continually, a practice that he followed all his life. He began taking drugs in high school for his allergies. He used amphetamines during the 1958–64 period as an aid to writing productivity. He also began to take medication for his arrythmic tachycardia. Not until the next period, 1964–72, did he use recreational drugs, led into this world by his fourth wife, Nancy. He experimented on some occasions with LSD, probably beginning about 1966. In a letter to a friend at that time he described the hallucinations he experienced and he commented on their parallel with the descriptions he had read in the *Tibetan Book of the Dead*. He also explored mescaline, and in a letter to Roger Zelazny on August 17, 1970, he said: "Three months ago I took some mescaline and had many insights, which, by the way, I've never gotten from acid. Out of these insights I wrote a novel (just the rough draft) in which the love that had been revealed to me, so to speak, appeared." He was referring to *Flow My Tears*. Although he occasionally smoked marijuana, amphetamines remained his preferred drug. During this period he took large doses of methadrine, as much as 1,000 pills a week. This heavy dosage contributed to the severe paranoia that often tormented him.

As with many topics, Dick made comments about drugs at various times throughout his life. These statements often contradict each other because his mind never held still. Having arrived at a conclusion, he tended to discard it and move on to find another. In the 1960s he was fascinated with the reality-altering possibilities of drugs. By the time he was released from X-Kalay in 1972, he violently opposed recreational drugs, insisting that they destroyed, not enhanced, reality. Despite this final view of street drugs, he continued to be a heavy user of various prescription drugs and did occasionally smoke marijuana.

Drugs first appear in his writing in *The World Jones Made,* published in 1956, long before a popular drug subculture existed. In this early novel the favored narrator is a secret service agent named Cussick whose wife, Nina, frequents a bar in San Francisco where drugs are served. She has become addicted to heroin. Years later Dick commented about how prophetic the novel was in its portrayal of heroin use even though at the time he knew so little about drugs that he had Nina taking heroin in capsule form.

Drugs appear in several other novels written during the late 1950s and early 1960s. In *The Man Who Japed* (1956), the protagonist, Allen Purcell, takes corto-thiamin capsules to counter his hangover, and his wife, Janet, uses sedatives and antianxiety pills. In *Vulcan's Hammer* (1960), Jason Dill regularly uses tranquilizers. The foreman of the plant where Frank Frink works smokes marijuana cigarettes in *The Man in the High Castle* (1962). Drugs tend in this early period to serve no greater purpose than adding detail to character development. But many of the novels that follow in the 1960s use drugs as an important part of the plot.

Pete Gardner, the favored narrator in *The Game-Players of Titan* (1963) first suspects that reality is unreliable and can easily be manipulated when he takes methamphetamines and alcohol. Under their influence, he visits Titan and talks with a vug psychiatrist in a hallucinatory experience that is convincingly real. He begins to believe that fake and authentic reality cannot be differentiated because in his hallucination he perceived qualities of the alien vugs that turned out to be true. Later in the novel the humans from Terra play a critical game with the Titan vugs and win because the psionic talents each side possesses have been made ineffective with drugs.

The key role of drugs in *The Three Stigmata* has already been noted, and in two novels published in 1966, drugs are an important element. Dr. Eric Sweetscent, the favored narrator in *Now Wait for Last Year* has a drug-addicted wife, Kathy. Because she regularly uses the hallucinogen JJ-180, she cannot ascertain what is real, what is illusion. She slips the drug in her husband's coffee and he also becomes an addict. He eventually learns that the drug was originally developed as a war weapon. The second part of *The Unteleported Man* records the experiences of the protagonist after he is shot by a dart tipped with LSD and trips out. Dick said on occasion that this work was the only fiction he ever wrote while under the influence of LSD. Although written in 1966, it was not published until after his death.

Dick drew on his LSD experiences the next year in writing *Counter-Clock World*. Sebastian Hermes, the operator of a vitarium, has a religious vision after taking LSD, and in this vision he talks with Anarch Peak, a religious leader who has died. In the powerful "Faith of Our Fathers" (1967), the plot turns entirely on hallucinatory drugs. In *The Zap Gun*, published the same year, Dick portrays two weapon designers who depend on drug-induced trances to give them their ideas for new weapons.

These citations of works where drugs play a critical part serve to show the growing use Dick made of drugs in his fiction as they became a consuming part of his personal life. For much of the decade of the 1960s, he explored the fascinating possibility that drug hallucinations were in truth closer to reality than the reality of common-sense perceptions. But he learned through painful experience how treacherous were the hallucinatory worlds created by drugs.

Flow My Tears deserves brief attention before we turn to examine *A Scanner Darkly* at greater length. The novel focuses on two characters: Jason Taverner, popular singer and artist who delights in his admiring fans, and Felix Buckman, a reclusive policeman. The novel tends to split, giving primary attention to Taverner in the first half and then moving on to study Buckman in the second half. This lack of unity is not surprising when we remember that Dick interrupted the novel after his wife Nancy left him in 1970 and did not complete it until several years later. He wrote eleven drafts, with version after version of the ending as he incorporated more biographical elements. He wanted to capture the sense of loss and grief and loneliness engulfing him after Nancy's departure.

The epigrams that head each of the four parts set the tone of darkness and loss. They are taken from "Lachrimae Antiquae Pavan," a song for four voices written by the sixteenth-century composer John Dowland. The song, sung by a man exiled into darkness, laments the loss of light and joy.

The cast of characters is relatively small, with two sets of *Doppelgängers*. First is Jason Taverner, who contrasts with Felix Buckman, the policeman educated as a lawyer. Buckman in turn contrasts with his twin sister, Alys, who is also his wife. His deep love for her torments him because she stands for everything he abhors. She uses drugs, has lesbian affairs, ruthlessly uses people for her pleasure, and delights in gratuitous destruction. The two sets of doubles join hands when Alys becomes infatuated with Jason Taverner and draws him for two days into a hallucinatory reality created by a powerful drug she has taken. Here Jason is a man without an identity. Suddenly he discovers he has fallen from a world where he is the most famous personality on TV to a world where no one has ever heard of him, where he seems never to have existed.

The drug eventually kills Alys, but only after she has given Jason a heavy dose of mescaline. Now Felix, her brother-husband, needs to create a scandal as a smokescreen so the press investigation of her death will be less likely to discover their marriage, their child, and her heavy drug use. He decides to accuse Jason of killing her and then before Jason can be brought to trial, to have him murdered. He recognizes the act is morally reprehensible, but feels it is a lesser evil than his losing his position if his incestuous relationship with Alys is discovered, for over the years he has often acted as a savior, using the power of his office to countermand the repressive actions of the bureaucracy. He has shut down forced labor camps and aided students in campus ghettos. His moral dilemma echoes that of Tagomi in *The Man in the High Castle*. He must kill one to save many.

Taverner escapes back to reality when Alys's death releases him from the hallucinatory world into which she dragged him. But the real world offers him no safety since he now finds himself charged with Alys's murder.

The final scene of the novel focuses on Felix Buckman as he drives home exhausted after his grief-filled day. Setting his quibble on automatic pilot, he falls asleep and dreams. In his dream he sees Taverner sitting alone in his house and then hears a shriek as the hit men come to kill him. Buckman awakes to a feeling of utter loneliness as he realizes that he has lost not only his beloved sister but his moral identity. Frantic to make some human contact, he stops at a gas station where he first talks briefly with a middle-aged colored man and impulsively hugs him. Then he drives on alone and full of sorrow. The Dowland epigram on the title page now carries a richer meaning for the reader:

> *Flow my tears, fall from your springs!*
> *Exiled forever let me mourn;*
> *Where night's black bird her sad infamy sings,*
> *There let me live forlorn.*

A brief epilogue to the novel traces the remainder of the lives of the principals. The final word of this epilogue deserves notice because it illustrates a practice Dick followed in the novels he wrote during this period. He embodied a key idea in the final word. Here the word is *love.*

A Scanner Darkly was written soon after Dick completed *Flow My Tears.* Its protagonist is also a policeman and again Dick makes use of the double, but with a variation from his method in *Flow My Tears.* There Buckman, representing law and order, was countered by Alys, a hedonistic, destructive individual. Now in *A Scanner Darkly* Dick incorporates these contrasting elements in a single character—Fred—and the story is told from his point of view. Like Buckman he also is a policeman, an undercover narcotics agent. To carry out his assignment of discovering drug dealers, he poses as Bob Arctor, an addict in the world of street drugs who lives only for sensual pleasure, as did Alys. The novel moves back and forth between two settings—the house of Bob Arctor, which he shares with four other junkies, and the police station where as officer Fred he goes to make periodic reports about his findings.

A technological device, the scanner, assumes a role in the novel almost as important as any of the characters. The police decide that Arctor's house needs surveillance when he is not present, so they install several scanners to film all activities round the clock. Officer Fred has the task of viewing these tapes, which include of course himself posing as Arctor. Thus through the scanners, he is able to watch himself dispassionately as a narcotics addict.

As Fred, he agonizes about what the scanners really see when "they" watch him. Do they see "into the head? Down into the heart? . . . Into me clearly or darkly?" He hopes it is clearly because he now only sees into himself darkly. The source for the idea of the scanner is, of course, one of Dick's favorite passages from Saint Paul's *1 Corinthians*: "We see through a glass, darkly."

The plot, straightforward and simple, contains none of the convoluted complexity we usually find in a Dick novel. Only at the very end does a twist of surprise startle the reader. Except for the device of the scramble suits worn by the narcotics agents, the novel is realistic fiction rather than science fiction. As the story begins, Officer Fred disguised as Bob Arctor lives with a group of junkies who are now beginning to pay a horrible price for their excessive use of drugs. Jerry Fabin stands in a hot shower for hours as he attempts to wash away the bugs which he believes contaminate him. Charles Freck·

stirs from the world of fantasy films that constantly roll in his head only when he needs more capsules of the drug Substance D on which he is hooked. Jim Barris makes Coke from Solarcaine and a psychedelic extract from mushrooms. Bob Arctor pops Substance D supplied by his girl friend Donna and listens to music on his elaborate sound system. Constantly fearful that they will be discovered by the police, the little group increasingly become suspicious of each other. Occasionally they venture into the streets to steal, find women, and obtain more drugs. The episodes Dick sketches so deftly combine to paint a powerful and frightening picture of the street drug scene.

Interspersed with these chapters are chapters portraying the police world where Fred/Bob goes regularly to report. His scramble suit distorts his features and thus protects his identity from his fellow police officers. Early in the novel his supervisor, Hank, asks him to take tests at the psychology testing lab because his erratic behavior suggests that the drugs he must use to maintain his disguise may be affecting his brain. The tests confirm that the two hemispheres of his brain are competing rather than performing cooperatively and as a result his perceptions are no longer reliable. His brain has been burned out by the drug. The remainder of the novel pictures his agony as he watches the deterioration of his own mind. Hank recommends that Fred turn himself into New-Path, a drug rehabilitation center, because a small chance exists that recovery is possible. Hank, hoping to offer solace, tells him his mental destruction has not been in vain because Jim Barris, a fellow drug addict at Bob Arctor's pad, has been arrested as a drug dealer, an arrest that would not have occurred without Fred's activities. Fred's girl friend Donna comforts him in the agony of the last hours before she takes him to New-Path.

The final chapters switch to the point of view of various policemen since Fred/Bob is now a vegetable without a mind. The reader discovers the complexity of the drug world where officer and addict perform their dance macabre together. It turns out that the police, always looking for those higher up in drug traffic, suspect that New-Path may be a cover for big drug activities. They have deliberately put Fred in a situation where he will become a drug addict and require admission to New-Path. They hope he will recover there and, now on the inside, be able to function once again as a narcotics undercover agent, collecting evidence they need to make arrests. Donna is really a federal agent who is part of the larger plot encompassing the small plot of which Fred/Bob had been aware. Deception layers deception. No one is authentically what he appears to be.

Donna muses in horrified reflection at what has happened to Fred/Bob. It is unjust, and yet it had to be done if the larger drug operation is to be destroyed. She reflects,

> It requires the greatest kind of wisdom to know when to apply injustice. How can justice fall victim, ever, to what is right? How can this happen? Because there is a curse on this world, and all this proves it; this is the proof right here. Somewhere, at the deepest level possible, the mechanism, the construction of things, fell apart, and up from what remained swam the need to do all the various sort of unclear wrongs the wisest choice has made us act out. It must have started thousands of years ago. . . . A long, long time ago. Before the curse, and everything and everyone became this way. The Golden Age, when wisdom and justice were the same. Before it shattered into cutting fragments. Into broken bits that don't fit, that can't be put back together, hard as we try.[1]

The suspicions of the federal agents turn out to be correct. In the last chapter Fred/Bob, who has been admitted to New-Path as Bruce, is sent to work on a farm facility in northern California. Now a zombie, he stares without comprehension as the farm manager instructs him in his task of hoeing corn. Then Bruce stoops to pick a small blue flower that grows everywhere. "You're seeing the flower of the future," the manager says, knowing Bruce cannot understand him. "*Mors ontologica.*" The flower of death. The flower from which Substance D is made. It is being grown behind a concealing shield of corn.

Mors ontologica. The name gives the clue to the novel's meaning—the death of being. For Dick, to exist is to think. When one can no longer think, he no longer exists. Thus, *A Scanner Darkly* is the ultimate novel about death since it pictures the death of the human spirit. No matter that the body survives if the brain cannot function. Reality exists because the human mind constructs it and Substance D has the power to destroy the function of the mind. Substance D is the drug of death.

The real drama of the novel lies not in the outer events portraying the struggle between police and drug criminals but in the inner struggle of the bicameral brain to maintain the cooperative

1. *A Scanner Darkly* (Garden City, NY: Doubleday, 1977), p. 187.

function of its twin lobes together, a struggle that ends in failure. Fred/Bob achieves the stature of a tragic hero because he is finally able to understand the evil he has done, and ironically he is his own victim. His recognition is more painful because it is prolonged. As the novel begins, Fred the policeman is in control, and he understands he is merely acting when he appears as Bob Arctor, the junkie. Then "the other side of his head opens up" and begins to speak to him, like another self. That other self gains more power. It "turns against him and acts like another person, defeating him from inside. A man inside a man. Which is no man at all." As the story continues, Bob Arctor, the drug addict, gains domination, and, finally, by novel's end, both halves of the brain are destroyed. Nothing remains but a physical husk named Bruce.

Can the human mind fuction as an observer, watching its actions at the same time as it performs them even though those actions eventually lead to the destruction of the mind? The answer seems to be yes, at least for the mind with a high level of self-awareness like Dick's. Always for him the detached observer remains, and in this novel the metaphor of that self-awareness is the scanner. Wired into the house of Bob Arctor, it records everything that happens, but never makes judgments. Later when Fred/Bob plays back the tapes, he is able to view them dispassionately and ponder over his action—both when he is with other people and when he is alone—now preserved on the tapes.

Similarly, the artist-as-observer consciousness of Dick seems to have been able always to separate itself, watch and record, even when Dick was undergoing the most painful of emotional experiences. Occasionally one wonders if he drove himself to the edge of emotional abysses so that Dick, the writer, might observe and record. Dick readily admitted that the material he used in *A Scanner Darkly* was primarily biographical. But we must never forget the difference between the character Fred/Bob which Dick models on himself and the real Philip K. Dick. The character finally becomes Bruce, a vegetable without a mind, who is confined indefinitely in a drug rehabilitation center. Dick himself left X-Kalay, the drug center where he spent several months, and rehabilitated himself enough so that a year later he was able to write *A Scanner Darkly*.

Did the act of writing the novel serve as some kind of catharsis? The question arises because it is the last novel in which the policeman figure appears—an important character in much of Dick's fiction over the years. Space does not allow intense study of Dick's use of the policeman character in his work; but brief points can be made. The policeman or secret agent does not appear often in the short stories of Dick's first period. One of the few is Security Commissioner Reinhart in "The Variable Man" (1953). He ruthlessly attempts to destroy a solitary inventor and tinkerer because he does not want the uncertainty that inevitably results from new inventions. He needs to be in absolute control.

The police figure is often associated with bureaucratic control either in the political or the industrial world. On the other hand, policeman are often sympathetically drawn. In Dick's first novel, *Solar Lottery,* the protagonist works within the law in carrying out orders to assassinate the President. But he finally recognizes the corruption of the law and refuses to obey the orders of his superiors. In *The World Jones Made* (1956) Cussick, an agent of the federal government, is the favored narrator. He is a sympathetic character because he supports a government that believes in relativism—that every individual has a right to his own opinion and that the responsibility of the government is to fight absolutism, be it religious or political. In contrast, in *The Man Who Japed*, published the same year, the favored narrator is Allen Purcell, a writer of propaganda for Morec (Moral Reclamation), whose founder is Major Streiter. Morec allows no deviation from its ideology. Allen is horrified to find that one night while he was drinking he desecrated a statue of Major Streiter. He has a hidden self which commits destructive acts against the establishment, which his conscious self supports. The character split in this early novel foreshadows the double character of Fred/Bob in *A Scanner Darkly* and suggests man's psyche may be divided—part law enforcer and part lawbreaker.

The most ruthless police characters are certainly the military elements of the Nazi government in *The Man in the High Castle* (1962). But in *Clanes of the Alphane Moon*, published just two years later, Chuck Rittersdorf, a CIA agent, is a sympathetic figure, as is Rick Deckard, the police officer in *Do Androids Dream of Electric Sheep?* and Officer Tinbane in *Counter-Clock World.*

Dick's comments about authority figures in various interviews would suggest a violent antipathy to them. He made statements like, "I'm terrified of Authority Figures like bosses and cops. . . . I enjoyed being thrown out of the University of California at Berkeley because I would not take ROTC—boy, an Authority Figure in a uniform is the Authority Figure." During the last year of his life he also described a dream about police figures in a series of interviews he gave to Greg Rickman (published in Rickman's *Last Testament*, 1985).

> I dreamed about a horse coming at me with tremendous speed. I was in a house, the walls of which were made of glass. And this horse, a race horse, at the last moment tried to leap over the house and clear it. I could see his eyes were kind of goggled out in each side. The horse went directly over the house without hitting it, so I wasn't hurt.
>
> I ran out the front door to see and the horse was lying on the ground and its legs were broken. It was dying. And the rider was a policeman, it was a cop. I just stood there and excoriated him in the most abusive terms for having killed the horse. Because that's in essence what he'd done, by trying to leap the house he'd killed the horse. He hadn't killed me. He was unhurt, and I was unhurt. The house was unhurt. The horse was crippled terribly.
>
> He looked at the cop with ferocious hatred, and I looked at the cop with ferocious hatred. There was hate by each of us on behalf of the other. The casualty was the horse.
>
> I never could fathom that dream. It was inscrutable to me. But it seemed to me like it was the most important dream I ever had, if I could only interpret it. The casualty—if I could just figure out what the horse represented. Life itself. The force of life. Horses are supposed to represent something like the life force.
>
> Because from that dream on I was in a state of utter grief, misery, and despair!

Actually, Dick, in the two novels we just examined, did create metaphors that work as keys to unlock the meaning of the dream. Felix Buckman, in *Flow My Tears*, is both a policeman and a lawyer. The law represents that social order necessary to fight the entropic powers forever cannibalizing culture and attempting to reduce it to chaos. His antithesis is Jason Taverner, the artist, whom he finally must accuse of murder even though he knows Taverner is innocent. He weeps as he gives the order to destroy Taverner because he senses he has now lost part of himself—that intuitive, feminine aspect which is also symbolized by his twin sister, Alys. Thus over the years Dick has moved from dramatizing political power struggles in the outer world to portraying the inner struggle between the two aspects of man's nature—the yin and the yang, or the feminine and the masculine. In *Flow My Tears* the two have become separated and the masculine prevails.

In the next novel, *A Scanner Darkly*, Dick reverses the pattern and the rational, masculine polarity fails to survive. Undercover police agent Bob Arctor watches his mental capabilities as they are first dulled and then destroyed by drugs. When the inner policeman of the self no longer functions, chaos and mental death result.

Policeman as oppressor? Policeman as insurer of law and order? Dick's answer in his fiction is clear. If the police control is external, it is oppressive. Order is necessary, but one must never give away to someone else one's freedom to control oneself. The policeman must always be an inner one. The artist creates in the dark, breaking old conventions, creating new forms. The forms wing through the dark underworld of the unconscious, gathering speed until they break through the surface into the world of light. There they must submit themselves to discipline, to reason, to order. Feminine must unite with masculine. Order and life are synonymous. When one loses touch with one's inner policeman, one destroys oneself as does Bruce in *A Scanner Darkly*, who at the end dumbly kneels to worship the blue flowers of death.

9
The Search for God and the *Valis* Novels

The fifth and final period of Philip K. Dick's writing dates from the end of the 1970s when be began working on *Valis* to his death in 1982. I have chosen to call this the Metaphysical Period because Dick's sole concern now was in reading, puzzling, and writing about the nature of God and the mystery of evil, suffering, and death. Dick himself called this his period of radical innovation, likening himself to Beethoven, who after an apprenticeship and a mature period, turned to the final quartets and their musical experiments. Because Dick began to experience an economic security he had never known before, he could afford to try new techniques and explore new subjects even though the results might not be accepted for publication. His royalties provided ample income to support his simple lifestyle. The sale of the film rights for *Do Androids Dream*, which was made into the film *Blade Runner*, netted a substantial sum. As his income continued to increase he was very generous in contributing large amounts to various charities and giving gifts to his friends in need.

Dick startled his public when *Valis* was published in 1981. They had not really expected another novel from him and certainly not one about God. They knew the drug world he had described in *A Scanner Darkly* was one where he had nearly destroyed himself. Many of them believed his statement that he would never write again and thought it was made because he had suffered so much brain damage that he was unable to write. A rumor spread that he was crazy, apparently a response of some persons to the tale he told them about his March 1974 mystical experience. His sincere belief in the vision was publicly confirmed when he gave a detailed report to Charles Platt for inclusion in *Dream Makers*, a collection of biographies of major science fiction writers published in 1980.

In 1974 I experienced an invasion of my mind by a transcendentally rational mind, as if I had been insane all my life and suddenly I had become sane. Now, I have actually thought of that as a possibility, that I had been psychotic from 1928, when I was born, until March of 1974. But I don't think that's the case. I may have been somewhat whacked-out and eccentric for years and years, but I know I wasn't all that crazy.

Platt, puzzled about how to assess Dick's story, explains in *Dream Makers:*

> I myself have never seen evidence to make me believe in any psychic phenomena of pseudoscience, from telepathy to UFO's. My faith is that the universe is random and godless. I am the last person to believe that there is a higher intelligence, and that Philip K. Dick has a private connection with it.
>
> I do believe that something remarkable happened to him, if only psychologically; and I do believe that the experience has inspired a rather beautiful vision of the universe and a strange, unique book which may enhance the lives of its readers. This is the minimum with which Dick must be credited. To debate his "mental stability" is missing the point; what matters is the worth of his insight, regardless of its source. There have been men far more deranged than Philip K. Dick who nevertheless produced great art of lasting relevance to the lives of millions of un-deranged people.
>
> Dick remains much the same personality as before his vision. He has not metamorphosed into a religious zealot. His perceptions, and his ironic, skeptical wit, are as sharp as ever.

At the time of the Platt interview, Dick had finished *Valis* (written in 1978 although it was not published until 1981) and he was already planning its sequel, to be titled *Valis Regained.* The title was changed to *The Divine Invasion* when it was published in 1981. He conceived of the project as a triology and planned a third novel. Apparently this would have been *The Owl in Daylight,* a novel on which he was working at the time of his death. *The Transmigration of Timothy Archer*, published posthumously in 1982, cannot be considered as the third in the trilogy because it is realistic fiction based almost entirely on the life of Bishop James Pike. Pike's *The Other Side* (1968) gives his account of the events that Dick tells in *Timothy Archer* and verifies how closely Dick followed Pike's experiences before and after his son's death.

By the time Dick began writing the Valis novels, he had

achieved some degree of inner peace. He said that "for the first time in my life I was able to live alone and enjoy it. It [*Valis*] was written not out of desperation in isolation but in compatability with isolation. I was living alone but not suffering. I just wrote it and enjoyed it. I had a lot of fun writing it."[1]

Readers and critics who regarded Dick's work as essentially political and social science fiction were distressed or disappointed at what they considered a radical change in subject matter. It is true that, at first glance, his 1974 theophany does seem to have changed the nature of his fiction. But a journey through his previous works turns up seeds for all the ideas that flower in *Valis* and *The Divine Invasion*. For example, in the very early short story "The World She Wanted" (1953), the protagonist speculates about the nature of reality. He concludes it is a private and unique thing for each person. Dick wrote another interesting story the next year when he was just twenty-six. It is "Jon's World," a time travel story that describes a disturbed child who has visions of a land where there are fields of green and people live peacefully. His vision is a sharp contrast to the war-devasted world where he actually lives. The protagonist, a man named Kastner, time travels to a future that grew from a past where the bomb and other destructive devices were not invented. This future is like Jon's beautiful vision. Kastner, fascinated with the possibilities he suddenly conceives, realizes "this opens up whole new lines of speculation. The mystical visions of the medieval saints. Perhaps they were of other futures, other time flows. Visions of heaven would be better time flows. Ours must stand some place in the middle. And the vision of the eternal unchanging world. Perhaps that's an awareness of non-time. Not another world but this world, seen outside time. We'll have to think more about that, too." He concludes, "Let's go find some people. So we can begin discussing things. Metaphysical things. . . . I always did like metaphysical things."

Dick, we recall, declared a major in philosophy during his brief college career at Berkeley. When he abandoned the university, he did not desert his philosophical reflections. Speculations about time and change and reality and illusion and evil weave through many of

1. Gregg Rickman, *In His Own Words* (Long Beach: Fragments West/ The Valentine Press, 1985), p. 200.

his novels. *The Cosmic Puppets* (1957) pictures alternate versions of reality and the struggle of Ormazd, the cosmic constructive power, against Ahriman, the deconstructor. *The Three Stigmata of Palmer Eldritch* (1964) and *Galactic Pot-Healer* (1969) also explore the question of evil in the cosmos.

A number of religious visionaries anticipate those that will appear in the Valis novels. There is Ignatz Ledebur in *Clanes of the Alphane Moon* (1964), Anarch Peak in *Counter-Clock World* (1967) and Wilbur Mercer in *Do Androids Dream* (1968).

At first glance *Valis* and *The Divine Invasion* appear very dissimilar. They seem to share only a concern with discovering *gnosis*, or knowledge, about the nature of God and the cosmos. However, thoughtful reflection and study of the two texts reveals why Dick regarded them as a single work. *Valis* portrays an anguished mind (Horselover Fat's mind) that has encountered God in a theophany. He then attempts through reason and the intellectual process to understand his theophany and the nature of God. After failing, Fat abandons the use of reason to build a theoretical construct explaining God's nature. In the second half of the novel, he sets out in search of the Savior. His quest succeeds briefly, but the Savior is accidently killed. As the novel ends, he is still searching to understand his theophany.

The Divine Invasion continues the story of man's encounter with God, but two hundred years have passed, and now God seeks out man. The protagonist, Herb Asher, has fallen into a lethargy near spiritual death. God appears and orders Herb to assume a part in the Second Coming of the Lord. In their journey to Earth both Herb and the divine child Emmanuel are injured. The mother is killed. The wounds destroy their knowledge of their pasts. Only anamnesis, or recovery of what they already knew, will allow them to heal the wounds and understand who they really are. What they have forgotten and thus lost is the female aspect of the divine. The novel traces their journeys of self-discovery. They are guided in their quests by Zina, a divine presence who gives them clues. The novel concludes as Herb and Emmanuel finally awaken to and thereby recover their true androgynous natures. They become their own saviors, healed by their own efforts.

A brief summary of the novels suggests that easy comprehension is possible. Not so. The novels—in typical Dickian mode—are an intricate and complex maze barring any but the most determined from penetrating to the secret at the center. Dick constantly uses paradoxes, contradictions, and reversals—his dialectic of the imagination. He creates an image of assertion and then deserts it as he creates an image portraying a counterassertion. The novels are full of allusions—literary, philosophical, theological, mythological, musical. Dick's erudition at this point in his life is impressive, as the allusions testify. He had been a constant reader over the years, and additionally, for the novels in this Metaphysical Period he did a great amount of research in Judaism and also Christian theology. Yet in expressing his ideas in the novels, he often uses the language of the vernacular. It is a strange combination—Gnostic and Jewish theology discussed in California street language! This is the unique world of Dick—intellectual madness. He delights in treating solemn subjects with a touch of insanity.

Beneath the web of complexities encountered on first reading, one finds a pattern of meaning dramatized in each novel. *Valis* pictures a mind driven almost to madness by its encounter with death. Not any death but death in its most inexplicable form, death of the young. First Gloria, a young woman who is apparently lucid and rational, commits suicide. Later Sherri, another young woman, dies from cancer. Phil Dick the writer is one of the major characters in the novel. He cannot understand or accept either of the deaths and becomes suicidal himself. (We need to remember that Phil Dick is a persona, a character in *Valis*. He should not be confused with author Philip K. Dick who is writing the novel.)

Then God reveals himself to Phil in a theophany—an hour-long encounter signaled by a strange pink light. The God so revealed is called Zebra and then later in the novel *Valis* (Vast Active Living Intelligence System). Phil's sanity is wounded by the theophany. How is an intelligent, rational man to understand such a theophany? The first nine chapters of *Valis* dramatize Phil's struggle against madness in the face of an experience that violates reason. Or is his theophany a sign that he is already mad? He is uncertain. Phil's method of coping with his crisis is to split out or project the mind that has experienced the theophany into a character named Horselover Fat. Fat's is a restless, inquiring mind obsessed with the need to understand his revelation. Phil Dick the writer gains objectivity by maintaining a distance from Fat. He listens to Fat's endless arguments and theories but he generally refrains from making a judgment. He does occasionally comment that he thinks Fat is crazy.

We have not finished with the splitting of characters. In the novel Phil Dick the writer splits himself into two. Author Philip K. Dick doubles the number and constructs a cast of four characters who are best understood as a dramatization of the inner state of a single mind. The first two characters, as we have noted, are Fat and Phil Dick. The others are Kevin, a nihilist who argues against the possibility of finding meaning in the universe, and David, who expresses the establishment position of the good Catholic. The four men endlessly debate theological questions. Primary are the questions of how one is to understand suffering and illness and death. The position from which each argues allows author Dick to cover the range of possible answers to these questions. Fat provides the energy that fires the discussions. He constantly adds fuel to the debate by tossing in passages from his private exegesis. David, the orthodox believer, and Kevin, the atheist, always attack the validity of the exegesis. Phil Dick is suspicious of its validity but generally withholds judgment. The reader of the first nine chapters of *Valis* has become involved in a fascinating process of infinite regress. At the heart of the process is Fat, struggling to understand the meaning of that beam of pink light and the information it gave him. Phil Dick the writer watches Fat with detachment, while Philip K. Dick the author of the novel, observes both Fat and Phil. We the readers—provided with enough biographical information to know that Philip K. Dick is writing of personal experiences—observe all three of the levels of the drama spread before us.

The death of Sherri pushes Fat to a suicidal attempt and he is hospitalized until he regains his sanity, whatever that may be. Those who are insane are out of touch with reality. But the definition of reality is uncertain. If what we perceive as reality is only an illusion (as the Gnostics and Fat maintain), then the person who believes in that reality is really insane. The person who rejects it is not. But it was Fat's divine revelation that alerted him to the truth about the illusory quality of our world. And this revelation may be mere fantasy. Phil thinks it is; Fat thinks it is not. Fat decides to prove his claim by going in search of the Savior.

The last six chapters of *Valis* are a reversal of the form used in the first part of the novel. They are more powerful because they sharply contrast with the long theoretical discussions between the four men in the first half of the novel. Those conversations, like Fat's exegesis, were a mulling over of abstractions. Now the novel moves from the abstract to the particular, the California world of the present where Kevin finds a strange underground science-fiction film called *Valis* and takes his friends to see it. It offers clues that suggest a hidden meaning. That secret, when finally decoded by the men (who now call themselves the Rhipidon Society), leads them to northern California. There they discover the Second Coming has occurred. The Savior has been reborn, this time as the little daughter of Eric and Linda Lampton, rock stars. She is called Sophia (Holy Wisdom). The wound of Phil Dick is healed as soon as he finds her. Fat, the tormented part of his psyche who attempted suicide twice, disappears.

Sophia instructs the little group to go out into the world and tell the kerygma with which she charges them. The days of the wicked are about to end. She instructs, "What you teach is the world of man. Man is holy, and the true god, the living god, is man himself."[2]

The novel has apparently reached a logical, happy conclusion. But a reader of Dick's works knows that such a conclusion never happens in a world created by his imagination. Now the unexpected occurs—a tragic occurrence. Sophia is accidentally killed by Mini, a friend of her parents who is experimenting with new electronic equipment. Fat reappears, driven back into existence by this new death and the doubts and confusion that again storm Phil's mind. He must ask all over again how he is to interpret his theophany. As the novel ends, Fat sets out in the world on another quest to find the Savior. Phil waits at home.

The Divine Invasion continues the story of man's experience of *gnosis*. Fat temporarily achieved a paradisiacal state of joy when he found Sophia, just as did the disciples of Christ. But he lost it when she was killed in the accident. The incarnation must be repeated if mankind is to be healed.

The quest to find God in *Valis* was an intellectual quest. It did not succeed. *The Divine Invasion* dramatizes another kind of quest—the quest of love. A reversal takes place in this second novel. Herb

---

2. *Valis* (New York: Bantam, 1981), p. 184.

Asher, the protagonist, does not search for God; God (Yah) comes to Herb and sends him on a mission to bring the Savior to Earth. Because the novel is concerned with love, not reason, its mode is very different from that of *Valis*. It is nonchronological. Its purpose is not to picture the process of ratiocination as did *Valis* but rather a transformation accomplished by love and wisdom. Consequently this novel uses metaphor as its dramatic device. Music and poetry, not theological disputation, serve as the language through which states of spiritual awareness are presented to the reader. It is as though *Valis* had been a creation of the left forebrain where reason and logic prevail, and now the right forebrain with its intuitive mode takes over.

The metaphor of the Black Iron Prison pictures the situation on Earth. Two oppressive authorities rule—the Christian Islamic Church and the Scientific Legate. The first is the religious establishment, the second the political establishment. Hand in hand, they control the population and allow no freedom. Although they give the appearance of cooperation, they secretly plot to destroy each other. This situation represents the Evil Forces that have entrapped the Earth and excluded the Godhead. The Savior, whose earlier attempts to save the Earth have been aborted, must return again. The Apocalypse is at hand.

Herb Asher is a metaphor for the imprisoned individual. Shut up in his little dome on the planet CY30–CY30B in the Formalhaut star system, he endlessly listens to Linda Fox tapes. He has cut himself off from other humans and lost concern for anyone but himself. He is irritated when he receives a request to help Rybys Romney, the attendant in a neighboring dome who is dying of multiple sclerosis. He does not want to be bothered.

The Divine Invasion also splits into two parts as did *Valis*. The first half portrays the preparation for and reenactment of the Advent. The Godhead appears to Herb first in the form of a local deity. Then as Elias, a reincarnation of the prophet Elijah, he tells Rhybys and Herb they are to be the parents of the next savior. More unlikely parents cannot be imagined. This is a bold stroke on Dick's part—his refusal to illuminate them with any divine gleam. To give a local habitation and a name to the wonderful is inevitably to trivialize it. Dick overcomes that limitation by accepting it and pushing it to the extreme, making both Herb and Rybys as commonplace as possible.

She vomits and complains during her pregnancy. He is resentful and moody.

The symbolic wound plays a key function in *The Divine Invasion* as it did in *Valis*. According to Dickian cosmogony, the Godhead was injured in the original Fall. The injury is repeated in this story. In an accident as they come to Earth, Herb is wounded and their child, called Emmanuel, is brain damaged and born prematurely. Rybys is killed. Herb is placed in cryonic suspension for ten years, and Emmanuel's injury causes him to forget who he really is. Thus the tale of the death of the female at the time of the creation of the universe, told in the "Two Source Cosmogony," written by Fat in his exegesis in *Valis*, has been enacted again. But here the Creator and the Savior do not split as they did in *Valis*. It is Emmanuel who comes to save the Earth.

The second half of the novel pictures the struggle of Herb and his divine son to remember who they are. Born into the reality of Earth, the individual suffers amnesia. He forgets his true nature. Anamnesis, or recovery of his memory, is necessary if he is to rediscover God. This view, taken from Plato, is a cornerstone of Philip K. Dick theology.

Another fundamental of Dick's theology is that the microcosm mirrors the macrocosm. What happens in one realm reflects what happens in the other. Emmanuel, the divine form, must learn who he is and in his task he is aided by a female companion, Zina. She gives him an electronic slate that allows him to receive cryptic communications from Valis, the divine ground of being. Part of the mystery Emmanuel must solve in order to understand his nature and purpose is to learn who Zina is. He will finally discover she is the female aspect of God, known by many names—Hagi Sophia, the Torah, Pallas Athena, Malkuth, Shekhina. She is that part of himself from which Emmanuel has become separated.

Analogously Herb, the microform, must also recall who he was before he was placed in cryonic suspension. The last half of the novel is constructed with a series of balanced scenes. In one series Emmanuel struggles to recover his divine memory. In the other series Herb labors to achieve knowledge of what he was before he came to Earth. Zina, the divine presence, also aids him.

As Emmanuel awakens to his true identity, he realizes his mission is to free humanity from the Black Iron Prison where it is trapped. He is an Old Testament God of indignation and wrath, and he believes in an eye for an eye and a tooth for a tooth. He plans to fight the Evil Empire. Zina, however, holds that to fight the empire is to become infected by its insanity. She knows Emmanuel is the creator of reality, but she can imagine a better one than the reality he has created. She suggests an alternative version where freedom, love, and compassion rule. She takes Emmanuel to visit her realm, the Palm Tree Garden, where evil has no power.

Then they make a wager. They will test his reality against hers, using Herb Asher as their pawn. Emmanuel will take Herb's fantasy of a love affair with Linda Fox and turn it into reality. Will Herb still be able to love her when he actually achieves his dream and discovers that because she is human she has blemishes and flaws?

The answer is yes. Herb not only loves her but sacrifices his dream of living with her when it becomes clear he must do this to protect her from the evil of Belial.

In the final chapter of the novel, Herb is united with Linda Fox (who is an earthly manifestation of Sophia-Christ). Simultaneously, Emmanuel finally identifies Zina as Shekhina, the part of the Godhead separated from him in the original Fall. To name is to know. When he experiences his gnosis, he and Shekhina are rejoined. The Old Testament wrathful God is now subsumed by a healed Godhead, containing both male and female polarities. Evil is banished. It is not defeated by Emmanuel but displaced by the love that creates another version of reality.

Dick displays a range of styles in the two novels. The first half of *Valis*, the philosophical ravings of a near madman, is written in a style quite different from that we have come to expect from Dick. It is erudite, full of literary allusions and long conversations. The reader who thrives on the bizarre and rapid action customary in a Dick novel may find this discursive mode heavy going and perhaps even dull. The reader with a bent toward metaphysical speculation will be fascinated. The long discussions about theology have an anguished necessity about them. This is not idle talk to pass the time. People close to Fat are suffering and dying. He himself has been driven to the madness of suicide. He reads endlessly because he is obsessed with the need to find answers. He writes endlessly in his exegesis because the answers he finds when he reads do not satisfy him.

The first half of *Valis* is unique, both to Dick's fiction and to the whole genre of science fiction. It reminds one of Dostoevski's *Notes from the Underground*, where the protagonist constructs a powerful logical argument to establish his point that man is irrational. Horse-lover Fat calls on reason to aid him in his fight against madness and, ironically, reason drives him closer to madness. This first part of the novel contains a distillation of Dick's most original thinking, and yet the writing is rescued from heaviness by humor and a sprinkling of street language. These are not scholarly discussions! The discrepancy between the language and the subject creates the kind of pained incongruity so often present in Dick's fiction.

This union of opposites also finds expression in the symbols Dick uses. He yokes the mundane and the sacred. There is Kevin's dead cat killed by a car. It is the symbol of everything he regards as "fucked up" in the universe. He wants to stick it in God's face and demand an explanation. Opposed to that is the beautiful gold fish pin that first sparks Fat's memory of who he really is. We learn the fish sign is like a section of the DNA spiral and thus a symbol for creativity and life. Another example of incongruity is the material means by which Valis or the Godhead reveals itself on Earth. It expresses itself in a beautiful poem written by Ikhnaton in ancient Egypt. It also appears in a science fiction film as a satellite that looks like a beer can run over by a taxi. The movie film, produced by a composer of contemporary music, provides clues to Fat in his search for God. So does Wagner's opera *Parsifal*.

The second half of *Valis*, when Fat and his friends set out to find the producers of the film, returns to the style typical of a Dick novel. It is comprised of dialogue and action—an antithesis of the expository style in the first part. Again, we are reminded of *Notes from the Underground*, which uses a similar pattern balancing exposition and action.

The Divine Invasion uses yet another style—a delicate, fragile one. It quite appropriately has the quality of a fairy tale since the key figure is Zina, who is a fairy. The long philosophical discussions of *Valis* are absent; instead poetry is quoted (Shakespeare, Dowland, Yeats). In commenting about the novel, Dick said he tried to evoke an atmosphere like that in *A Midsummer Night's Dream*.

The point of view is also different in the two novels. *Valis* uses the first person; Phil Dick, the writer, narrates the story. Phil is as objective and sane as the reader likes to believe he is. Phil makes the judgment the reader would have been forced to reach had Fat been the narrator of the story. Fat is crazy. Because Phil makes that judgment, the reader is spared the task and thus freed to move on to speculation about the possibility that Fat may be the only really sane person in the novel.

The Divine Invasion returns to the use of the multiple points of view Dick mastered and used when he wrote the great novels of his second period. He uses three narratives with a narrative center for each. Herb's relations with Rybys and Linda are told from his point of view. Cardinal Harms is the center for the political narrative about the Church and the Legate. Emmanuel provides the point of view for the third story, the one focusing on his education. In this novel we have escaped the mundane world built by reason which provided the setting for *Valis*. Here the limitations of time and space no longer apply since according to Dick they are constructs of the logical mind, and the world of *The Divine Invasion* can be reached only when the imagination is awakened.

Music, always important in Dick's fiction, has never played a larger role than in this pair of novels, particularly in *The Divine Invasion*. Since *Valis* primarily uses the discursive mode, music is of less significance, although Mini's Syncronicity music gives subliminal cues about meaning when the Rhipidon Society goes to see the film, and Wagner's *Parsifal* suggests the wound and the quest.

The Divine Invasion uses three kinds of music, each for a particular purpose. The sappy, soupy strings playing music from *Fiddler on the Roof* and *South Pacific* represent the counterfeit world that locks most people in the mental prison house they assume is reality. In contrast, the lute songs of John Dowland as sung by Linda Fox represent true reality. The music unites the awakened intelligence of mankind on all the planets. Dowland, a contemporary of Shakespeare, was both a composer and a virtuoso performer on the lute. The texts of several Dowland songs are quoted in the novel. Gustav Mahler's Second, or *Resurrection*, Symphony is also used to suggest the awakened consciousness. One music critic has described this symphony, a favorite of Dick's, as portraying "a human being grappling with the concept of immortality through earthly suffering, joy and passion." For Herb the symphony represents the complexity, profundity, and beauty for which he yearns as an escape from the sappy, soupy string music of the illusory reality he experienced in cryonic suspension.

The third use of music is the bells that signal the Palm Tree Garden. This is Zina's springtime world of dancing and joy and peace. It is the world Emmanuel has forgotten because of the wound he received when he fell. She must lead him again to it. She reminds him, "You heard the bells and you know that their beauty is greater than the power of evil."

Music provides more than cues to signal various states of spiritual awareness. Dick's method in weaving together a number of related ideas into a harmonious whole is reminiscent of the fugue, that Renaissance musical form in which a number of voices combine in stating and developing a single theme. The main idea of a fugue is that one voice contrasts with others; all the voices do not move together. It is descended from the contrapunctual music of the Middle Ages, where one voice is played against another. The theme is first stated, then developed, and finally resolved. In *Valis* Horselover Fat is the lone anguished voice crying out the theme: Given suffering and death, how is man to understand God and reality? By the end of *The Divine Invasion*, the question has been resolved.

A single reading of the novels rewards the reader with subliminal sparks of meaning, as did the movie *Valis* for its viewers. But as the Rhipidon Society returned again and again to the movie to study its intricate parts and to understand its clues, so must the reader of these complex novels. Gradually seven major themes emerge.

First and most important is the theme of the wound and the quest for healing. Man suffers from physical illness and death and worse, a wounded or dead psyche. This is the state of every man, a result of his having been born into this world. According to Dick, we live in an irrational world and our suffering is a result of that irrationality. Man's task, having identified his wound, is to set out on a quest that will bring healing. In defining this wound, Dick draws on *Parsifal*, which tells the story of Amfortas, the wounded leader of the Grail knights. Finally healing occurs when Parsifal, the pure fool, "abolishes the delusion of the magician Klingsor and his castle." The apparent evil in the world was actually an inner wound which caused Amfortas to see a false reality.

The Parsifal legend is retold in the novels. Emmanuel's wounded mind is finally healed and the Black Iron Prison of Evil vanquished when Zina convinces Emmanuel that he should create her alternate vision as a new reality. Evil is not defeated because the confrontation of Emmanuel and Belial never takes place. Evil just fades away. In the final brief scene of the novel, Linda and Herb go to view the broken remains of Belial. Nothing is left but what looks like a great luminous kite—pieces of damaged light. He has returned to his original shape—Lucifer, the brightest of the angels, who fell to earth.

A second theme, and also a very important one, is the theme of *gnosis*, the Greek word for knowledge. Dick is to be regarded as a contemporary thinker in the Gnostic tradition because he holds that salvation through self-knowledge is the only means possible to man to heal his wounded psyche. His views follow those of such men as Simon Magus, Paracelsus, Boehme, and Bruno. These mystical thinkers all experienced theophanies in which secret knowledge about the nature of God was revealed to them. They formed secret societies like the Friends of God and the Brothers of the Rosy Cross, to which reference is made in *The Divine Invasion* (96). Not only does Dick create a character, Horselover Fat, who is a present-day Gnostic, but Fat draws heavily on Gnostic literature as he writes his *Tractates Cryptica Scripture* (hidden writing) and develops his cosmogony. See, for example, entries number 11, 17, 21, and 48 in the *Tractates*.

The original Gnostics were a religious movement of the early Christian Era, the first two centuries following Christ's death. Because the movement involved many different sects, their beliefs cannot be summarized easily. A leader of one of the major sects was Valentinus, and Dick has drawn heavily on his views.

The early Catholic church claimed that humanity needed a divine way beyond its own power to approach God. The church offered this way to salvation and claimed there was no other. In contrast, the Gnostics accepted no such institution or authority. Their claim was that humanity, from its own inner potential, must discover for itself the revelation of truth. For the Gnostic, exploring the psyche was a religious quest. The more radical Gnostics rejected any religious institutions at all.

Once the Catholic church was well established, its leaders began to label this kind of thinking as heretical and to ban the gospels of the Gnostics. These gospels were texts the church founders had decided not to include in the New Testament. Little was known about these writings except in oblique references by the early church fathers as they attacked them, until the discovery at Chenoboskion, Egypt, in 1945 of a library of fifty-two Gnostic writings. (The usual English transliteration of the town's name is Nag Hammadi and so the texts are occasionally referred to by that name.) Entry number 24 in Fat's exegesis makes reference to the texts and they play a key part in the novel. They are symbolized as the pot where Fat found God. For him the language of the texts is alive. Language or information, which he calls the plasmate, is God or Valis.

The Valentinian Gnostics held that each individual is a spirit, or pneuma, a fallen particle of the true God. He is trapped in the prison of material existence. He is asleep and ignorant of his condition. God sends messengers to call the sleeping spirit to awaken and remember its true destiny. *Gnosis* comes as a theophany, an intuitive process of knowing. To know oneself is to know human destiny.

Theodotus, a Gnostic teacher, wrote that when one achieves *gnosis*, he understands "who we were, and what we have become; where we were . . . wither we are hastening; from what we are being released; what birth is, and what is rebirth."[3]

In Dick's cosmogony, reason is of prime importance, indeed synonymous with God. Here, too, he draws on the Gnostic tradition. Silvanus, a writer whose *Teachings* were found at Nag Hammadi, advises: "Bring in your guide and your teacher. The mind is the guide but reason is the teacher. . . . Live according to your mind. . . . Acquire strength, for the mind is strong. . . . Enlighten your mind. . . . Light the lamp within you." To do this, he says, you must "knock on yourself as upon a door and walk upon yourself as upon a straight road. For if you walk on the road, it is impossible for you to go astray. . . . Open the door for yourself that you may know what is. . . . Whatever you will open for yourself, you will open."[4]

Third is the theme of evil. Dick's view is dualistic in that he holds evil does exist and is a power in its own right. It is a result of an accident when the universe was created. The One created a pair of twins which were in turn to divide into the Many through their

3. Elaine Pagels, *The Gnostic Gospels* (New York: Random House, 1979), p. xix.

4. Pagels, p. 153.

dialectical interaction. Hyperuniverse I developed according to the original plan. Hyperuniverse II was damaged in an accident symbolized by the Fall and as a result became deranged. We live in Hyperuniverse II and thus partake of its madness and irrationality, manifest as illness, suffering, and death. Salvation or escape is possible only as each individual, awakened to his true consciousness by *gnosis*, returns to the rationality of Hyperuniverse I. Belial is the name Dick gives to the irrational force in its macrocosmic dimension. He uses the symbol of the Black Iron Prison or the Empire for its microcosmic, or earthly, expression (see *Tractates* entry 41). Opposed to Belial are the forces for good which rule in Hyperuniverse I and will eventually heal Hyperuniverse II. These powers are symbolized by the Palm Tree Garden—the original unfallen state of God.

A fourth theme draws on a parallel between the macrocosm and the microcosm. Emmanuel, born on Earth as a man, is able to experience the Hermetic transformation because "the truth is that what is above is like what is below and what is below is like what is above, to accomplish the miracle of the one thing."[5] The original wound when the universe, the macrocosm, was created is experienced by "each of its microcosmic pluriforms: ourselves."[6] Each individual is a little world. *The Divine Invasion* dramatizes this relationship of macrocosm and microcosm. When the accident occurs to the flycar as Rybys and Herb come to Earth, Emmanuel, the macrocosm, is injured. So is Herb, the microcosm, who falls into a trance from which he will not awaken for ten years—not until the time when Emmanuel has almost recovered his memory.

A fifth theme is that of anamnesis. Following Gnostic tradition (which on this point draws from Plato), Dick holds that most of mankind is asleep and thus deprived of the memory of its true identity. As a result, we regard the pseudoreality of this world as the true reality. Actually it is *maya*, a veil of illusion. Gradually anamnesis, or a reversal of our amnesia, can be accomplished. Dreams and the imagination aid us in our quest, and if we persevere we may experience a theophany, a divine revelation of our true identity. We discover that "all history is one immortal man who continually

5. *The Divine Invasion* (New York: Timescape Books, 1981), p. 91.
6. *Valis*, p. 124.

learns."[7] Thus Fat discovers he is Thomas, the disciple who lived in Rome in the first century. This is not to be understood as reincarnation, since in Dick's cosmogony time does not exist. His tractate explains: "The universe is information and we are stationary in it, not three-dimensional and not in space or time. The information fed to us we hypostatize into the phenomenal world."

The significance of the sixth theme, androgyny, is not easy to understand until the reader has grasped the first five themes just outlined. The Godhead is both male and female—a polarity similar to the Taoist concept of the yin and the yang. The two aspects became separated in the primordial Fall. The female part remained with the fallen world. She has a number of names in *The Divine Invasion*: Diana, Pallas Athena, Hagia Sophia, the Torah, Malkuth. But she is more—she is Shekhina, as the female aspect of the Godhead was known to the Jews. When Emmanuel is finally able to recognize and name her as the other half of himself, the split in the Godhead is healed.

For this view of the androgynous Godhead, Dick goes to the literature of the Cabala, the structure of Jewish mysticism that developed during the Middle Ages. He makes reference to the *Zohar,* the bible of Cabala, where the account of the severed Godhead is given. It holds that for God to be One and Whole, the masculine aspect must be united with Shekhina, the feminine half.

Information (language) is sacred to Dick because he believes it is the divine plasmate. Its finest expression is the Torah, the Creator's instrument. The Torah is the living soul of the world. Elias explains to Herb that the Torah is "the totality of divine disclosure by God; it is alive; it existed before Creation. It is a mystic, almost cosmic, entity."[8] Another Cabala text, the *Sepher Yezirah*, holds the same idea about the mystical power of language. According to the story of creation given in this text, God used the twenty-two letters of the Hebrew alphabet. Elias draws on this account in the *Sepher Yezirah* in explaining to Herb the power and mystery of the Torah.

The seventh and final theme is that of games, play, and children. In *Valis* this theme is submerged beneath others. True, Sophia, the Savior, is only two years old, but she does not survive. The world of

7. Ibid., p. 216.
8. *The Divine Invasion*, p. 97.

Valis is essentially the adult world searching for God through the use of reason. In *The Divine Invasion*, in contrast, we enter the world of children and play. Emmanuel first points out this aspect of God's nature to Elias, insisting that "He enjoys games and play. It says in the Scripture that he rested but I say that he played." Herb, watching his ten-year-old son after he has awakened from his long sleep, recognizes the element of playfulness in Emmanuel's nature. He realizes that "the part of him that derived from his mother is ten years old. And the part of him that is Yah has no age; it is infinity itself. A compound of the very young and the timeless."[9]

Zina takes Emmanuel to her imaginative world in the Palm Tree Garden where the wind blows through the bamboo and joy reigns. She is a fairy child who leads him into the world of enchantment. And it is through a trick that Zina causes Emmanuel to make Herb's dream world into a reality. At the end of the novel Emmanuel marvels that he has finally been reunited with the female half of himself. Zina tells him how she accomplished this awakening. "My love of games. That is your love, your secret joy; to play like a child. To be not serious. I appealed to that."[10] To be serious, to pursue truth with reason as did Horselover Fat, is not enough. One needs also to be a child, to dream and imagine and play. To believe in fairies. True reality lies beyond the grasp of reason alone.

Dick writes in the tradition of the mystics, drawing on the Gnostics and the writings of Cabala, as noted. Yet his goal is to do more than rejoice in revelation; he wishes to understand it. He insists that the theophany experienced by the mystic must be comprehended before it can be accepted. What he is really attempting to do in these novels is to reconcile revealed religion and rational philosophy.

Dick's cosmogony in summary form appears as entry number 47 in Fat's exegesis—the "Two Source Cosmogony." It draws on, incorporates, and finally subsumes all past philosophies and saviors. He is strongly influenced but by no means limited by the thinking of Heraclitus, Plato, and Spinoza. As the title "Two Source Cosmogony" indicates, Dick's view is bitheistic. He sees two elements of the Godhead in dialectical combat and identifies one as an irrational,

9. Ibid., p. 138.
10. Ibid., p. 199.

even demonic, will, which struggles against wisdom and rationality, that is, the Logos.

According to his view, the cosmos is thought—a vast active living intelligence system. Each of us is a part of the cosmic mind. What we experience as a physical material world is, when properly seen, the thoughts of Valis (God). These thoughts take the form or arrangements of physical reality into information. This "physical reality" is not physical reality at all, but rather mental concepts. Valis literally thinks our spatiotemporal world.

For Dick, the fact that Valis's thoughts take the form of arrangements of physical reality is the most important discovery that can be made about what the universe really is and what/who Valis is—the entity who thinks the thoughts. Time, as experienced by the human mind, is an occluding factor. When time is removed as a factor, our world is properly seen as a conceptual arrangement in which nothing perishes.

However, part of the conceptual arrangement (Valis) was damaged in an accident and is therefore irrational. This is the universe where we live. Christ as the Logos comes to this decomposing creation to form his own universe in its place. Thus the rational has invaded the irrational and is assimilating it into its own body. Therefore, the universe is moving from chaos to order, from irrationality to rationality.

What Dick has done in his concept is to replace a static deity with a dynamic, process deity. He conceives of that deity as a vast unitary brain and the physical world is that brain and necessary for the mind to exist. As we need a brain to think, so does the deity; our universe is that deity. The deity (the mind) contacts the brain (the physical world), arranges it, impinges on it, imprints information, processes information in/on it. The mind is the music; the brain (the physical universe), the groove.

What are the implications for the individual (the microcosm) of this view of the macrocosm? He needs to experience an awakening of his true nature. This is the task of each individual and no institution can do it for him. The concept of individual freedom and responsibility is very important to Dick and explains why he is so strongly attracted to the writings of the Gnostics. The awakening comes when you realize that the world you experience is your creation, that you are the Pantocreator. In a letter Dick explains further:

This world that you see— it is an objectification of your own prior thought-informations; it is substantial now, but originally it consisted of ideas; that is, it has two modes of existence; first as ideas in a mind—and it is your mind—and then as objective, substantial creation coming back at you-as-percipient. Thus you are not what you thought you are, and you have an origin and nature different from what you supposed; you have a history, and if that history is followed backward in time (and up the ladder of ascending ontology) you arrive at the Absolute, call it Ch'ang Tao, or Braham, or God, or the One, or the Good, or the Prime Mover—names do not matter; perhaps it has no name. This realization is the Awakening, but it leads, after a time, to further realizations equally great, which inelectably follow, and carry equal weight; if you came from this Absolute, it follows that you will inevitably return; this is something that cannot be doubted; it is understood to be indubitable. It is as indubitable a truth as the truth of your origin.[11]

During the last years of his life, Dick often talked about his *Valis* trilogy, and so *The Transmigration of Timothy Archer*, published several months after his death, tends to be accepted by his readers and critics as the final work of the trilogy. I do not believe this is the case. My conversations with Dick as he worked on these metaphysical novels as well as my reading of *Timothy Archer* suggest to me that *The Owl in Daylight*, the novel in progress when he died, was to be the final work in the trilogy. The writing of *Timothy Archer* gave him a chance to catch his intellectual breath, to retrace his creative leap in moving from the depression of *Valis* to the transcendence of *The Divine Invasion*. We recall that he saw the two novels as analogous to *Paradise Lost* and *Paradise Regained*.

At the end of *Timothy Archer*, Angel Archer finally understands the wound to her psyche that incapacitated her so that she sat passively and watched while the three persons closest to her died. Having gained that understanding, she is healed and ready to act. I suspect the writing of the novel served the same purpose for its author as it did for his protagonist. It allowed him to review the territory over which he had traveled in his *Valis* novels and to prepare for the third work in the trilogy.

The Owl in Daylight, I believe, was to be that novel—a work that would be the third ring uniting the rational and mystical modes of

11. Dick to Warrick, August 31, 1981.

thinking with which he had dealt in the first two novels. A letter Dick
wrote in June 1981 supports this view:

> My novel-in-progress assumes that the three realms of Dante's *Com-*
> *media* are three ways of viewing reality, *this* life, not the next; I got this
> idea from reading comments by Dante on the *Commedia*; he said that
> the three realms are in this world. This is a Sufi notion, a very mystical,
> very secret comprehension that now we are dead and in a kind of prison.
> *Inferno* is characterized by metal, by dark clouds, the smokey red light,
> immutable cause-and-effect, total repetition, total karmic control, total
> recycling of everything forever, as if time has stopped. . . . Karma has
> power but can be broken by the right acts. When you perform the right
> act, instantly the karmic fetters loosen. The colors lighten. Brightness
> enters. The mode is flying, not walking. Time flows forward; there is
> constant newness. [Dick continues as he explains his 1974 visionary
> experience.] I was transferred out of Purgatorio, or at least into one of
> the higher levels, perhaps even the highest level, that of Earthy Delight,
> the Palm Tree Garden; I heard what Dante reports: the lady singing,
> and I drank from the fountain of anamnesis. All this fits in with Sufi
> mysticism, not with Christian or for that matter any other that I know
> of, but Dante was strongly influenced by the Sufis. This is why *The*
> *Divine Invasion* has an optimism that is virtually absent in all my
> previous writing; in that novel I am experiencing the Garden. . . . All
> this will show up in my new novel, *The Owl in Daylight*.[12]

The novel was never committed to paper. Dick indicated he had
it worked out in his mind and "the next thing to do was to sit down at
the typewriter and I just fell flat on my face. I could not lift my hands.
I could not go from the notes to the typewriter. I had everything. The
plot, the theme, the characters—everything! and I just crapped
out."[13] The problem was the complexity of the task Dick had set for
himself. He wanted to do something innovative, to "write the most
ambitious science fiction novel I could write." The major character
was to be based on Beethoven and the plot on Goethe's *Faust*. The
character has reached the end of the third period, just as Beethoven
did in his music, and wants to go to a fourth period. Dick's task, then,
was to figure out what Beethoven's fourth period would have been,
had he lived to compose it. Like Beethoven, Dick did not live to
wrote the last work he planned.

12. Rickman, pp. 253–54.
13. Rickman, p. 238.

While *Timothy Archer* cannot be read as the final work in a trilogy, it does work as an exegesis on the two completed novels in the opus. It also allowed Dick to accomplish something for which he had yearned since the beginning of his career—to write a literary novel for which he had a publisher. Further, the novel was an answer to those critics, and especially Ursula LeGuin, who piqued him when they said he was unable to create a sympathetic, convincing woman in his fiction. The narrator and protagonist is female (a point of view never before used by Dick except for parts of *Confessions of a Crap Artist* and *Mary and the Giant*). Angel Archer is intelligent, witty, lonely, sane, overeducated, warm, occasionally spiteful—as when she says of her visits to her friend Kirsten in the hospital, "I always made sure I brought her something she couldn't eat or something she couldn't wear." Angel uses the speech patterns of contemporary California to tell her tale about madness, suicide, and death.

The title of the novel would suggest, however, that Timothy Archer, not his daughter-in-law, Angel, is the protagonist. Dick's comments indicate the book is a thinly disguised biography of his friend James Bishop Pike. On first appearance, it seems to be just that. Timothy Archer, controversial bishop in the Episcopal church, is tried by his colleagues for heresy. Angel, married to his son Jeff, introduces the bishop to her friend Kirsten Lundborg. Kirsten is herself the mother of a grown son, Bill, who suffers from schizophrenia. Kirsten soon becomes Tim's mistress and offers comfort and companionship during the trial as he successfully defends himself against the heresy charges. He and Kirsten go to England to be on hand as translators unravel the language of the Zadoke Documents recently found in Israel. These documents at first promise to be as important to Christianity as the Dead Sea Scrolls. But when finally translated, they threaten to destroy Christianity because they contain the teachings to which Christ gave voice, and yet they were written two hundred years before his birth. Christ may be a fake. Timothy Archer's faith is shaken. He cannot continue to preach and to offer communion if Christ is not the Son of God and if Christ's promise of immortal life is questionable.

While he is in England, his son Jeff commits suicide. Afterward, Tim and Kirsten begin receiving messages from him—from beyond the grave, and the bishop is so moved by this evidence of life after death that he begins to write a book about it called *Here, Tyrant*

Death. Tim and Kirsten, accompanied by skeptical Angel, go to a California medium for aid in contacting Jeff. The medium has fearful news for the pair: death awaits them. Kirsten accepts the sentence; Tim does not.

Kirsten's subsequent death from cancer goads Tim into a desperate attempt to learn the answer about immortality. Does life after death really exist? He now believes the answer lies in a cave in Israel where the Zodakites hid it away after they learned it. He is obsessed with the need to search for the evidence but still rational enough to recognize his obsession. He asks Angel to accompany him as a stabilizing force. She refuses, convinced that his quest is madness and so he goes alone to Israel.

Tim's death, when Angel hears it on the news, devastates her. She feels her soul die and she then turns into a mere machine. She is still able to function physically, to understand intellectually, but without a heart that also understands, she is not really alive.

Thus ends the plot of *Timothy Archer*. But the real story belongs to Angel, not Timothy Archer. The real quest is not Tim's search for the secret life after death hidden in the desert caves, but Angel's quest to escape from the death-in-life where she lives as the novel opens. The structure of the novel reveals the meaning. All the events of Tim's life are told as flashbacks in a single day of Angel's life as she attends a seminar on Arabic mysticism, conducted by one Edgar Barefoot and held, ironically, on the day of John Lennon's death. The first chapter of the novel portrays the seminar, which she feels compelled to attend even though she regards mysticism as nonsense. But somehow, she recognizes, she must break free from her ossification and face the madness inherent in the deaths of Jeff, Kirsten, and Tim. She must understand why they "went the way they collectively went, volunteering to die, each of them, like Parsifal, a perfect fool." Angel must journey back in time if she is ever to journey forward. Her recollection of things past, when completed, allows her finally to understand her failure. She recognizes herself as a mere Berkeley intellectual, locked into her world of books, where she endlessly reads the works of others, skeptically discusses their ideas, and never believes in anything herself. She has been a record, passively repeating—just like the merchandise she sells in her record shop.

The structure of *Timothy Archer* echoes that of *Valis*, as Dick recognized. He saw both books as analyses of religious mania, but in

Valis, the character Phil Dick is much less hostile to Horselover Fat and his mania than is Angel Archer to Tim Archer and the Dionysian madness that drives him to his death.[14] Yet, at the end of the novel, Angel affirms Tim's mania for mysticism as she accepts it, yokes it with her rational mode, and transcends both.

The four-chambered metaphor again offers the most workable model to understand the complexity of Dick's bipolar concepts. The metaphor pictures a fictional world where each character, once he defines his polarity, moves toward its opposite, either by reason or mysticism—except for those two characters who opt for suicide, Jeff and Kirsten. Timothy Archer, who believes in mystical experience, has as his antipode Angel, who, like her husband, Jeff, argues against what they both regard as the bishop's madness. The negative of Tim's position, as the novel opens, is Bill Lundborg, who lives in the totally real world of the senses, symbolized by cars. He is unable to engage in any kind of abstract thinking, a secular madness (in contrast to Tim's divine madness) that sends him periodically to mental institutions. He cannot rise above the literal in his attempts at theological discussions with the bishop.[15] He continually insists that if something does not make sense—cannot be perceived by the senses—its existence is an impossibility.

In this complex metaphor, Kirsten also functions as the negative of Tim's view just as does her son. She believes so completely in the power of the occult that she passively accepts the judgment of death given by the California medium, and then, ironically, flees to death through the madness of suicide. Tim, in contrast, fights death by facing it and going to search in the desert for the answer that will vanquish death.

Angel's quest through the past as she sits on the houseboat at Sausalito produces a series of epiphanies, each allowing her to see into the nature of her former selves. Jeff escaped into books, struggling to establish a parallel between Wallenstein in the Thirty Years' War and Hitler in World War II. Both, he maintained, destroyed their country because in times of crisis they relied on the occult rather than reason. Like Jeff, she has become a professional student with a

---

14. Ibid., p. 215.

15. *The Transmigration of Timothy Archer* (New York: Timescape Books, 1982), chap. 8.

word sickness. She is lost in meaningless words, a merchant of words, with no real contact with life. She concludes that "I am a metaphor junkie, over-educated and smart. I think too much, read too much, worry too much" (195).

Like Tim, she failed to respond to Jeff's silent call for help. Not until after Jeff's death did Tim become concerned with his son, and even then, Angel concludes, he saw Jeff only as "an instrument, a device for learning; he is converted into a talking book! Like all these books that Tim forever reaches for, especially in moments of crisis" (145).

Finally, after speculation about the books she has read and the people, now dead, she has loved, Angel relives the moment of her ultimate failure—the moment when she refused to respond to Tim's cry for help. Chapter 13 dramatizes the crisis that has led to Angel's spiritual death. The bishop, after a long silence, contacts Angel and asks her to go with him to the desert wadi, where he believes he will find the *anokhi*, which is Christ. He wants her to drive the car for him because of her excellent sense of direction. In her sanity, she recognizes he is mad to believe that a mushroom growing in a cave can give immortal life. Christ spoke in metaphors, not literally as Tim now insists. Even recognizing his condition and the insanity of what he proposes to do, she refuses to accompany him to Israel, preferring the safety of Berkeley and her record shop. She knows her presence and good judgment would be a steadying influence, but she is not willing to take the risk.

Looking back now and recalling, she at last realizes the gravity of that refusal to act, an action that might have prevented Tim's death. Her refusal to act has locked her into a rut and she has become a machine that cannot change. Her recollections end with this last epiphany, and she returns to the present of the Sufi seminar she is attending on the houseboat.

Edgar Barefoot closes the novel as he opened it. He introduces Angel to one of his students. It is Bill Lundborg, transformed into a Parsifal, a perfect fool whose madness has become divine. For he claims to be Timothy Archer, a *bodhisattva*. Rather than attaining Nirvana, Bill/Tim has chosen out of compassion to come back to this world to aid others. And although he says he did not find the *anokhi* in the desert, he offers Angel a mushroom, telling her it is his body and blood, and that it will give immortal life.

Does Angel believe him? Has she found salvation? The Dickian ending is typically ambiguous. She invites Bill to come home and live with her, manipulated by Edgar into making the offer because he says it will be good for her. In trade, Edgar gives her a collector's record she covets. Not bad, she concludes shrewdly as she thinks about how much she can sell the record for and how she has bested Edgar since he led her only to do what she intended to do anyway—ask Bill to live with her.

When Dick finished writing the book, he delighted in his success in finally creating a rounded, convincing female character while at the same time he mourned that he must lose Angel since he no longer needed to speak in her voice. Perhaps, however, he did not lose her but incorporated into his own being that female aspect of himself from which he felt he had been separated at the death of his infant twin sister. Angel, with her skeptical wit and love of words often sounds like the Philip Dick many of us knew—ever the rational intellectual. And Bill Lundborg, the Parsifal-like divine fool whom she invites to come and live with her, suggests another Phil Dick, one I never met: the one who could write the following letter to his agent, Russell Galen, a few months before he died:

> Seven and a half years ago the voice that speaks to me—I call it, as in *Valis*, the AI voice—told me that a new savior would be born, and, as you know, it has added further details from time to time, the most recent statement coming about two years ago when it said, "The time you've waited for has come. The work is complete; the final world is here. He has been transplanted and is alive." After that it said only one more thing: that the savior would be found on an island. After that the voice fell silent. I have asked it repeatedly to tell me where the savior is and his name. Two nights ago the voice broke its silence. Here is a summation.
>
> The savior is named Tagore _____. I could not catch the other part of the name. He was born—or lives now—in Ceylon, in the rural countryside.
>
> . . .
>
> This is the information I have been waiting for, but I got more than information, more than words by the AI voice; I actually saw Tagore, although imperfectly. The vision will remain with me forever.

Let me hasten to counter this letter, which tests one's credulity, with a series of letters Dick wrote to me during January through

October of 1981—long, typed, single-spaced letters. They are remarkable letters, philosophical disputations aimed at erecting a
rational explanation of his visionary experiences. In one of the first
ones, dated January 13, 1981, he says:

> My belief in Valis, being based on experience, has passed through
> almost seven years of analysis and scrutiny and out of this there arises in
> me, based on the enormous exegesis that I have brought into existence,
> a conviction that ultimately I will be able to find a *rational*, rather than a
> supernatural, explanation for March 1974. My experience was unusual
> and perplexing, but that does not make it ad hoc incomprehensible. It
> may have been incomprehensible to me at that time, but so were the
> results of the Michelson-Morley experiment. An inexplicable experi-
> ence—encounter—with reality, that is, reality behaving inexplicably in
> affront to all known laws, is a challenge to the reasoning human, the
> human who is dignified by an innate curiosity; he wants to know what
> the hell caused it, what the hell happened.

The letters that follow are intense explorations of Dick's visionary experience that draw on Plato, Plotinus, Pythagoras, Joachim del
Fiore, Spinoza—the list is endless—in an attempt to erect a rational
structure that will explain the experience, which in turn requires an
explanation of ultimate reality.

When Dick had worked out an explanation that satisfied him,
the letters ceased for a few weeks. Then they began again as he
discarded that answer as unsatisfactory and started once again to
build another theory. On September 11, 1981, he wrote: "I have
wound down my exegesis, at last, realizing that in the seven and a half
years that I have worked on it I have learned relatively little. . . . My
study of Plato, Pythagoras, and Philo (among others) indicates that
what I saw in March, 1974 that I call VALIS is real, but what it is I
simply do not know, nor do I expect ever to know." But his mind
could not rest in this conclusion.

On September 15, 1981, he began again: "I have it and this time
I truly have it." Another metaphysical theory followed. On October
2, in the last letter he wrote to me on the subject, he concluded, "I am
onto it at last, and it *is* Gnosticism—radically redefined, but still
Gnosticism."

Had he lived, he would have been still theorizing about ultimate
reality, still working out his ideas in his exegesis, still sharing with us

in his fiction the bizarre possibilities he imagined. His restless mind rejected the comfort of a final answer. For his death to have occurred when he was in the process of writing another novel seems appropriate. He would have wanted it that way.

10
Philip K. Dick's Moral Vision

This critical study of Dick's fiction is a work without a concluding chapter—and appropriately so. To summarize his ideas, to categorize his work, to deliver the final word would be to violate Dick's vision. He saw a universe of infinite possibility, with shapes that constantly transformed themselves—a universe in process. He had not delivered his final word when he died on March 3, 1982, because for him the Word was truly the Living Word, the power that creates and re-creates patterns. Trapped in the stasis of a final statement, the Word would have been defeated by entropy and death.

But if we cannot make a final statement, we can at least note the significance of his opus of fiction for the times in which we live. Great creative personalities often see the essence of an age with a clarity denied to the mass of people. Their vision is so vivid that when subsequent events confirm it, humanity, slower at arriving at a realization of its present, hails them as prophetic. I believe that Dick may well be one of those creative personalities whom we hail as visionaries. The claim seems a strange one, considering the literary form in which he worked. Blake, Wordsworth, Yeats—the Romantics with the elegance of poetic diction make up the visionary company, not writers working in a prose form often regarded as trash. But let us for the moment ignore the form in which he was forced to write and consider instead his vision.

He had a remarkable sense of the cultural transformation taking place in the last half of the twentieth century. He pointed out the cracks in our institutions, our ideologies, and our value systems that would inevitably lead to their collapse. He understood that what had been functional in an industrial age would not work as our culture transformed itself and moved into an Information Age. Such changes often march in with violence. As Dick's fiction declares again and again, the late twentieth century is a time at war with itself, not with an external enemy. To fight against what one abhors without realizing it lies within is to destroy all. Dick warns us against doing this to ourselves. The cloud of chaos inevitably hangs above the Dickian landscape, a reminder that a like chaos will descend on the real world and envelop us if we continue to make war.

Dick's fiction calls up our basic cultural assumptions, requires us to reexamine them, and points out the destructive destinations to which they are carrying us. The American Dream may have succeeded as a means of survival in the wilderness of early America; it allowed us to subdue that wilderness and build our holy cities of materialism. But now, the images in Dick's fiction declare, we live in a new kind of wilderness, a wasteland wilderness, because those cities and the culture that built them are in decay. We need a new American dream to overcome this wasteland. Dick's ubiquitous wasteland landscape is a moral mirror asking us to journey within and explore the universe of mind and psyche where all the forms that shape the outer world are created. The critical journey of discovery is into the mysterious realm of inner space. Just as Dick's Fomalhaut Cosmos was a universe created by his imagination, so the universe in which we live is constructed of our ideas about it. To change it we must change our ideas.

Dick's work makes no new declarations about our time; we knew early in the twentieth century that ours was an Age of Anxiety. But the gift of his powerful mythmaking ability is to give us the stories that help us see both what we are and what we may become as we move into the Space Age. His novel contribution is the bizarre images he creates that so vividly picture our anxieties. Phantasmagoric shapes, the Dickian protagonist often calls them, as he muses about the swirl of awesome possibilities sweeping through his mind. They are disorienting images—without clear boundary, inconsistent, contradictory, fragmented, at war with one another. They force us to reconsider our conventional conception of reality. Dick said that "science fiction is uniquely a kind of semi-reality. It is not a statement that 'this is,' but a statement, 'What if this were.' The difference is crucial in every respect." Frightening as are some of the futures Dick imagines for mankind, they are not fixed. We are Leo Buleros, we are "choosers," Dick tells us in *The Three Stigmata of Palmer Eldritch*"; and *The Divine Invasion* envisions another future than nuclear destruction that we can choose.

We have noted Dick's wide acquaintance with the classics. But much as Dick loved classical literature, he did not draw on this source in creating his characters. The Dickian fictional world is a world without Titans or Heroes; instead it is a world cut off from the gods. It is filled with little people lacking in power or wisdom, who daily face the dilemma of trying to survive in the face of the inexplicable destructive forces that constantly try to snuff them out. Yet they are not the conventional antiheroes of modern fiction. Perhaps the oxymoron *heroic antihero* best describes Dick's protagonist. Finally, the Dickian hero acts. He may writhe and struggle to escape, but in the end he accepts the burden of his existential freedom. Daily, he finally learns, he must choose once again to push the boulder of moral responsibility up the hill of right action. Freedom thus becomes of highest value in Dick's code. The individual must be free to make moral choices, even though he may often fail to make the right choice. Dick declares again and again, for the individual to be turned into a machine programmed to carry out the decisions of others is "the greatest evil imaginable; the placing on what was a free man who laughed and cried and made mistakes and wandered off into foolishness and play a restriction that limits him, despite what he may imagine or think, to fulfilling an aim outside his own personal—however puny—destiny."[1]

Our study of Dick's writings has traced the journey of his restless mind, watching as it grasped an idea, created a metaphor for it in a fictional pattern of antinomies, discarded it for another idea—always spiraling forward albeit often in a wobbling, erratic course. Yet from the beginning one element remains constant in all the fiction—Dick's faith in the power of empathy. The idea was not well developed or labeled when it first appeared. We see empathy in two of his early short stories as through a glass darkly. He has not yet given it a name. Instead, his characters act it out, and only later does he recognize what his fiction has said. In "Roog" Dick pictures a dog who guards the garbage can of his owners against the garbage men who come to collect it each week. The dog is driven crazy because he cannot offer protection to his owners against these weekly raids. Years later, Dick commented on the story, explaining that he was describing an actual

1. "The Android and the Human," in *Philip K. Dick: Electric Shepherd.* Ed. Bruce Gillespie. (Melbourne: Norstrilia Press, 1975), p. 85.

dog owned by a Berkeley neighbor. "I watched the dog suffer, and I understood a little of what was destroying him, and I wanted to speak for him. That's the whole of it right there. Snooper couldn't talk. I could. In fact I could write it down, and someone could publish it and many people could read it. Writing fiction has to do with this: becoming the voice for those without voices. It's not your own voice, you the author; it is all those other voices which normally go unheard."[2]

"Beyond Lies the Wub," Dick's first published story, also dramatizes the concept of empathy. It tells the story of a piglike alien captured and eventually eaten by a crew of space adventurers despite the fact that the wub possesses human characteristics. Captain Franco and his men lack the ability to see beneath the wub's appearance. Twenty years later Dick said of the story:

> The idea I wanted to get down on paper had to do with the definition of "human." The dramatic way I trapped the idea was to present ourselves, the literal humans, and then an alien life form that exhibits the deeper traits that I associate with humanity: not a biped with an enlarged cortex—a forked radish that thinks, to paraphrase the old saying—but an organism that is human in terms of its soul.
>
> I'm sorry if the word *soul* offends you, but I can think of no other term. Certainly, when I wrote the story back in my youth in politically-active Berkeley, I myself would never have thought of the crucial ingredient in the wub being a soul; I was a fireball radical and atheist, and religion was totally foreign to me. However, even in those days I was casting about in an effort to contrast the truly human from what I was later to call the "android or reflex machine" that looks human but is not. The germ of the idea lies in this my first published story. It has to do with empathy, or, as it was called in earlier times, caritas or *agape*.
>
> In this story, empathy (on the part of the wub who looks like a big pig and has the feelings of a man) becomes an actual weapon for survival. Empathy is defined as the ability to put yourself in someone else's place. The wub does this even better than we ordinarily suppose could be done: its spiritual capacity is its literal salvation. The wub was my idea of a higher life form; it was then and it is now. On the other hand, Captain Franco (the name is deliberately based on General Franco of Spain) looks on other creatures in terms of sheer utility; they are objects to him, and he pays the ultimate price for this total failure of empathy. So I show empathy possessing a survival value; in terms of

2. Unpublished introduction to "Roog."

inter-species competition, empathy gives you the edge. Not a bad idea for a very early story by a very young person!

Two years after writing "The Wub," Dick again explored the concept in "The Last of the Masters" (1954) and now he named it and actually called it empathy. In the story a young freedom fighter, Silvia, finally encounters the head of the coercive government and discovers he is a robot. She says in horror, "My God, you have no understanding of us. You run all this, and you're incapable of empathy. You're nothing but a mechanical computer."

By the second period of Dick's fiction when he writes his great novels in the 1960s, empathy is regularly used as the key element defining the authentic human being. The concept is made concrete most vividly in "The Little Black Box," published in 1964. Dick then incorporates the black empathy box into *Do Androids Dream* where those like J. R. Isidore who use it regularly gain the strength to climb up through the difficulties of their daily lives. Beyond that, the power of empathy frees the individual from the prison house of his own consciousness and allows him to slip through the mirror forever reflecting back his own image. Once beyond, he sees the world from an alien consciousness to which he gives the same rights and worth as his own awareness. All life, not just his own, becomes sacred.

At first glance, Dick seems to be a contemporary writer who in many ways espouses an old-fashioned moral view that places him in the long tradition of humanistic writers. From the beginning, his writing insists that each individual has a responsibility to act in a moral way, even though that early fiction makes no reference to God. And of course by the end of his career, the novels focus on the major concepts of the Judeo-Christian tradition. While these concepts are never accepted in their entirety—in fact they are almost always revised—they are never denied or negated.

A closer examination of Dick's moral code, however, shows us that given the complexities of the contemporary world, the values of traditional Christian humanists are too simple to be workable. He develops a code of valor that is much more demanding. Choice is no longer a choice between good and evil, as the moralist in an earlier age would have declared. Today the problem facing each man is that even when he practices empathy and yearns to make the right moral choice, he often finds himself in a moral dilemma where in order to do right he must also do wrong. Again and again the Dickian hero is faced with this tragic choice: to do the right thing he must violate his own moral nature: for example, Tagomi, Glen Runciter, Joseph Adams, Joe Chip, Rick Deckard. The moral road is not an easy one. The critical metaphor for this arduous journey is the upward climb— Wilbur Mercer on the hill, Joe Chip on the stairs.

In an interview near the end of his life Dick once again reinforced his belief that moral values are ultimate values: "In a sense what I'm saying is that all life is a moral issue. Which is a very Jewish idea. The Hebrew idea about God is that God is found in morality, not in epistemology. That is where the Almighty exists, in the moral area. It isn't just what I said once, that in Hebrew monotheism ethics devolve directly from God. That's not it. It's that God and ethics are so interwoven that where you have one you have the other."[3]

Dick is an iconoclastic literary figure. His fiction refuses to conform to the characteristics of any particular category. Because he uses many of the techniques of science fiction, he is customarily labeled as a writer in that genre. But the strong, often overwhelming, elements of realism in his fiction—novels like *Martian Time-Slip* and *Dr. Bloodmoney*, for example—make that label somewhat inaccurate. In many ways he seems to fit into the tradition of Absurdist literature, and he readily admitted the influence in his formative stage of Beckett, Genêt, and other Absurdist dramatists. The typical Absurd hero inhabits a grotesque world whose structures violate reason and common sense but are nevertheless true. He is constantly frustrated, muddled, or horrified by inexplicable events that seem to happen only to him and finally lead him in paranoiac panic to decide that Fate is deliberately playing pranks on him. Not the Fall of Man but his pratfalls are the concern of the Absurdist writer. So, too, are pratfalls often Dick's concerns. Yet in a fuller assessment, we find that Dick does not fit neatly into this category because he refuses to give in to the nihilism of the French Absurdists.

Dick on occasion proclaimed himself a writer in the Romantic tradition who was particularly influenced by German Romanticism. He read Goethe and Schiller when he was young, and the works of Beethoven and other German romantic composers were among his

3. Gregg Richman, *In His Own Words* (Long Beach: Fragments West/ The Valentine Press, 1985), p. 47.

favorites. His intuitive mode of creativity and his emotional excesses characterize him as a romantic, as does his rebellion against all institutions that violate individual freedom. "I'm a *Sturm and Drang* romantic," he himself declares in one interview.

When we continue to look for Dick's literary ancestors, we discover that the ones from which he is rooted most directly are the metaphysical poets. Dick claimed them as among his favorite poets and uses quotations from Vaughan and Marvell and Donne in his fiction. For example, he quotes Donne's Holy Sonnet XIV, "Batter my Heart, three person'd God," in its entirety in *Timothy Archer*. His four chambered metaphors resemble metaphysical conceits with their concentrated images that involve an element of dramatic contrast, or strain, or of intellectual difficulty. Like Donne, he uses a colloquial style. Both writers are obsessed with the idea of death and treat it again and again in their works. So, too, do both writers blend wit and seriousness, intense feelings and vast erudition.

A discussion of literary influences is not a discussion of the essence of Dick's fiction because his literary voice is unique. He is an eclectic, choosing and using ideas, techniques, and quotations from the literary tradition as he creates in his own distinctive form. He is a synthesizer but never an imitator. The bibliography accompanying *Timothy Archer* demonstrates the wide range of literature that yielded material to him: the Bible, works of Aeschylus, Plato, Vergil, Dante, Shakespeare, Donne, Vaughan, Goethe, Schiller, Yeats, to name the major writers. In this final novel Dick felt free to reveal his debt to and use of the great literary tradition, a use that he hid under cryptic allusions in most of his science fiction.

Time must be the judge of Dick's literary worth. If, as some of us suspect it will, Time does declare him one of the major writers of the twentieth century, he will be hailed as the synthesizer of a new literary form yoking realism and the fantastic. The novels to which I have given major attention in this study (with the possible exception of *A Scanner Darkly*) all succeed in this new form, for which I have chosen the term *quantum-reality fiction*. Dick's fiction gives too little emphasis to science to be called true science fiction. It gives too much emphasis to the real world to be called fantasy. It violates common-sense reality too often to be called realistic fiction. He sees with a new vision as he creates imaginary worlds for his reader—a vision that declares all worlds to be fictions, brought into existence by the consciousness of the creator. Man faces the void and keeps it at bay only by the power of his intelligence to create forms.

The universe where Dick's characters live when they fall out of commonsense reality is built on concepts that are a part of quantum physics. As physicists describe it, quantum reality is evasive and seems forever to hide beyond direct observation. Quantum physicists do not entirely agree about the nature of quantum reality, except in labeling it as bizarre. A contemporary physicist notes, "If we take the claims [of some outspoken physicists] at face value, the stories physicists tell resemble the tales of mystics and madmen. . . . Not ignorance, but the emergence of unexpected knowledge forces on us all new visions of the way things really are."[4] Quantum theory holds that all elementary events occur at random, governed only by statistical laws. And Heisenberg's famous uncertainty principle forbids an accurate knowledge of a quantum particle's position and momentum. Beyond that, the prevailing quantum theory holds that there is no reality without the act of observation. Dick's fiction catches the essence of this quantum reality, and he is probably the first writer of fiction to have done so.

In addition to his creation of quantum reality fiction, Dick also deserves recognition for the development of the complex four-chambered metaphor that allows him to picture the dialectical mode of the human mind as it moves in the process of thinking.

Beyond his accomplishments as a writer, Dick merits recognition for his accomplishments as a human. He struggled to live by his code of valor. In the face of great adversity, he survived and created. He was a tortured genius, condemned to live within a brilliant mind that compulsively drove itself to gather up and live out all the anxiety, pain, and torment of our age. Perhaps he needed so to suffer before he could transform our shared experiences into literature. Perhaps he did not choose but worked heroically in the shadow of a mental illness from which he had no escape. He is not the first writer to be so tortured. I recently reread a biography of Virginia Woolf which describes her struggle to write in the face of repeated nervous breakdowns, and I noted how similar Dick's life was in this respect. He was less fortunate than she; he had no lifetime spouse like Leonard Woolf

4. Nick Herbert, *Quantum Reality: Beyond the New Physics* (Garden City, NY: Anchor Press/Doubleday, 1985), p. 16.

to shelter him economically and emotionally and to publish his works.

Dick's life was a quest for meaning, a struggle with the great metaphysical problem of our time—how to reconcile what he knew in his head with what he knew in his heart. He identified himself with his little men, unheroic protagonists who endure in the face of great adversity, going quietly about their work. His work was writing and he, too, went about it quietly, eschewing publicity. Through all the mental and physical illness he never stopped writing for more than a brief time. He never lost faith in the power of the word to create reality for the individual and the power of literature to create a shared consciousness for the community of men. Looking at our strife-torn world, he said:

> The key is this. We must shape a joint dream that differs for and from each of us, but it must harmonize in the sense that it must not exclude and negate from section to section. How this is to be done I can't of course say; maybe it can't be done. But . . . if two people dream the same dream it ceases to be an illusion; the sole prior test that distinguished reality from hallucination was the consensus gentium, that one other or several others saw it, too. This is the idios kosmos, the private dream, contrasted to the shared dream of us all, the koinos kosmos. What is new in our time is that we are beginning to see the plastic, trembling quality of the koinos kosmos—which scares us, its insubstantiality—and the more-than-merrier-vapor quality of the hallucination. Like science fiction, a third reality is formed half way between.

In his writing Dick shared with us his private dreams and his nightmares about this new reality in the future toward which we move. He said he was disturbed by those reviewers who found only bitterness and pessimism in his fiction because his mood was one of trust. "Perhaps," he said, "they are bothered by the fact that what I trust is so very small. They want something vaster. I have news for them; there is nothing vaster." For Dick all that one could trust was the capacity of the ordinary person to act with courage when courage is required. He explained, "To me the great joy in writing a book is showing some small person, some ordinary person doing something in a moment of great valor, for which he would get nothing and which would be unsung in the real world. The book, then, is the song about his valor."

Perhaps this book can be regarded at least in part as a song about the valor of Philip K. Dick. For he continued to write over the years, hounded by poverty, often depressed, and ignored by the mainstream literary world where he hoped for recognition. He lived in a sea of emotional disaster, he was often ill, he used drugs, he alienated his friends, he destroyed five marriages. . . . Yet incredibly he wrote well over forty novels and one hundred short stories, and at least eight of those novels, the ones we have examined in detail, seem likely to become classics. He was one of the most courageous of writers, a man who lived by his own code of valor.

Bibliography
Index

Philip K. Dick: A Bibliography

Novels

Blade Runner. See Do Androids Dream of Electric Sheep?

Clanes of the Alphane Moon. New York: Ace, 1964 pb.

Confessions of a Crap Artist. New York: Entwhistle, 1975. (Mainstream. Written in 1959.)

The Cosmic Puppets. New York: Ace, 1957 pb.

Counter-Clock World. New York: Berkley: Medallion, 1967 pb.

The Crack in Space. New York: Ace, 1966 pb.

Deus Irae. Garden City, NY: Doubleday, 1976.

The Divine Invasion. New York: Timescape Books, 1981 pb.

Do Androids Dream of Electric Sheep? Garden City, NY: Doubleday, 1968. (Filmed under the title *Blade Runner.*)

Dr. Bloodmoney, or How We Got Along After the Bomb. New York: Ace, 1965 pb.

Dr. Futurity. New York: Ace, 1960 pb.

Eye in the Sky. New York: Ace, 1957 pb.

Flow My Tears, the Policeman Said. Garden City, NY: Doubleday, 1974.

Galactic Pot-Healer. New York: Berkley, 1969 pb.

The Game-Players of Titan. New York: Ace, 1963 pb.

The Ganymede Takeover (with Ray Nelson). New York: Ace, 1967 pb.

Humpty Dumpty in Oakland. London: Victor Golldncz, 1986. (Mainstream. Written in 1960.)

The Man in the High Castle. New York: Putnam, 1962.

The Man Who Japed. New York: Ace, 1956 pb.

The Man Whose Teeth Were All Exactly Alike. Willimantic, CT: Mark Ziesing. (Mainstream. Written in 1960 and published posthumously.)

Martian Time-Slip. New York: Ballantine, 1964 pb.

Mary and the Giant. New York: Arbor House, 1987. (Mainstream. Written in 1954–55.)

A Maze of Death. Garden City, NY: Doubleday, 1970.

In Milton Lumky Territory. Pleasantville, NY: Dragon Press, 1985. (Mainstream. Written in 1958 and published posthumously.)

Now Wait for Last Year. Garden City, NY: Doubleday, 1966.

Our Friends from Frolix 8. New York: Ace, 1970 pb.

The Penultimate Truth. New York: Belmont, 1964 pb.

Puttering About in a Small Land. Chicago: Academy Chicago, 1985. (Mainstream. Written in 1957 and published posthumously.)

Radio Free Albemuth. New York: Arbor House, 1985. (Written circa 1976 and published posthumously.)

A Scanner Darkly. Garden City, NY: Doubleday, 1977.

The Simulacra. New York: Ace, 1964 pb.

Solar Lottery. New York: Ace, 1955 pb.

The Three Stigmata of Palmer Eldritch. Garden City, NY: Doubleday, 1965.

Time out of Joint. Philadelphia: Lippincott, 1959.

The Transmigration of Timothy Archer. New York: Timescape Books, 1982. (Mainstream. Written in 1981 and published posthumously.)

Ubik. Garden City, NY: Doubleday, 1969.

Ubik: The Screenplay. Minneapolis: Corroboree Press, 1985. (Written in 1974 and published posthumously.)

The Unteleported Man. New York: Ace, 1966 pb. (Reprinted in 1983 with missing material restored. Reprinted in 1984 with revisions and titled *Lies, Inc.*)

Valis. New York: Bantam, 1981 pb.

Vulcan's Hammer. New York: Ace, 1960 pb.

We Can Build You. New York: DAW, 1972 pb. (Serialized in 1969.)

The World Jones Made. New York: Ace, 1956 pb.

The Zap Gun. New York: Pyramid, 1967 pb.

Short Fiction

"A. Lincoln, Simulacrum." *Amazing* (Nov. 1969, Jan. 1970).

"Adjustment Team." *Orbit Science Fiction* (Sept.–Oct. 1954).

"The Alien Mind." *F&SF* (Oct. 1981).
"Autofac." *Galaxy* (Nov. 1955).
"Beyond Lies the Wub." *Planet Stories* (July 1952).
"Beyond the Door." *Fantastic Universe* (Jan. 1954).
"Breakfast at Twilight." *Amazing* (July 1954).
"The Builder." *Amazing* (Dec. 1953, Jan. 1954).
"Cantata 140." *F&SF* (July 1964).
"Captive Market." *Worlds of If* (Apr. 1955).
"Chains of Air, Web of Aether." In *Stellar #5*. Ed. Judy-Lynn Del Rey. New York: Ballantine, 1980 pb.
"The Chromium Fence." *Imagination* (July 1955).
"Colony." *Galaxy* (June 1953). Collected in *The Best of Philip K. Dick*.
"The Commuter." *Amazing* (Aug.–Sept. 1953).
"The Cookie Lady." *Fantasy Fiction* (June 1953).
"The Cosmic Poachers." *Imagination* (July 1953).
"The Crawlers." *Imagination* (July 1954).
"The Crystal Gift." *Planet Stories* (Jan. 1954).
"The Days of Perky Pat." *Amazing* (Dec. 1963).
"The Defenders." *Galaxy* (Jan. 1953).
"The Electric Ant." *F&SF* (Oct. 1969).
"Exhibit Piece." *Worlds of If* (Aug. 1954).
"The Exit Door Leads In." In *The Best Science Fiction of the Year #9*. Ed. Terry Carr. New York: Ballantine, 1980 pb.
"Expendable." *F&SF* (July 1953).
"Explorers We." *F&SF* (Jan. 1959).
"The Eyes Have It." *Science Fiction Stories 1* (1953).
"Fair Game." *Worlds of If* (Sept. 1959).
"Faith of Our Fathers." In *Dangerous Visions*. Ed. Harlan Ellison. Garden City, NY: Doubleday, 1967.
"The Father-thing." *F&SF* (Dec. 1954).
"Foster, You're Dead." In *Star Science Fiction Stories 3*. Ed. Frederik Pohl, New York: Ballantine, 1955.
"Frozen Journey." *Playboy* (Dec. 1980).
"A Game of Unchance." *Amazing* (July 1964).
"A Glass of Darkness." *Satellite Science Fiction* (Dec. 1956).
"The Golden Man." *Worlds of If* (Apr. 1954).
"The Great C." *Cosmos* (Sept. 1953).
"The Gun." *Planet Stories* (Sept. 1952).
"The Hanging Stranger." *Science Fiction Adventures* (Dec. 1953).

"Holy Quarrel." *Worlds of Tomorrow* (May 1966).

"The Hood Maker." *Imagination* (June 1955).

"Human Is." *Startling Stories* (Winter 1955).

"If There Were No Benny Cemoli." *Galaxy* (Dec. 1963).

"The Impossible Planet." *Imagination* (Oct. 1953).

"Imposter." *Astounding* (June 1953).

"The Indefatigable Frog." *Fantastic Story Magazine* (July 1953).

"The Infinites." *Planet Stories* (May 1953).

"James P. Crow." *Planet Stories* (May 1954).

"Jon's World." In *Time to Come*. Ed. August Derleth. New York: Farrar, 1954.

"King of the Elves." *Beyond Fantasy Fiction* (Sept. 1953).

"The Last of the Masters." *Orbit Science Fiction* (Nov.–Dec. 1954).

"The Little Black Box." *Worlds of Tomorrow* (Aug. 1964).

"The Little Movement." *F&SF* (Nov. 1952).

"A Little Something for Us Tempunauts." In *Final Stage*. Ed. Edward L. Ferman and Barry N. Malzberg. New York: Charterhouse, 1974.

"Martians Come in Clouds." *Fantastic Universe* (June–July 1953).

"Meddler." *Future* (Oct. 1954).

"Midadjustment." *Science Fiction Quarterly* (Feb. 1957).

"The Minority Report." *Fantastic Universe* (Jan. 1956).

"The Mold of Yancy." *Worlds of If* (Aug. 1955).

"Mr. Spaceship." *Imagination* (Jan. 1953).

"Nanny." *Startling Stories* (Spring 1955).

"Not by Its Cover." *Famous Science Fiction* (Summer 1968).

"Novelty Act." *Fantastic* (Feb. 1964).

"Null-O." *Worlds of If* (Dec. 1958).

"Of Withered Apples." *Cosmos* (July 1954).

"Oh, to Be a Blobel!" *Galaxy* (Feb. 1964).

"Out in the Garden." *Fantasy Fiction* (Aug. 1953).

"Paycheck." *Imagination* (June 1953). Collected in *The Best of Philip K. Dick*.

"Pay for the Printer." *Satellite Science Fiction* (Oct. 1956).

"Piper in the Woods." *Imagination* (Feb. 1953).

"Planet for Transients." *Fantastic Universe* (Oct.–Nov. 1953).

"Precious Artifact." *Galaxy* (Oct. 1964).

"The Pre-Persons." *F&SF* (Oct. 1974).

"A Present for Pat." *Startling Stories* (Jan. 1954).

"The Preserving Machine." *F&SF* (June 1953).
"Prize Ship." *Thrilling Wonder Stories* (Winter 1954).
"Progeny." *Worlds of If* (Nov. 1954).
"Project: Earth." *Imagination* (Dec. 1953).
"Prominent Author." *Worlds of If* (May 1954).
"Psi-Man, Heal My Child!" *Imaginative Tales* (Nov. 1955).
"Rautavaara's Case." *Omni* (Oct. 1980).
"Recall Mechanism." *Worlds of If* (July 1959).
"Retreat Syndrome." *Worlds of Tomorrow* (Jan. 1965).
"Return Match." *Galaxy* (Feb. 1967).
"Roog." *F&SF* (Feb. 1963).
"Sales Pitch." *Future* (June 1954).
"Second Variety." *Space Science Fiction* (May 1953).
"Service Call." *Science Fiction Stories* (July 1955).
"Shell Game." *Galaxy* (Sept. 1954).
"The Short Happy Life of the Brown Oxford." *F&SF* (Jan. 1954).
"The Skull." *Worlds of If* (Sept. 1952).
"Small Town." *Amazing* (May 1954).
"Souvenir." *Fantastic Universe* (Oct. 1954).
"Stand-by." *Amazing* (Oct. 1963).
"Strange Eden." *Imagination* (Dec. 1954).
"A Surface Raid." *Fantastic Universe* (July 1955).
"Survey Team." *Fantastic Universe* (May 1954).
"Time Pawn." *Thrilling Wonder Stories* (Summer 1954).
"Tony and the Beetles." In *Orbit 2*. Ed. Damon Knight. New York: Putnam, 1967.
"To Serve the Master." *Imagination* (Feb. 1956).
"The Trouble with Bubbles." *Worlds of If* (Sept. 1953).
"The Turning Wheel." *Science Fiction Stories 2* (1954).
"The Unreconstructed M." *Science Fiction Stories* (Jan. 1957).
"The Unteleported Man." *Fantastic* (Dec. 1964).
"Upon the Dull Earth." *Beyond Fantasy Fiction 9* (Nov. 1954).
"The Variable Man." *Space Science Fiction* (Sept. 1953).
"Vulcan's Hammer." *Future 29* (1956).
"War Game." *Galaxy* (Dec. 1959).
"War Veteran." *Worlds of If* (Mar. 1955).
"The War with the Fnools." *Galaxy* (Feb. 1969).
"Waterspider." *Worlds of If* (Jan. 1964).
"We Can Remember It for You Wholesale." *F&SF* (Apr. 1966).

"What the Dead Men Say." *Worlds of Tomorrow* (June 1964).
"What'll We Do with Ragland Park?" *Amazing* (Nov. 1963).
"A World of Talent." *Galaxy* (Oct. 1954).
"The World She Wanted." *Science Fiction Quarterly* (May 1953).
"Your Appointment Will Be Yesterday." *Amazing* (Aug. 1966).

Short Story Collections

The Best of Philip K. Dick. Ed. John Brunner. New York: Ballantine, 1977.
The Book of Philip K. Dick. New York: DAW, 1973.
The Collected Stories of Philip K. Dick. Columbia, Pa: Underwood/Miller, 1987.
The Golden Man. Ed. Mark Hurst. New York: Berkley, 1980.
A Handful of Darkness. London: Rich & Cowan, 1955.
I Hope I Shall Arrive Soon. Ed. Mark Hurst and Paul Williams. Garden City, NY: Doubleday, 1985.
The Preserving Machine. New York: Ace, 1969.
Robots, Androids, and Mechanical Oddities. Ed. Patricia S. Warrick and Martin H. Greenberg. Carbondale: Southern Illinois UP, 1984.
The Variable Man. New York: Ace, 1957.

Index

Aeschylus, 200
"A. Lincoln, Simulacrum" (1969), 66
Allusions, musical and literary, 84, 130, 177–78
Amazing magazine, 66
"Android and the Human, The" (Vancouver speech, 1972), xiii, 112–13, 117, 135, 152
Androids. *See Do Androids Dream of Electric Sheep?*, androids in
Apostolides, Kleo. *See* Dick, Kleo Apostolides
Archer, Angel (*Timothy Archer*), 19, 185, 188, 189–92
Art Music, Dick's employment at, 7–8
"Aunt Flo" stories, xxi

Bach, Johann Sebastian, 93
Bardo Thol, 34
Beckett, Samuel, 34, 199
Beethoven, Ludwig van, 4, 93, 166, 186, 199
Berkeley: Dick living in, xxi, 6–7; radical decade in, 5–6: as setting for end of *Dr. Bloodmoney*, 83, 86
Berman, Morris, 24
"Beyond Lies the Wub" (1952), xxi, 99–100, 197–98

Bindswangler, Ludwig van, 64
Blade Runner (film), xvi, 11, 166
Bohlen, Jack (*Martian Time-Slip*), 15, 20, 69, 70, 72, 73–75, 76, 144
Bohr, Niels, 21, 23
Boucher, Anthony, 8, 12
"Breakfast at Twilight" (1954), 81
Bring the Jubilee (More), 33
Broglie, Louis de, 21
Brown, Ray, 13n
Bulero, Leo (*Palmer Eldritch*), xiii, 98, 102–6, 107, 108, 110–12, 137, 195
Busby, Leslie. *See* Dick, Leslie Busby

California State University—Fullerton, Special Collections Library, Dick manuscripts sold to, xiv, xxiii, 153
Camus, Albert, 122
Capra, Fritjof, 24, 26
Characters: aliens, 20; based on Bishop Pike, 11, 147, 167, 187; children, 19, 38, 63, 64, 104, 168; in *Confessions of a Crap Artist*, 63; in *Counter-Clock World*, 147–48, 156, 163, 169; in *Do Androids Dream*, 20, 117–18, 119, 120–21, 123–29,

Characters (*cont.*)
130, 131, 136, 163, 198; in *Dr.
Bloodmoney*, 80, 81, 83–86, 87,
88, 136; in *Eye in the Sky*,
64–65; female, 19, 77, 107, 136,
145, 191; in *Flow My Tears*,
157–58, 164; ideas as, 107; idiot
savant, 20, 130; little man, 20,
32, 34, 89; male, 19–20, 136; in
Man in the High Castle, 9, 19,
20, 33, 40, 41–42, 47, 48, 51,
53, 56–57, 98, 158; in *The Man
Who Japed*, 38–39; in *Martian
Time-Slip*, 15, 19, 20, 38, 59,
63, 64, 67–69, 70, 72, 73–75,
76–77, 122, 136, 144; obsessed
with death, 136; in *Our Friends
from Frolix 8*, 61; in *Palmer
Eldritch*, xiii, 19, 96, 98, 102–6,
107, 108, 110–12, 136, 137, 195;
policemen, 163–64, 165;
religious visionaries, 169;
scientists, 20; in *A Scanner
Darkly*, 159–60; in *The
Simulacra*, 88, 91–92; in *Solar
Lottery*, 34–35; sources for,
196; in *Timothy Archer*, 19, 20,
185, 188, 189–91; in *Ubik*, 19,
137, 138, 139–44, 146; in *Valis*,
xvi, 170–71; in *The World
Jones Made*, 38
Chip, Joe (*Ubik*), 20, 137, 138,
139–44
Clanes of the Alphane Moon
(1964), 17, 65, 163, 169
Cold war, influence on Dick, 4
"Commuter, The" (1953), 100
Confessions of a Crap Artist:
Anne as prototype for Faye in,
9; idiot savant in, 20, madness
examined in, 63; publication of
(1975), xiv, xxiii, 9; writing of
(1959), xxii, 9, 63
"Cookie Lady, The" (1953), 135
Cosmic Code, The (Pagels, 1982),
24n

Cosmic Puppets, The (1957), xxii,
11n, 98, 119–20, 169
Counter-Clock World (1967):
compared to *Ubik*, 147; drug
use portrayed in, 156–57;
·Sebastian Hermes in, 148, 156;
policeman in, 163; themes
examined in, 15, 136, 147;
Anarch Thomas Peak in, xiv,
147–48, 169
Cryonics Society of California,
137

Dancing Wu Li Masters (Zukav),
26
Dangerous Visions (Ellison,
1967), 113
Dante, 200
Davidson, Grania, xxii, 134
"Days of Perky Pat, The" (1963),
95–96, 110
Death and entropy, as theme
examined by Dick, 15, 135–36,
140, 146–47, 149, 152, 161–62
"Defenders, The" (1953), 118
del Fiore, Joachim, 192
Deus Irae (with Roger Zelazny,
1976), 134
Dick, Anne Rubenstein (third
wife): daughters of, 9, 34;
Dick's writing while married to,
9–10, 12, 33, 66, 82; marriage
to Philip, xxii, 9–10, 34, 97,
133; as prototype for Faye in
Confessions of a Crap Artist, 9;
as source of information on
Dick's writings, 83
Dick, Christopher (son of Philip
and Tessa), xxiii, 10, 153
Dick, Dorothy Kindred (mother),
xxi, 6–7
Dick, Isolde ("Isa"; daughter of
Philip and Nancy), xxii, 10, 134
Dick, Jane (twin sister), xxi, 6,
11, 86, 131

Dick, Jeanette Marlin (first wife), xxi, 8, 12
Dick, Joseph Edgar (father), xxi, 6–7
Dick, Kleo Apostolides (second wife), xxi, 8, 9, 12
Dick, Laura Archer (daughter of Philip and Anne), xxii, 9
Dick, Leslie Busby ("Tessa"; fifth wife), xxiii, 10, 11, 12, 153
Dick, Nancy Hackett (fourth wife), xxii, 10, 12, 134, 150, 152, 154, 155, 157
Dick, Philip Kindred: antipathy toward authority figures, 163–64; anxiety about nuclear warfare, 80–81; and cats, xv, 20; as character in *Valis*, xvi, 170; childhood of, 4, 6–8; as Civil War buff, 33; compared to Shakespeare, 70, 71; death of (1982), xvi, xxiii, 11, 166, 193; education of, 4, 7, 8, 168; employment of, 7–8; function of literary art for, 57; health problems of, 11; impact of World War II on, 2, 4, 5, 33, 40, 80; income of, 34, 166; interest in mushroom hunting, 83; life phases of, 6–11, 12; literary ancestors of, 199–200; mental health problems of, 8, 9, 10, 11, 63, 64, 84, 131, 133, 150, 166; multiple personalities of, 6; mystical experience of (1974), xv, xvi, xxiii, 10–11, 16, 153, 166, 168, 191–92; reputation of, 1, 199; as social observer, 6, 194–95; suicide attempts by, xxiii, 10, 11, 15, 133, 135, 150, 152, 153; use of drugs by, 10, 11, 12, 95, 97, 133, 134, 153, 154–55, 156–57
—writings of: apprenticeship novels, 34; autobiographical elements in writings, 3–4, 6, 9,

12, 136, 153, 156–57, 162, 171; characters created by (*see* Characters); corpus of writing, xiv, 1, 8, 82, 133–34, 194; cosmogony of, 180, 183–84; creative method of, xiii–xiv, 12–14, 33–34, 97; critical reception for, 1, 3, 102, 138, 154, 199; death and entropy examined in, 15, 135–36, 140, 146–47, 149, 152, 161–62; doubles used, 84, 87, 119–20, 123, 130, 131–32, 157; drug use examined in, 16, 95, 152, 154, 155–58, 159–62, 160, 165, 166; evil examined in, 98–99, 109, 110, 111–12, 113–14, 121–22, 180–81; fictional cosmos of, 16–19; hiatus in writing, xiv, 11, 152, 153, 166; illusion and reality examined in, 15, 96, 99–102, 104–6, 109–11, 129–30, 132; madness examined in, 14–15, 62–65, 73–74, 77–78, 80, 85, 88, 91; mainstream novels of, xiv, xxii, 9, 137; manuscripts destroyed (1971), xxii, 10, 135; metaphors used by, 2, 3, 15, 21, 26, 29–31, 57, 59, 67, 77, 82, 87, 90, 93, 118, 120, 124, 131, 140–41, 142, 145, 162, 164, 173, 196, 198, 199, *Fig. 2*; misuse of power examined in, 14, 32–33, 46–47, 59–60; moral code delineated in, 198–99; nuclear holocaust examined in, 80–83; quantum reality in, 25–26, 200–201; realistic (literary) fiction of, 8, 9, 11, 12; religion examined in, 108–9, 116, 166, 172–75, 179–80, 183–84; religious novels of, 12, 16; science fiction novels of, xiv, 8; short stories of, xiv, 12, 32, 63–64, 99–100, 131, 196; speeches by, xiii,

Dick, Philip Kindred (*cont.*)
xxiii, 26, 109, 112–13, 117, 132,
135, 145–46, 150–51, 152;
themes examined by, 14–16,
32, 37, 39, 48–51, 59–60;
writing periods of, 11–16;
writing style of, 21, 33, 34, 40,
41–42, 47–48, 51–57, 86, 119,
148, 175–77. *See also* names of
individual works
Dirac, Paul, 21
Divine Invasion, The (1981):
relationship to *Valis*, xxiii, 11,
167, 169–70, 172–75, 176–78,
178–79, 181, 183, 195
*Do Androids Dream of Electric
Sheep?*: allusions to music, art,
and literature in, 130; androids
in, 117–18, 124, 125–29, 131;
based on *We Can Build You*,
66, 117; Rick Deckard in, 20,
119, 120, 123–26, 163; doubles
used in, 119, 120, 123, 130; evil
examined in, 121–22; illusion
and reality examined in,
129–30; John R. Isidore in, 20,
120–21, 123–24, 125, 126, 130,
136, 198; made into film (1981),
xvi, xxiii, 11, 166; messiah in,
122–23; metaphors in, 29–30,
118, 120, 121, 124, 125, 131,
142, 198; plot of, 120, 125–29,
Fig. 3; publication of (1968),
xxii, religious visionary in, 169;
single point of view in, 119;
structure of, 121, *Fig. 3*; themes
examined in, 15, 117, 121–22;
writing of (1966), 10, 12, 117
*Dr. Bloodmoney, or How We Got
Along After the Bomb*: based
on *Voices from the Street*, 80;
Dr. Bruno Bluthgeld in, 81, 85,
87; characters in, 80, 81, 83–85;
children in, 19, 83–84; the
Dangerfields in, 85, 86, 87, 88,
136; Hoppy Harrington in, 84,
85–86, 87, 136; madness in, 80,
85; mankind's survival in,
93–94; multiple narratives used
in, 86; musical and literary
allusions in, 84; nuclear
holocaust examined in, 15, 80;
omniscient point of view of, 84;
paired elements in, 84, 87; plot
of, 85–86, 87; publication of
(1965), xxii, 97; regarded as
utopian, 83; subtitle of, 88; as
twin to *The Simulacra*, 80, 88;
writing of (1963), 9–10, 12, 80,
83, 97
Donne, John, 200
Doppelgänger (doubles), Dick's
use of, 84, 87, 119–20, 123,
130, 131–32, 157
Dostoevski, Fëdor M., 120, 176
Doubles, use of. *See*
Doppelgänger
Dowland, John, 93, 157, 158, 176,
177
Dream Makers, The (Platt, 1980),
xv, 166–67
Drugs, Dick's use of, 10, 11, 12,
95, 97, 133, 134, 135, 153,
154–55, 156–57. *See also* Dick,
Philip Kindred, writings of,
drug use examined in

Einstein, Albert, 21
"Electric Ant, The" (1969),
131–32
Eliot, T. S., 93
Ellison, Harlan, 113
Empathy, 131, 196–97
Entropy. *See* Death and entropy,
as theme examined by Dick
Ettinger, R. C. W., 137
"Exhibit Piece" (1954), 64
"Expendable" (1953), 63–64
Eye in the Sky (1957), 64–65
"Eyes Have It, The" (1953),
26–29

"Faith of Our Fathers" (1967),
113–15, 157

Fantastic magazine, 82
Fantastic Stories magazine, 12
Fantasy and Science Fiction
   magazine, 12
"Father-thing, The" (1954), 64
Fermi, Enrico, 81
Finnegan's Wake (Joyce), xvi
*Flow My Tears, the Policeman
   Said*: Felix Buckman and Jason
   Taverner in, 157–58, 164; John
   W. Campbell Jr. Award for
   Best Novel (1974), xxiii;
   doubles used in, 157;
   publication of (1974), xxiii, 152;
   writing of (1970–73), xxii, 11,
   150, 153, 155, 157
Fomalhaut Cosmos, 16–19, 195,
   Fig. 1
Free Speech movement, 5

Galactic Pot-Healer (1969), 15,
   17, 98–99, 169
Galaxy magazine, 12
Galen, Russell, 191
Game-Players of Titan, The
   (1963), 59, 101–2, 136, 156
Game theory, in *Solar Lottery*,
   35, 36
Ganymede Takeover, The (with
   Ray Nelson), xxii, 134
Genêt, Jean, 199
Gilbert and Sullivan, 93
"Glass of Darkness, A," 98
Glenn, John, 83–84
Goebbels Diary, The (Shirer), 40
Goethe, Johann Wolfgang von, 4,
   93, 99, 186, 199, 200
Golden Man, The (Hurst, 1980),
   6n, 29
Gribbin, John, 24n
Guevara, Che, 39

Hackett, Marion, 134
Hackett, Nancy. *See* Dick, Nancy
   Hackett
Haight-Ashbury, drug culture in,
   5

"Hanging Stranger, The" (1953),
   63
Heine, Heinrich, 119
Heisenberg, Werner, 21, 22
Heisenberg's Principle of
   Uncertainty or
   Indeterminacy, 22, 26
Heraclitus, 183
Hiroshima, atomic bomb
   explosion at, 2, 80
Hoffman, E. T. A., 119
Hollis, Herb, 7, 8, 84
Hugo Award, for *The Man in the
   High Castle* (1962), xxii, 9
Huxley, Aldous, 95, 154

I Ching (Book of Changes), in
   The Man in the High Castle, 34,
   40, 41, 42, 43–44, 46–47, 60
Idios kosmos, 202
"If There Were No Benny
   Cemoli" (1963), 59
Illusion and reality, as theme
   examined by Dick, 15, 96,
   99–102, 104–6, 109–11, 129–30,
   132
Imagination magazine, 12
"Imposter" (1953), 82, 118
In Search of Schrodinger's Cat
   (Gribbin, 1984), 24n
Isidore, John R. (J.R.) (*Do
   Androids Dream*), 20, 120–21,
   123–26, 127–29, 130, 132, 136,
   198

Jary, Alfred, 130
John W. Campbell Jr. Award for
   Best Novel, for *Flow My Tears,
   the Policeman Said* (1974), xxiii
"Jon's World" (1954), 168
Joyce, James, 93
Julius Caesar (Shakespeare), 93
Jung, Carl, 26, 34, 64, 99

Kafka, Franz, 93
Kennedy, John F., 4, 97
Koinos Rosmos, 112, 202

Korean War, 4

Laplace, Pierre de, 22
"Last of the Masters, The"
    (1954), 198
Last Testament (Rickman, 1985),
    164
"Lateral Time Tracks and Other
    Realities." *See* Metz speech
Leary, Timothy, 154
"Little Black Box, The" (1964),
    198
London speech (1976), 117, 132,
    145, 150–51
Lucretius (Titus Lucretius Carus),
    xiv, 93

McCarthy, Joseph, 4
McNelly, Willis, xxiii, 10, 152–53
Madness, as theme examined by
    Dick, 14–15, 62–65, 73–74,
    77–78, 80, 85, 88, 91
Mahler, Gustav, 93, 177
"Man, Android, and Machine"
    (London Speech, 1976), 117,
    132, 145, 150–51
Man in the High Castle, The:
    autobiographical elements in, 9;
    castle metaphor in, 57–58;
    characters in, 9, 20, 33, 40,
    41–42, 48, 51; Robert Childan
    in, 42, 50, 51, 53; drug use
    portrayed in, 156;
    foreshadowed in *The World
    Jones Made*, 38; Frank Frink
    in, 9, 20, 33, 42, 47, 51, 53;
    Juliana Frink in, 19, 42, 51,
    56–57; *The Grasshopper Lies
    Heavy* in, 42, 48, 49, 51, 56–57;
    Hugo Award for (1962), xxii, 9;
    I Ching in, 34, 40, 41, 42,
    43–44, 46–47, 60; inspiration
    for, 33; misuse of power
    examined in, 14, 32–33, 46–47;
    multiple narrative structure of,
    40, 41–42, 47–48, 51–57;
    Nazism in, 33, 40–41, 42–43,
    54, 163; plot development in,

54; publication of (1962), xxii,
    9; in relation to Dick's other
    novels, 33, 48, 59; research for,
    58; Mr. Tagomi in, 41, 48, 51,
    53–56, 98, 158; Taoism in, 40,
    43–47, 50; themes examined in,
    48–51; Warrick's article on, xiv;
    writing of (1960), 9, 12
Man Who Japed, The (1956),
    38–39, 81–82, 156, 163
*Man Whose Teeth Were All
    Exactly Alike, The* (1984), 137
Marlin, Jeanette. *See* Dick,
    Jeanette Marlin
Martian Time-Slip: Jack Bohlen
    in, 15, 20, 63, 67–68, 69,
    73–75, 144; Leo Bohlen in, 59,
    67, 73; characters in, 67–69, 70,
    76–77; confrontations in, 69,
    70; demands on reader, 76; as
    favorite novel, 66; Arnie Kott
    in, 59, 67, 68, 69–71, 73, 75;
    madness examined in, 14–15,
    62–63, 73–74, 77–78; Martian
    setting of, 17, 63, 67;
    metaphors and symbols in, 77;
    misuse of power examined in,
    59; moral wisdom of, 78;
    multiple narrative structure of,
    68–69, 76; plot of, 69–76;
    publication of (1964), xxii;
    Shakespearean aspects of, 70,
    71; Manfred Steiner in, 19, 38,
    63, 64, 69, 72, 73–75, 122, 136;
    themes examined in, 49, 67;
    writing of (1962), 9, 12, 62, 80
Marvell, Andrew, 200
Maze of Death, A (1970):
    multiple points of view in,
    148–49; Bishop Pike's influence
    on Dick in writing of, 147;
    themes examined in, 15, 136,
    149–50
Me First age, 6
Messiah theme in novels. *See*
    individual titles
Metz speech (1977), xxiii, 26, 109,
    145–46

Midsummer Night's Dream, A
(Shakespeare), 176
More, Ward, 33
Mozart, Wolfgang Amadeus, 93,
126–27
Munch, Edvard, 122, 130
Mushroom hunting, Dicks's
interest in, 83

Nagasaki, atomic bomb explosion
at, 80
Narrative, multiple. *See Man in
the High Castle, The,* multiple
narrative structure of
Nazism: in *Man in the High
Castle,* 33, 40–41, 42–43, 54,
163; in *The Man Who Japed,* 38
Nelson, Ray, xxii, 134
New Doors of Perception
(Huxley, 1954), 154
Newton, Sir Isaac, 24
Newtonian (mechanistic) physics,
22
Nietzsche, Friedrich Wilhelm, 41
Nixon, Richard M., 6
Notes from the Underground
(Dostoevski), 120, 176
"Novelty Act" (1964), 82
Now Wait for Last Year (1966),
60, 136, 138, 156
"Null-O" (1956), 82–83

Offenbach, Jacques, 119
Only Apparently Real (Williams),
11n
Order out of Chaos (Prigogine,
1984), 24n
Ornstein, Robert E., 119
Our Friends from Frolix 8 (1970),
35, 61, 115, 150
Owl in Daylight, The (unwritten),
167, 185–86

Pagels, Heinz R., 24n
Pascal, Blaise, 93
Pauli, Wolfgang, 21, 26

"Paycheck" (1953), 119
"Pay for the Printer" (1956), 83,
135
Penultimate Truth, The (1964), xiv,
32, 59, 60
Pike, Bishop James: Dick
characters based on, 11, 147,
167, 187; Dick's friendship
with, xxii, 10, 134; suicide of
son of, 133, 147
Planet Stories magazine, 99
Plank, Max, 21
Plato, 183, 192, 200
Platt, Charles, xv, 166–67
Plotinus, 192
Point Reyes Station: Dicks living
in, 9; use of in *Dr.
Bloodmoney,* 83
Power, misuse of: as theme
examined by Dick, 14, 32–33,
46–47, 59–60
"Precious Artifact" (1964), 29,
97–98
Prigogine, Ilya, 24n
Prospect of Immortality, The
(Ettinger), 137
Proust, Marcel, xvi, 93
Pythagoras, 192

Quantum physics, 21–25
Quantum-reality fiction, 200

"Rautavaara's Case" (1980),
115–16
Reenchantment of the World, The
(Berman, 1981), 24
Religion, as theme examined by
Dick, 12, 16, 18–19, 116, 166,
172–75, 179–80, 183–84
Remembrance of Things Past
(Proust), xvi
Richter, Jean Paul, 119
Rickman, Greg, 164
Rise and Fall of the Third Reich
(Shirer), 40
Rolling Stone magazine, Dick
interviewed in, 135

"Roog" (1952), 8, 100, 196–97
Rubenstein, Anne. *See* Dick,
  Anne Rubenstein
Runciter, Glen (*Ubik*), 137, 138,
  139, 141–44

"Sandman, The" (Hoffman,
  1814), 119
Sanity, *See* Madness
Sartre, Jean Paul, 122
Scanner Darkly, A:
  autobiographical elements in,
  153, 162; characters in, 159–60;
  death examined in, 161–62;
  Fred/Bob Arctor in, 159;
  metaphors in, 162; plot of,
  159–62; publication of (1977),
  152; research for, 154; title of,
  98; use of drugs examined in,
  16, 152, 154, 159–62, 165, 166;
  writing of (1973), xxiii, 11, 12,
  153, 159
Schiller, Friedrich von, 4, 199,
  200
Schizophrenia. *See* Madness
Schrodinger, Erwin, 21
Schubert, Franz, 119
Science Fiction Commentary,
  Dick's letters to, 54, 55n, 150,
  153
Science-Fiction Studies, special
  issue on Dick (1975), 154
Scott Meredith Literary Agency,
  xxi, 11
"Second Variety" (1953), 118,
  119
Shakespeare, William, 70, 71, 93,
  176, 200
"Shell Game" (1954), 64
Shirer, William, 40
Siebenkäs (Richter, 1796), 119
Simulacra, The: exploitive power
  examined in, 32, 59; focus on
  events leading to nuclear war,
  81, 88; Richard Kongrosian in,
  88, 91–92; madness in, 80, 88,
  91; mankind's survival in, 93;

metaphors in, 90, 91, 93;
  musical and literary allusions
  in, 93; plot of, 88–93; political
  satire in, 89–90, 93; publication
  of (1964), 82; scene from
  "Novelty Act" in, 82; as twin
  to *Dr. Bloodmoney*, 80, 88;
  unwritten subtitle for, 88;
  writing of (1963), 80
"Skull, The" (1952), 119
Sladek, John, 153
"Small Town" (1954), 100–101
Smetana, Bedrich, 58
Solar Lottery (1955), xxii, 8, 26,
  34–37, 60, 163
Spinoza, 183, 192
Star Wave (Wolf, 1984), 24n, 25
Steiner, Manfred (*Martian
  Time-Slip*), 19, 38, 64, 69, 72,
  73–78, 136, 137

Tagomi, Mr. (*Man in the High
  Castle*), 20, 41, 42, 47, 51, 53,
  56, 57, 98, 158
Tales of Hoffman (Offenbach),
  119
Taoism, in *The Man in the High
  Castle*, 40, 43–47, 50
Tao of Physics, The (Capra,
  1975), 24, 26
Teller, Edward, 81
Theodotus, 180
Theophany. *See Valis*, theophany
  in
*Three Stigmata of Palmer
  Eldritch, The*: based on "The
  Days of Perky Pat," 95–96;
  Leo Bulero in, xiii, 98, 102–6,
  108, 111–12, 137, 195;
  characters in, 19, 103, 107;
  critical reception for, 102; drug
  use protrayed in, 95, 156;
  Palmer Eldritch in, 96, 102,
  103–6, 110–11; evil examined
  in, 98, 109, 110, 111–12, 169;
  exploitive power examined in,
  32, 59, 108; illusion and reality

examined in, 15, 96, 99–102, 104–6, 109–11; inspiration for, 95; as LDS novel, 95; loss of control in, 97; Martian setting of, 17, 67; Barney Mayerson in, 98, 102–6, 111–12, 136, 137; memo in, xiii; multiple narratives used in, 97; omniscient point of view in, 97, 107; plot of, 97, 102–7; publication of (1964), xxii; religion examined in, 108–9, 116; settings for, 102–3; themes in, 107–12; writing of (1963–64), 10, 12

Tibetan Book of the Dead, 145, 155

Time out of Joint (1959), 39, 101

Transmigration of Timothy Archer, The: Angel Archer in, 19, 185, 188, 189–91; based on Bishop Pike, 11, 167; Bill Lundborg in, 20, 189, 190, 191; metaphors in, 189; plot of, 187–88, 189–91; posthumous publication of (1982), xxiii, 11, 167, 185; structure of, 188–89; writing of (1981), 185, 191

Twin sister. *See* Dick, Jane

Ubik: characters in, 137, 138, 146; Joe Chip in, 137, 138, 139–44; differing interpretations of, 144; entropy and death examined in, 15, 136, 146–47; metaphors in, 140–41, 142, 145; Jory Miller in, 19, 137; plot of, 138–44; publication of (1969), xxii; Glen Runciter in, 137, 138, 139, 141–44; success of, 146; themes of, 137; Ubik in, 141, 143–44, 145; writing of, 10, 12, 133, 136–37

University Radio, Dick's employment at, 7–8

Unteleported Man, The (1966), 17, 32, 95, 156

"Upon the Dull Earth" (1954), 119, 131

Valis: autobiographical elements of, 171; character Phil Dick in, xvi, 170; characters in, 170–71; compared to *The Divine Invasion*, 169–70; evil examined in, 181; germ of idea developed in "Man, Android, and Machine," 132; first-person point of view in, 176–77; manuscript of, xv–xvi; messiah in, 172; plot of, 170–72; publication of (1981), xxiii, 11, 166, 167; religious themes examined in, 16, 169–70; sequels to, 167, 185; themes examined in, 178–83; theophany in, 170; writing of (1978), xxiii, 166, 167–68; writing style of, 175–77

Valis Regained. See Divine Invasion, The

Valor, Dick's code of, 196–97, 198–99, 201, 202–3

Vancouver speech (1972), xxiii, 112–13, 117, 135, 152

"Variable Man, The" (1953), 20, 163

Vast Active Living Intelligence System. *See Valis*

Vaughan, Henry, 200

Verdi, Giuseppe, 93

Vergil, 200

Vertex magazine, Dick interviewed in, 40

Vietnam War, 4, 6, 133

Voices from the Street (1952–53), xxii, 8, 80

von Neumann, John, 35

Vulcan's Hammer (1960), 19, 39–40, 156

Vysehrad castle, 57–58

Wagner, Richard, 93, 176, 177, 178–79

Watergate scandal, 6
We Can Build You: as basis of
  *Do Androids Dream of Electric
  Sheep?*, 66, 117; publication of
  (1969), 117; writing of (1962),
  62, 65–66, 117, 150
Williams, Paul, 135
Wolf, Fred Alan, 24n, 25
Woolf, Virginia, 201
World Jones Made, The (1956),
  37–38, 136, 155–56, 163
"World of Talent, A" (1954), 64,
  138

"World She Wanted, The"
  (1953), 100, 168

X-Kalay, Dick's drug treatment
  at, 10, 135, 152, 155

Yeats, William Butler, 93, 176,
  200

Zap Gun, The (1967), 60, 136,
  157
Zelazny, Roger, 134, 155
Zukav, Gary, 26

Patricia S. Warrick is a professor of English at the University of Wisconsin Center-Fox Valley. She is the author of *The Cybernetic Imagination in Science Fiction* (MIT Press, 1980). She has also edited or co-edited books on science fiction and has written numerous articles on science fiction and technology.